How to SAVE TAXES Through ESTATE PLANNING

By
Robert J. Pinto

DOW JONES BOOKS
PRINCETON, NEW JERSEY

This publication is designed to provide accurate and authoritative information in regard to the subject matter covered. It is sold with the understanding that the publisher is not engaged in rendering legal, accounting, or other professional service. If legal advice or other expert assistance is required, the services of a competent professional person should be sought.

From a Declaration of Principles jointly adopted by a Committee of the American Bar Association and a Committee of Publishers.

First Printing December 1976
Second Printing March 1977
Third Printing May 1977
Fourth Printing August 1977
Fifth Printing December 1977
Sixth Printing July 1978
Seventh Printing September 1978
Eighth Printing June 1979

Published by Dow Jones Books
P.O. Box 300, Princeton, NJ 08540

Printed and bound in the United States of America
10 9 8 7

Library of Congress Cataloging in Publication Data

Pinto, Robert J
  How to save taxes through estate planning

    1. Inheritance and transfer tax—United States.
I. Title.
KF6584.P53 1979   343'.73'053   79-15228
ISBN 0-87128-576-2 pbk.

ACKNOWLEDGEMENT

There are many who generously offered their time and encouragement in the writing of this book, but I would especially like to recognize the contributions made by Kennedy-Sinclaire, Inc. who have provided much technical information and illustrative material including the fifty State Inheritance Tax Tables; James Misciagna for his photography, Joyce Fitzpatrick for her illustrations, and a special thanks to my "personal critic," secretary and wife, Marilyn for her help and encouragement.

ROBERT J. PINTO

Lawyer, lecturer and bank trust officer, Robert J. Pinto brings a wealth of practical knowledge to the important subject of personal financial planning.

In hundreds of appearances before laymen's groups throughout the country, Mr. Pinto has guided and counselled thousands of businessmen, executives and retirees. Thanks to this experience, he is able to present authoritative information on estate planning in down-to-earth terms.

Mr. Pinto is a regular lecturer at meetings sponsored by Ford Motor Company for its dealers around the country. As one Ford executive has said, "None of our other guest speakers has ever stimulated the interest and response from our dealers as did Mr. Pinto's presentation on wills, estate planning and taxes. To many who believed they were well-protected in these areas, it was a revelation and to many who hadn't yet done so, it provided the necessary stimulant to take actions they had neglected."

Mr. Pinto has also served as a guest speaker at various state automobile dealers' conventions. In addition he is a lecturer on wills and trusts at the Rutgers University Institute for Continuing Legal Education and before chapters of the American Institute of Banking and has appeared on the Nationally televised Public Broadcasting System's show, "Consumer Survival Kit" discussing Estate Planning.

In his former position as First Vice President and Trust Officer of a bank trust department, his responsibilities included presentation of estate planning seminars before residents of retirement communities, small business owners and executives throughout the state of New Jersey. Mr. Pinto presently maintains a private law practice in Princeton, New Jersey.

TABLE OF CONTENTS

INTRODUCTION

Why write a book about estate planning?

I've asked myself this question many times. There is, already, much material available about estate planning—mostly prepared by insurance companies, banks and investment counseling firms. But two failings are readily apparent in much of this material: It is seldom prepared by the most competent, most objective authorities in the field; and the material usually is presented in language incredibly difficult for a layman to understand.

There is a great deal of confusion that exists in the areas of wills, trusts, estates, Federal Estate Taxes, Federal Gift Taxes and State Inheritance Taxes. This confusion comes naturally because of misunderstandings, lack of sufficient knowledge in complex areas, and the lack of any logical process in our tax laws.

Despite the difficulties, however, most of us need to understand more about estate planning because we all face the same basic problems in trying to accumulate capital and retain some of it for our heirs. To do this—and save money, time and trouble in the process—requires sound financial planning.

Therefore, one motivation in preparing this book is the obvious importance the subject has in people's lives. Another is the desire to communicate useful information which can be profitably used. Still another is the conviction, based on my experience in working with automotive dealers of Ford Motor Company, that the problems of financial planning are manageable.

In HOW TO SAVE TAXES THROUGH ESTATE PLANNING, I have set out the basic facts that will help you cut through the confusion of a subject that is admittedly complex. It will point the way, too, I trust, to some solutions of fairly common problems.

I have made marginal notations throughout the book calling special attention to certain areas which will require the advice of your financial planning advisers. I have also noted those areas which are especially complex; space is provided in these places for you to make notes on points that may have special application to your circumstances.

I have included Financial Planning work-forms for use in listing assets at their fair market values. This will aid in the determination of Federal Estate Taxes and State Inheritance Taxes. To provide a means of calculating these taxes, there is also included a Federal Estate Tax Table and the inheritance tax rates for the fifty states.

To give some indication of the possible executor and trustee fees which one will incur, I've added a table of average fees for each of the fifty states.

Included too, is a glossary of the more important estate planning terms and phrases with easy-to-understand definitions.

For several years now, Congress has been talking about possible changes in the Federal Estate Tax and Gift Laws. These changes became a reality with the passage of the Tax Reform Act of 1976, signed on October 4, 1976, which becomes effective on December 31, 1976.

Before December 31, 1976, the Gift Tax Law applied only against lifetime transfers which exceeded the Gift Tax exemptions. One of the changes is to eliminate the two separate taxes, the Federal Gift Tax and the Federal Estate Tax, and provide in their place one tax which would apply to all transfers of property whether they were made during lifetime or by way of testamentary transfer. Also, there has been the introduction of a tax credit which substantially increases the present exemptions from tax. The marital deduction is also increased to $250,000 or half the adjusted gross estate in the decedent's estate, whichever is greater.

Still another change is the capital gains treatment of property held by the decedent. Under the pre-December 31, 1976 Law, all property acquired a new basis at the date of death of the decedent for purposes of the income tax. Under the new Law, a capital gains tax would be applied on the difference between the fair market value of the asset when sold by the beneficiary and the value of the asset as of December 31, 1976 or if the asset was acquired after December 31, 1976, its cost. The 1976 Act has been followed with the Revenue Act of 1978 which attempts to clarify some of the changes made by the 1976 law. These changes included estate tax relief for husbands and wives who operate businesses jointly, exclusion of death benefits payable in a lump sum from a qualified pension or profit sharing plan under certain circumstances, and a more liberal approach in the application of the 15-year period available for the payment of estate tax on closely held businesses.

Perhaps the most significant provision of the Revenue Act of 1978 was the three-year postponement of the effective date of the carryover basis law introduced by the 1976 Tax Reform Act. This means that the old stepped up basis law, i.e., fair market value on the date of death or six months from the date of death will continue in effect for anyone dying before December 31, 1979. These are only some of the new provisions.

In addition to the tax information, the basic measures of gathering financial information, formulating objectives, selecting competent advisors, applying the marital deduction, gift-giving programs, and other estate planning techniques outlined in this book, will provide useful information in the formation of your estate plan.

One thing should be made clear: This is not a complete "do-it-yourself" estate planning book. You will need competent professional help from your attorney, trust banker, insurance counsellor and accountant to put a sound financial program into full effect.

HOW TO SAVE TAXES THROUGH ESTATE PLANNING will, however, help you set your estate planning objectives and better understand the tax and legal advice you will need. It will also assist you in taking full and profitable advantage of estate planning strategies.

Chapter I

SAVING ESTATE TAXES

In any framework used for talking about taxes and estate valuations one must also discuss the United States' economic picture, past and present. In discussing this topic, the simplest indicator is a review of the value of the dollar from 1940 down to the present time.

In 1940, for example, the dollar was worth just about 99.8 cents in terms of its purchasing power. Looking at that same dollar in 1950 we found that its value had diminished to 56 cents in terms of its ability to purchase goods and services. Today, with the spiralling inflation we contend with, the dollar of 1940 is worth less than 37 cents in terms of its purchasing power.

You may be wondering at this point what the depreciation of the dollar has to do with estate planning. Well, it has much to do with it when you consider that the living conditions of a surviving spouse are directly connected with the amount of dollars left to her by her deceased husband and the ability of invested dollars to earn income.

Let's use an example: If a person in 1940 had passed away leaving an estate of $137,519, assuming the value of the dollar at 99.8 cents, he would have left purchasing power to his family annually of some $5,000. If that same person had died in 1950, he would have to leave an estate of $260,000 in order to duplicate that same $5,000 purchasing power and, again, if the individual passed away at the present time, he would have to leave in excess of $300,000 because of the 37.5 cent dollar in order to leave $5,000 worth of purchasing power.

So realistically, we're seeing inroads made upon the ability to conserve and accumulate dollars.

Not only is there inflation, but we also have the Federal Income Tax to contend with. Both erode our ability to accumulate dollars and leave them to our loved ones. Not only do we have income tax and inflation, but we also have the Federal Estate Tax and State Inheritance Tax of our respective states, which can be quite substantial.

Let's look at the Federal Estate Tax on a typical estate. In order to understand the impact of the taxes let's presume a certain kind of Will. Let's presume the kind of so-called simple Will which says, "after the payment of debts and expenses I leave everything outright to my wife" and "in the event my wife predeceases me, then I leave my entire estate to my children, to be divided equally among them."

Assuming that kind of simple Will, let's look and see what happens to a $400,000 estate. Immediately on this $400,000 estate (as shown in Figure #1) there is approximately $32,000 taken out at the time of the decedent's death for what is known as estate settlement costs. You will note that this $32,000 represents 8% of the $400,000

OUTRIGHT DISTRIBUTION

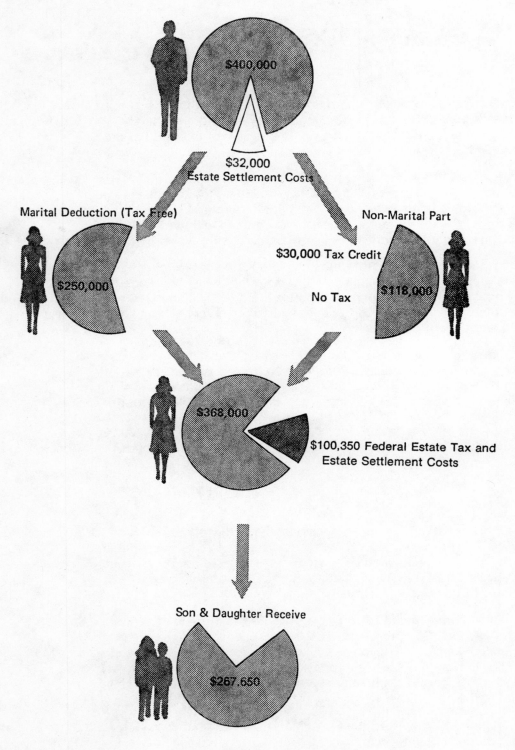

$400,000

$32,000
Estate Settlement Costs

Marital Deduction (Tax Free)

Non-Marital Part

$30,000 Tax Credit

No Tax

$250,000

$118,000

$368,000

$100,350 Federal Estate Tax and
Estate Settlement Costs

Son & Daughter Receive

$267,650

Figure 1

Well, what are estate settlement costs? Estate settlement costs are (1) an average amount of debts and expenses of the last illness, (2) debts due and owing at the time of death, (3) the attorney's fee, which is not set by law, (4) executor's fee, which in most cases is set by law, and (5) there is even a factor in here for some dissident individual who says "before Mr. Able passed away, I did him a lot of favors and he promised to leave me something in this Will." If Mr. Able does not leave him something in the Will, there is an action brought by the individual against the estate which produces corresponding legal fees to defend against that action. This 8%, or $32,000, is a national average. It may be more or less in the particular state in which you are a resident.

All right, what happens after subtracting these so-called estate settlement costs? Well, the Federal Government, under what is known as the Marital Deduction, says that after subtracting the estate settlement costs from the gross estate of $400,000, we come up with what is known as the adjusted gross estate or taxable estate. Under the Marital Deduction a husband can leave his wife $250,000, or one half of his adjusted gross estate, whichever is greater, tax free. Now, under these particular circumstances, using a $400,000 estate as a model, the wife receives $250,000 as her Marital Deduction. If the adjusted gross estate was $500,000 or $700,000 or $1,000,000, she would still receive one half completely tax free under the Marital Deduction. Now, the remainder of the $400,000 estate will pay no tax as a result of a tax credit of $30,000 available to persons dying in 1977. The Tax Reform Act actually provides for a $47,000 credit to be phased in over the next few years as follows:

In the case of decedents dying in:	
1977	$30,000
1978	34,000
1979	38,000
1980	42,500
1981	47,000

We really could have drawn an arrow directly from the $400,000 to $368,000 in Figure #1 because this is the amount that the wife will receive net after the payment of the estate settlement costs of $32,000.

When the wife eventually passes away, what happens then? The wife no longer has the Marital Deduction. Her husband has predeceased her. Therefore, the entire $368,000 will be taxable in her estate and, assuming she leaves children at her death, there is going to be some $100,350 in Federal Estate Tax and estate settlement costs coming out of that $368,000. Therefore, the children of this marriage will receive $267,650.

I'm sure many of you will say that is not too bad. Two children, $267,650, that is $133,000 plus for each. That is not too bad at all, if we don't consider the original amount of the estate. We started with $400,000 and we're down to $267,650. We've lost some $132,350 in estate settlement costs and taxes. There ought to be a better way for programming an estate and there is.

There are many different ways of reducing the so-called "bite" of Federal Estate Tax, but certainly, one of them is by changing the type of Will. Instead of an outright distribution, let's talk in terms of a planned distribution. You will recall that the Will that we were talking about before said "I leave

The marital deduction use may not always be desirable.

PLANNED DISTRIBUTION

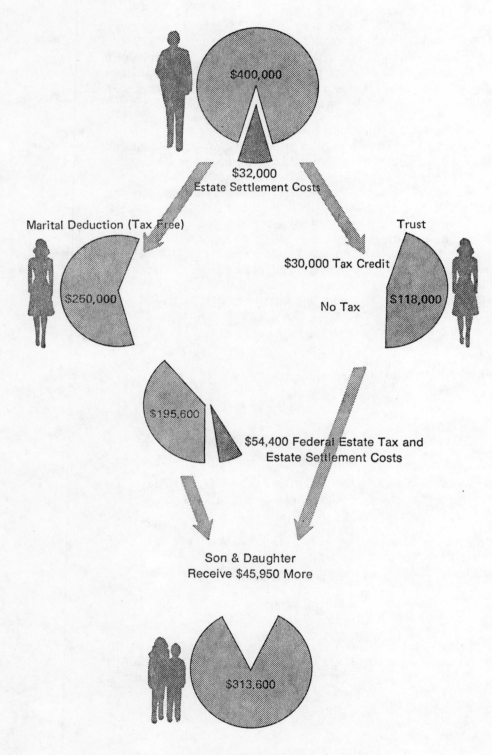

$400,000

$32,000
Estate Settlement Costs

Marital Deduction (Tax Free)

Trust

$250,000

$30,000 Tax Credit

No Tax

$118,000

$195,600

$54,400 Federal Estate Tax and
Estate Settlement Costs

Son & Daughter
Receive $45,950 More

$313,600

Figure 2

everything outright to my wife and if she predeceases me, I leave everything to my children be to divided equally among them."

Under the new Will we are going to change that. We are going to say "leave $250,000 to my wife, that part commonly known as the Marital Deduction. Then with the remainder of my estate, let's put that into a trust."

Now, let's look at Figure #2 and see how that works. We are again involved with the same $400,000 estate and estate settlement costs of 8% of the total amount. We again take $250,000 of the estate, that part commonly known as the Marital Deduction, and pay this portion outright or in trust to the surviving spouse. The remainder of the estate will be going into a trust under the Will, a so-called modern flexible trust. Again we have no Federal Estate Tax because the available tax credit exceeds the tax, but unlike our first example, the remaining $118,000 won't go directly to the spouse. Instead, it will go into a trust which will provide that its main purpose be for the benefit of the surviving spouse.

The trustee of the trust, a bank or an individual, is given the authority to invest the funds in this trust in stocks, bonds, and other investments. The Will also provides that the entire income from this trust will be payable to the wife during her lifetime. In addition to income, the trustee will also be empowered to pay her so much of the principal as is necessary to cover emergencies and to keep her in the style that she was accustomed to living.

The trustees powers should be carefully spelled out.

Let me digress a moment. I was sitting in my office one day giving the same kind of flow chart explanation of a planned estate with a husband and wife sitting before me. When I got to this part, I said, "Now we will take this other half of the estate and put it in trust and pay you, the surviving spouse, so much of the income as is necessary, or all of the income and so much of the principal as is necessary to keep you in the style in which you have been accustomed to living."

The wife sat bolt upright in her chair. She looked over at me and said, "Wait a minute; I want to live much better than that!"

All too often people feel that somehow this type of trust is going to be too restrictive. A wife might get the impression that her husband really doesn't have confidence in her. It appears he is trying to severely restrict her when, in reality, he is trying to provide a financial secretary (in the form of a trustee). The "secretary" will manage the funds, see that the beneficiary gets income from these funds, plus principal necessary to keep her in the style she is accustomed to, principal necessary for any emergency expenses, medical expenses. The trustee will even allow for the payment of nursing home fees if they are required and further expenses of the education of the children. In other words, this trust acts as a source of income as well as a reservoir for any emergency.

Under certain circumstances, although a greater tax savings will be realized at the death of the first spouse, a higher tax may be levied at the death of the surviving spouse because fewer assets will find their way into the non-marital trust.

I've been explaining thus far about this trust in terms of its positive effect of providing income and also reserve for emergencies. There is also another benefit, however. That is a tax benefit. Under this program, at the time that the wife passes away, the only portion of her husband's estate which is includable in her estate for tax purposes is that portion which came to her tax free when he passed away, the so-called Marital Deduction. The taxes and the estate settlement cost on this portion at her death will be $54,400, not that $100,350 bite. This means that she will leave to her children at her demise

$195,600. Now, what happens to the trust? The trust passes completely tax free at the wife's death to the children. If the trust has appreciated by virtue of the trustee's expert management to $218,000, then $218,000 goes directly to the children, completely tax free. On the contrary, if it diminishes from $118,000 downward because of the inroads made upon it for emergencies or the wife's requirements necessary to keep her in the style to which she was accustomed to living, or for emergency expenses, or what have you, then whatever amount is left in the trust at the wife's death would pass tax free to the surviving spouse or children.

We have a tremendous tax advantage in setting up the so-called Marital Deduction Will. We have all the advantages of a financial secretary and all of the advantages of substantial savings in taxes.

At the wife's demise the trust can terminate and all of this money go directly to the children. Or there are several other choices available. You could provide that in the event the husband and wife died in a common disaster, then this trust will continue for the benefit of the children until such time as they meet certain stipulated ages. For example: "At age 21 I wish each of my children to receive one-third of their respective share; at 25 I wish each of them to receive one-half of the balance of their respective share, and at age 30 I wish the trust to terminate, and they receive the balance of their respective share." There is no magic with respect to the 21, 25 and 30 ages. It can be 30, 35 or 40. I have seen some trusts where the postponement was way into the 50's, which I don't think was a good idea. But that is purely a personal matter and that has nothing to do with the tax savings involved.

It would appear rather simple to take advantage of the use of a tax savings trust under a Will. However, there are some complications. The problem centers around probate and non-probate assets. Probate assets are those assets in a person's individual name. These assets are also the only assets controlled by a Will. Non-probate assets include any asset in joint name with the right of survivorship and life insurance made payable to a named beneficiary.

I can recall two examples of very well-drafted Wills with all the necessary tax savings trusts clearly spelled out, which, unfortunately, were completely ineffectual because no one had bothered to take an accurate survey of how the assets in the particular estate were owned. One estate was as follows:

$250,000	Series E Savings Bonds in joint name.
340,000	Savings accounts in various banks in joint name with wife with the right of survivorship.
300,000	Stock in business in joint name of husband and wife.
12,000	Hess Oil Company in husband's individual name.
$902,000	

Notwithstanding the fact that the individual in this case had a well-drafted Will, only $12,000 of his assets, the oil company stock, were controlled by it. This would mean that only $12,000 would find its way into the tax savings non-marital trust and the remainder of the estate would be taxed again at his wife's subsequent demise.

Let me give you one other example: To the extent that Mr. Able with $400,000 has joint ownership, he is not going to be able to get that amount into this tax saving trust. This is because one of the facets of joint ownership is that at the death of one of the joint owners the other joint owner immediately becomes

Check the technical requirements of the non-marital trust.

A trust can be very flexible in this area.

There are other assets which may be non-probate.

the owner of that property, notwithstanding anything that was said in the Will. In other words, if there was a statement in the Will that said "My jointly held stock with my wife I leave to this trust," that provision of the Will would absolutely fail.

The wife brought into the ownership of that particular item a survivorship clause, so to speak. That property would immediately pass to the joint owner, in this case to the wife, outside of the trust. This would make this asset totally outside the reach of any of the tax savings that could have been achieved had the asset been in the husband's individual name. Another means of savings could have been achieved had the joint assets been split right down the middle, half to the wife and half to the husband.

The important point to remember is that the Federal Estate Tax is a progressive tax. The larger the estate the larger the percentage. The so-called tentative tax, computed before the application of the tax credit, starts at 18% and continues to a maximum tax of 70%. If we apply the trust format to estates, the savings achieved are really between your children and the Federal Government, not between your wife and the Federal Government. The better the estate plan the greater the tax savings. You'll note that the Outright Distribution chart and the Planned Distribution chart were absolutely the same up to this point. The savings really occur at the wife's subsequent death. The money saved is going to your children as opposed to going to the Federal Government. It is a substantial amount of dollars.

Something else should also be noted. We're presuming in every one of these situations that the man dies first. That is because actuarial computations tell us that on average the man dies first.

Now, if we presumed that the wife passed away first and we've got this same kind of set up, all the tax savings will go right down the drain, no question about it. But there are certain circumstances where, if the husband and wife have equal estates, which is very rare, there are other programs which can achieve equal or greater tax savings.

This program is the so-called equalization of estate plan. Under this plan either the husband and wife both have assets because they have both been employed or one of them has received an inheritance. Their assets in their individual names are usually equal or are very close to equal. Through the use of gifts the estate might even be made more equal.

In order to achieve maximum Federal Estate Tax savings each of them would have drafted by their attorney a Will which would provide that after the payment of debts, due and owing at the time of death, debts incurred as a result of the last illness and payment of Federal Estate and State Inheritance Tax, that all the rest, residue and remainder of the estate be left in trust for the benefit of the surviving spouse. The trust income would be payable to the surviving spouse and the trustee would be directed to pay so much of the principal to the surviving spouse as was necessary to keep him or her in accustomed style.

There would also be provisions for the invasion of the principal in the event of emergencies such as medical expenses of the surviving spouse and nursing home fees, if they were required. There could also be inserted within the trust provisions a so-called 5 × 5 clause which would allow the surviving spouse, after receiving all of the income and so much of the principal as needed in the trustee's discretion, to invade the principal of the trust to the extent of 5% or $5,000 of the trust, whichever amount was greater. The only restriction on the use of this clause is that the 5% or $5,000 invasion provision is a non-cumulative right. This means that if three years went by without the surviving spouse invading the principal of the trust, she would not be entitled to 15% or $15,000 of the trust principal but would only have the right to 5% or $5,000 in a particular year.

This trust would continue for the life of the surviving spouse. At the surviving spouse's death the trust would terminate and be divided equally among the surviving heirs.

No use of the Marital Deduction is made under this program. Since both spouses have left their assets in trust, none of their assets will be comingled during their lives or during the life of the survivor of them.

If we assume a $500,000 estate for each of them, let's use three sets of computations to demonstrate the greatest estate tax savings available. In the following set of computations we will assume that each left a so-called Simple Will. Note the amount which is ultimately left to their children (Figure 3).

In the second set of computations we will provide a Marital Deduction Will for each. Under these circumstances there would be a substantial savings in taxes (see Figure 4).

The final set of computations assume the non-use of the Marital Deduction and the equalization of estate program, (see Figure 5), previously described. The program offers the greatest tax savings in that each estate is taxed only once.

One other estate planning tool available to certain individuals with large insurance coverage is the so-called Life Insurance Trust. Life insurance is a so-called non-probate asset, i.e. an asset not controlled by one's will. The Life Insurance Trust and its advantages can best be explained by envisioning the trust as a double spouted coffee urn.

Figure A

The first step in effecting the tax savings offered by an Insurance Trust is to have all life insurances policies, both personal life insurance and group insurance, made payable to the trustee of the Insurance Trust.

SIMPLE WILL

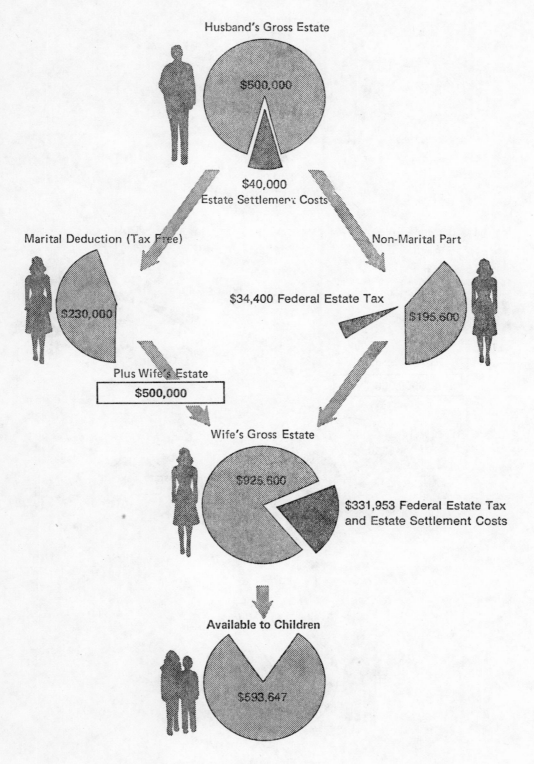

Husband's Gross Estate

$500,000

$40,000
Estate Settlement Costs

Marital Deduction (Tax Free)

Non-Marital Part

$34,400 Federal Estate Tax

$230,000

$195,600

Plus Wife's Estate

$500,000

Wife's Gross Estate

$925,600

$331,953 Federal Estate Tax
and Estate Settlement Costs

Available to Children

$593,647

Figure 3

MARITAL DEDUCTION WILL

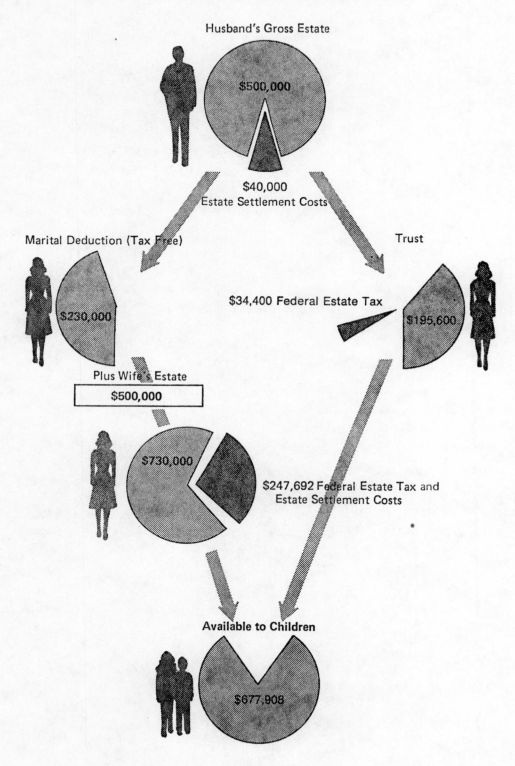

Husband's Gross Estate

$500,000

$40,000
Estate Settlement Costs

Marital Deduction (Tax Free)

Trust

$230,000

$34,400 Federal Estate Tax

$195,600

Plus Wife's Estate

$500,000

$730,000

$247,692 Federal Estate Tax and
Estate Settlement Costs

Available to Children

$677,908

Figure 4

EQUALIZATION OF ESTATES PROGRAM

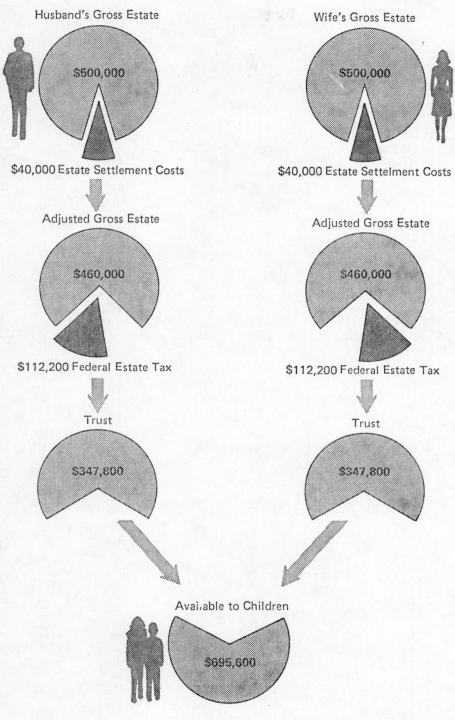

Figure 5

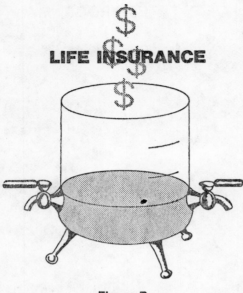

Figure B

Secondly, if the individual is employed by a corporation which provides a pension plan, the beneficiary designation on the pension death benefit is changed to reflect payment to the Insurance Trust

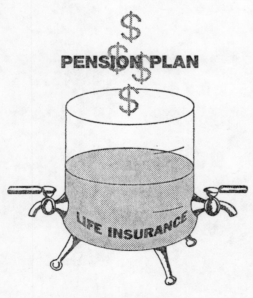

Figure C

Some companies, either in addition to a pension plan or in lieu of it, provide a profit sharing plan. The profit sharing plan will also usually provide a death benefit and therefore the beneficiary designation should also be changed in order that it be made payable to the Insurance Trust.

Figure D

Thus far, we have coordinated all of the individual's non-probate assets into one vehicle of distribution. Or, to put it another way, we have coordinated all of the individual's assets not controlled by his Will.

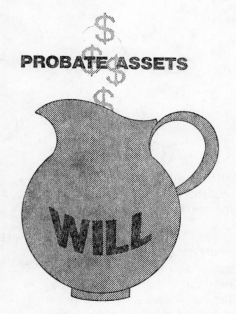

Figure E

The next step is for the individual to execute what is commonly known as a Pour-Over Will, which can be best depicted by a pitcher.

A Will, as you know, controls all those assets which a person holds in his individual name. These assets are also known as his probate assets. After the Will provides for payment of debts, expenses, and taxes, it will direct the executor to pour-over all the remaining assets of the estate into the Insurance Trust. Now, the Insurance Trust as the main vehicle of distribution will take over the disposition of all the assets in the estate.

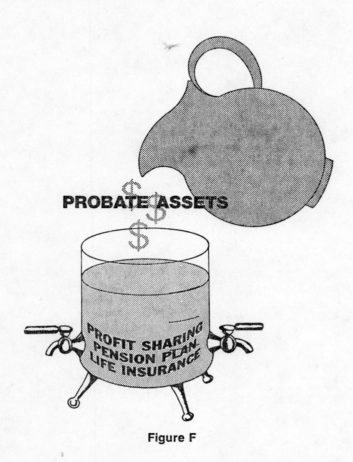

Figure F

In order to take maximum advantage of the Marital Deduction, the trust will direct that $250,000 or one half of the taxable estate, whichever amount is greater, be made payable directly to the surviving spouse, either outright or in trust. This part is commonly known as part A.

There are other technical requirements to the marital deduction.

The remaining assets in the estate will pass into part B, sometimes labeled as the non-marital trust or Residuary Trust. Similar to the non-marital trust under a will, part B will be held in trust for the benefit of the surviving spouse by making all of the income payable to her during her lifetime. In addition to the income, the trustee is empowered to invade the principal of the trust for (1) keeping the wife in the style she was accustomed to living, (2) providing for emergency expenses, medical expenses and the like, and (3) for any educational expenses of the children. Under the foregoing circumstances, at the wife's death, all those assets in Trust B will pass to the children completely tax free as provided under the Federal Estate Tax laws.

These are sometimes referred to as "sprinkling provisions."

**MARITAL
DEDUCTION**   **NON-MARITAL
TRUST**

Figure G

Before too many of you readers become disinterested in further exploration of this estate planning program on the theory that you do not qualify because your estate isn't large enough, you ought to spend a few minutes reviewing the recapitulation schedule of the Federal Estate Tax Return (Form 706) reproduced on the following page.

All real estate in your name is taxable. Its taxable value is the fair market value as of the date of death or six months from the date of death, whichever value is lower. In addition there will be a capital gains tax on the difference between the fair market value of all assets valued on December 31, 1976 and the value of these assets as of the beneficiary's date of sale. The valuation on these assets or cost basis as of December 31, 1976 will be adjusted by the Federal and State death taxes attributable to the appreciation of these assets.

All stocks and bonds owned by you are also taxable at fair market value on date of death or six months from the date of death.

Mortgages owed to you or debts and cash are taxable as well as life insurance. It is a common misconception that life insurance is not part of

Sched-ule	Recapitulation		
	Gross estate	Alternate value	Value at date of death
A	Real Estate		
B	Stocks and Bonds		
C	Mortgages, Notes, and Cash		
D	Insurance on Decedent's Life		
E	Jointly Owned Property		
F	Other Miscellaneous Property		
G	Transfers During Decedent's Life		
H	Powers of Appointment		
I	Annuities		
	Total gross estate		

Figure 6

one's taxable estate when in reality it is. The test is whether the decedent held the so-called incidents of ownership at his death.

Perhaps the most common misconception is in the area of jointly owned property. The Federal Government and the State Inheritance Tax authorities at one time took the position that the first joint owner to die owned the whole amount for Federal Estate Tax and State Inheritance Tax purposes, unless the surviving joint owner could demonstrate by clear and convincing evidence that the survivor contributed something or some portion of the jointly-held assets. Recent legislation has modified this position. Now where property is held jointly by husband and wife with rights of survivorship and this ownership arose out of a gift that is taxable, the jointly-held asset will be treated as being only 50% taxable in the decedent spouse's estate, if the joint ownership was created after December 31, 1976.

All of the foregoing estate planning programs, the Marital Deduction Will, the equalization of estate program and the Life Insurance Trust and Pour-Over Will are all methods of saving taxes and reaching one's objectives. They are by no means the only ways. There are many variations to the basic forms and there are companion moves in the areas of trusts, lifetime gifts and ownership of property which may greatly enhance the tax savings of any program. We will explore these in the chapters to follow.

Chapter II

LIFE TIME GIFTS: ANOTHER WAY TO REDUCE TAXES

We have learned that you can reduce a taxable estate through proper wills and trusts. Another method of saving is transfers of assets during lifetime through gifting. Gifts reduce one's taxable estate for purposes of computing the Federal Estate Tax and State Inheritance Tax.

However, a sweeping change in the Federal Gift Tax Law effective December 31, 1976, makes gifting of assets somewhat less attractive. Under the old law there were three basic exemptions:

1. **The $3,000 annual exclusion**
2. **The $30,000 lifetime exemption**
3. **The Gift Tax Marital deduction**

Under the new laws the $3,000 annual exemption is still available, but there has now been introduced a single, unified tax rate schedule to be applied to both lifetime gifts as well as testamentary transfers by will or trust (see Unified Tax Table in Appendix).

The $3,000 annual exclusion gives one the opportunity to gift to any number of people $3,000 without incurring any gift tax. The common misconception is that this exclusion applies only to gifts to family members. Actually, it applies to any transfers from one person to another. For example, the annual exclusion means that if I wanted to, or had the ability to make a gift of $3,000 to every person reading this book, I could do this every year and not pay any gift tax. One must remember that the gift tax, if any, is on the donor, the person making the gift, and not the donee, the person receiving the gift. Furthermore, there is no income tax on the amount of the gift received by the donee. Conversely, it is also not an income tax deduction for the person making the gift. Gifts are made with after income-tax dollars or other real or personal property and in most cases they are motivated by a desire to reduce one's Federal Taxable Estate or State Inheritance Tax.

In addition to my $3,000 annual exclusion my wife also has her own $3,000 exclusion. Under the provisions of the Federal Gift Tax law she may allow me to make use of her $3,000 annual exclusion and therefore make me capable of gifting $6,000 each to as many people as I wish. It is also important to remember that this is an annual exclusion, and revives itself each year indefinitely.

The 1978 Act provides that in computing the consenting spouse's estate tax, such gifts are excludable in determining the amount of gifts made during her lifetime.

19

20

The $30,000 lifetime exemption is specifically repealed under the new tax law and in its place there has been instituted a credit against taxes due on gifts. Ultimately the credit will be $47,000, but it is to be phased in as follows:

After December 31, 1976, and before July 1, 1977	$ 6,000
After June 30, 1977, and before January 1, 1978	30,000
After December 31, 1977, and before January 1, 1979	34,000
After December 31, 1978, and before January 1, 1980	38,000
After December 31, 1979, and before January 1, 1981	42,500
After January 1, 1981	47,000

The gift tax marital deduction which formerly was defined as one-half of the value of any gift made from one spouse to another has now been increased. Under the new law, a spouse will be allowed a marital deduction of $100,000 plus 50% of any gifts over $200,000. The $100,000 gap between the first part of the new marital deduction and the $200,000 will be taxed under the new unified gift tax schedule. Furthermore, the gift tax marital deduction will now be integrated with the estate tax marital deduction and any gifts will cause an adjustment downward in the estate tax marital deduction.

Gifts may be made with anything of value. Cash is by no means the only medium to use. Real estate or partial interests in real estate, stocks, bonds, life insurance, annuities, income from a trust, creation of a joint bank account and articles of personal value are just a few other examples of gifting. The forgiveness of a debt owed can also be a gift. It should also be noted that gifts of $3,000 or less will not be challenged as a gift made in contemplation of death under the new tax law.

If the gift is $3,000 or less there is no necessity to file a gift tax return. However, it is necessary to file a return for any gift over that amount even though you and your wife each are charged with only $3,000 of the gift. Under a recent change in the gift tax law, effective for gifts made after 1976, a gift tax return must be filed for the first quarter of the year during which the total cumulative taxable gifts made during the calendar year for which a return had not been filed exceed $25,000. If the total amount of taxable gifts made during the calendar year did not exceed $25,000, only one return will be necessary for the calendar year, rather than separate quarterly returns.

In order to more clearly see the impact of the gift tax exclusions and exemptions, let's assume a husband makes a $150,000 gift to his wife. Let's first deduct $100,000, the marital deduction, which than leaves a balance of $50,000 taxable. Now subtract the annual exclusion of $3,000 to reduce the taxable gift to $47,000. Now assuming there have been no prior taxable gifts made, the gift tax on $47,000 will be $9,880. This computation is arrived at by consulting the Unified Rate Schedule for Estate and Gift Taxes in the Appendix. Of course, this tax could be eliminated by applying a portion of the phased in tax credit of $47,000 as shown in the Appendix. The use of a portion of this credit would then reduce the credit when applied to the Federal Estate Tax payable at the husband's death.

GIFT TO SPOUSE (ASSUMES NO PRIOR GIFTS)

Value of Property Given	$150,000
Marital Deduction (Tax Free)	$100,000
Taxable Balance	$ 50,000
Annual Exclusion .... $3,000.	
Subject to Tax	$ 47,000
Tax	$ 9,880

For purposes of computing the gift tax, the donor, the person making the gift, must compute tax on all gifts made since June 6, 1932 including those gifts made in the current year and then compute the tax on all taxable gifts except the current year. The difference between these two figures would be the current gift tax due. In other words, a person's taxable gift rate will be greatly affected by the amount of net taxable gifts made in prior years. The sought-after objective of the Federal Government is to make continuing gifts subject to progressively higher gift taxes.

Let's take another example of a husband and wife wishing to make maximum gifts to their four children. You will recall that both parents have available to them the $3,000 annual exclusion. Gifts to children or to any third parties are taxed as if the husband and wife each made a gift of one-half the total gift.

Under this example each of the four children would receive $6,000 in gifts tax free by the combined use of the $3,000 annual exclusion for a total gift by the parents of $24,000. Under this arrangement each child would receive $6,000.

the change in the law makes all transfers subject to the same tax rate.

Husband	**Wife**
$12,000 ($3,000 x 4 children)	$12,000 ($3,000 x 4 children)

Total Tax Free Gift $24,000

It should be remembered that a corporation may not make a gift and to the extent it attempts to do so is really declaring a dividend. For example, a father may not gift stock to his son but retain the dividends for his use. Any attempt to do so would make the value of the stock taxable in the father's estate at the time of his death.

Corporate charitable gifts are permissable.

A word should be directed to those husbands and wives living in so-called community property states. Community property is owned equally by each spouse and when a gift is made by one spouse it is as if each made a gift of one-half the object gifted. Also, anytime a gift is made to a spouse only one-half the value is considered transferred, for tax purposes.

A word of caution before everyone runs out and begins making gifts to his or her spouse. It may not be the best thing to do in all circumstances. You will recall in our earlier discussion of the estate tax marital deduction we said that the first $250,000 of the adjusted gross estate or one-half the adjusted gross estate of the first spouse to pass away would pass free of Federal Estate Tax. So, if we make the $150,000 gift as shown in the gift to spouse illustration, and left the $150,000 in the estate, the entire amount would have passed tax free under the Marital Deduction anyway. Do not make gifts in a vacuum. Check all the circumstances of your estate. Weigh each move before you make it. Many times, unfortunately, people will over use the gift method of attempting to reduce their estate only to regret their actions at a later time.

As we've already discussed, one of the motives for making gifts is that the estate is reduced for the payment of Federal Estate Tax purposes, to the extent that the $3,000 annual exclusion and the gift tax Marital Deduction has been used. However, Uncle Sam has a little hook in this apparent give-away. He says that if you die within three years of the making of a gift he will automatically include the value of the gift in your estate. Nobody is going to physically take the gift back from a donee, but the dollar amount will be put into the estate to compute the Federal Estate Tax just as if no gift had been made. Furthermore, in determining the amount of your gross estate, the gift taxes paid in connection with these gifts will be included in your estate for Federal Estate Tax computations.

Let me give you an example of an unusual gifting program involving a closely-held corporation. The company is a manufacturer in the clothing business. The only stock holders are the father and son. Over the years the father, who presently maintains a major stock interest in the corporation, has been gifting stock to his son within the allowable gift tax exemptions. The motivation on the part of the father for these gifts is the desire to keep his son interested in the business and give him an incentive to work harder. A by-product of course, is the reduction of the father's estate for Federal Estate Tax and State Inheritance Tax purposes. If the stock is dividend paying, it could also mean a reduction in income tax.

Recently consideration has been given by the father to a very substantial gift of stock to the son. The motivation is the father's desire to take a much less active part in the management of the business. The father also recognizes that the son has demonstrated a keen aptitude for the successful management of the business. The contemplated gift would cause the payment of a very substantial gift tax but it will save a substantial amount in the State Inheritance Taxes.

This is an excellent example of the tax savings possible through gifting.

There are other problems associated with gifting. Some estate planners will argue that the prospective savings in Federal Estate Taxes can be seriously diminished by the loss of earning capacity of the large amount of gift taxes paid in any substantial transfer. Their argument is that the dollars used in paying the gift tax put at interest could earn a substantial amount between now and the donor's death, or conversely, since the large gift tax is paid now, the loss in earning power could be so substantial it would significantly diminish the savings in Federal Estate Taxes. I'm sure in some cases this might happen. The point earlier made is again illustrated: Nothing can be done without first examining the consequences of the gift.

SPECIAL PROBLEMS IN GIFTING LIFE INSURANCE

Life insurance is historically a major area considered as an asset used for gifting, and is perhaps the most well-known subject for a gift. The reason for its notoriety is probably the vast marketing effort of the life insurance industry in the general area of estate planning and the specific area of transfer of ownership of insurance policies.

There are two different ways to gift life insurance. The first is to have someone purchase a life insurance policy on his life where the beneficiary is someone other than his estate and he retains no reversionary interest in it himself, nor does his estate. The second method would be to transfer a policy already purchased, including the cash surrender value in the policy again without retaining any reversionary interest. If in either of the above-described examples he continues to pay the premium on the policy he will be considered to have made a gift to the extent of the premium.

The usual and more basic of insurance policy gifts is the transfer of an ordinary existing Whole Life insurance policy. Assuming that the cash surrender value of the policy is $2,500 the transfer to a spouse will neither incur a gift tax nor the necessity of filing a gift tax return since the amount of the gift is less than $3,000. It should be noted that the cash surrender value of a policy is not the amount of premiums paid under the policy, but is the amount which the insurance company will return to the owner of the policy should he desire to cancel the policy. Premiums for the policy must be paid by the new owner from an independent source of income. In my experience I have found a number of individuals who followed the advice of their insurance agents and transferred their life insurance policy or policies to their spouse. However, they either continued to pay the insurance premiums out of their own checking account or are under the mistaken impression that as long as their wife signs the check for the premium payment out of their joint checking account they had effectively transferred the policy.

A problem which is most often presented is that the wife does not have any independent source of income. In order to provide the necessary funds for the premium payment it will probably be necessary to have the husband transfer assets to the wife by way of gift during the year, preferably not coincident with the date of premium payment. Although the issue of what constitutes the effective transfer of insurance policies remains, the foregoing method would appear to be the best under existing federal court decisions.

Thus far our discussion of gifting of life insurance policies has dealt only with the assignment of personal life insurance policies. However, the controversy is even more volatile in the area of the attempted transfer of group insurance policies, though not for gift tax reasons. Many individuals are covered by group insurance policies. These policies are term insurance because they have no cash surrender value nor will they ever acquire any. The individual is covered under the policy as long as he is in the employ of the company and upon his termination of employment the insurance usually ceases except in cases of retirement where the coverage usually decreases over a period of years to a percentage usually equal to 50% of the coverage while the individual was employed. In many instances group insurance may be a substantial portion of one's estate. In some group programs it can be as much as three and one-half times annual salary, although in most instances coverage amounts to one and one-half to two times salary.

In any event, the transfer of group insurance was somewhat impeded because many states had no laws either approving or prohibiting transfer of such policies. Unlike the usual policy of whole life, there are no gift tax consequences because the policies have no cash surrender value.

Caution: rules on insurance taxation are complex.

An uncertain legal area.

OTHER GIFT PROBLEMS

Having already discussed the available gift tax exemption and exclusions, the next logical discussion should center around the income tax implications of making a gift. We have already noted that one of the accepted lifetime motives of making a gift is the lessening or total avoidance of paying income tax. I believe the illustration of this concept is best made by assuming a gift of stock, under the following example:

"A" purchases 100 shares of Divot International at $60 per share. This $60 per share price is his cost basis. He holds the stock for several years and then decides to gift 50 shares to his son. At the time that he transfers the stock its market value is $180 per share. For purposes of computing the value of the gift the stock is valued at $180 per share and the available exemptions and gift tax if any are applied using this value. The son receives the stock and does not sell it for a period of one year at which time he sells 25 shares at $200 per share. As in any sale of stock held for more than a twelve-month period the tax will be assessed at a capital gains rate on the difference between the cost basis of the stock and the selling price.

The key question is what is the son's basis for purposes of computing his tax? Some, I am sure, will look to the value of the stock per share at the time he received it, namely $180 per share. Wrong. For income tax purposes the son acquired the father's cost basis of $60 at the time the gift was made, thus the son's capital gains tax will be paid on the difference between his $60 cost basis and the $200 selling price or on a profit per share of $140.

A major change in capital gains tax has been enacted under the Revenue Act of 1978. Now only 40% of the gain will be taxed rather than 50%.

One little known nuance of gift giving involving income tax consequences is the gifting of Government Savings Bonds. At the time of transfer the donor is liable for the income tax on these bonds just as if he had redeemed the bonds. Reissue of the bonds in the donee's name requires that the donor report at the time of the transfer the interest that is accrued or not yet reported. The income tax liability of the donee is limited to the interest accruing on the bond after the date of transfer.

An area of so-called "unintentional" gifts is worth mentioning. The joint savings account can cause gift tax problems. The usual circumstance surrounding the establishment of a joint account is that, although it is in joint names coupled with the right of survivorship, it is usually funded with the husband's earnings. Under this account, however, both husband and wife are in a position to withdraw funds. The Federal Government has taken the position that although both names are on the account no gift is made by the husband when he makes deposits to the account. However, the government's position is that when the wife withdraws funds from the account for her use a gift taxable event occurs. Naturally, there won't be any gift tax liability as long as the amount of the withdrawal falls within the allowable exclusion and gift tax marital deduction.

WHEN NOT TO MAKE A GIFT

Unfortunately some people are bedazzled by the possibility of savings in taxes and they torture their objectives to save taxes. I have seen some cases where parents who could ill afford to make a substantial gift to their children make such gifts only to regret the move later. One example of such a situation was the couple whose total assets were approximately $200,000. They were retired and living on social security and a small pension from the husband's former employer. The buying power of the pension had grown smaller of late because of the ravages of inflation. They had been advised by friends and also through articles in periodicals of the available gift tax exemptions. The couple had two children who were in the throes of raising a family and about to embark upon the great American dream, the purchase of their first home. The parents decided that they would help the children along by making a gift of $30,000, $15,000 each to the children to help with the purchase of the home. This left them an estate of approximately $170,000, some of which was not income-producing.

As time went on, the portion of the estate which was income-producing began to decline in a bear market and hasty decisions on changes in investments reduced the income of the couple still more. It became apparent that they sorely needed the $30,000 which they had impulsively gifted away. The children could have better afforded to struggle because their incomes were likely to rise with the inflationary economy whereas the retired couple were in a fixed income situation, living on a pension and social security.

Another example was a man who decided to use a portion of his gift tax marital deduction to establish a $60,000 irrevocable trust. Under the terms of the trust the income was payable to the man's wife during her lifetime and upon her death the trust terminated and the trust assets were divided among the children of the marriage. This result would occur although the husband could very well outlive the wife. During their joint lives the husband was not really relinquishing a great deal because presumptively he could share in the income his wife was receiving from the trust. However, at her death he would lose this source of income.

When the gift was made both husband and wife were very enthusiastic about it. However, after the realization by the husband that at his wife's death he would no longer have the income he began to demonstrate an inordinate concern over every word in the trust agreement. He began to realize that he had completely lost control over these assets and now is obviously very unhappy over having made the gift. I have purposely not indicated the size of this man's estate. I wanted to illustrate the point that no matter the size of an estate the donor should be comfortable with the gift, otherwise he should not make the transfer. He had an estate of over $700,000.

Even where no gift tax consequences result, the problem of inter-spousal gifts must be viewed from another standpoint. With the advent of increasingly liberal divorce laws in the various states and the introduction of the concept of "equitable distribution" being introduced in the area of distribution of marital assets, the estate planner as well as the individual is well advised to look carefully into the idea of gifting. Over-gifting may cause one who is subsequently involved in marital discord to find himself on the short end of a property settlement. In some cases even where the situation does not deteriorate to the point of divorce, a husband (pardon my chauvinistic tendencies) may find that he no longer controls the financial destiny of his household.

All of the gifts discussed thus far have been from one adult to another. Somewhat different problems arise when gifts are made from adults to minors. The first problem is the legal definition of a minor. Because of recent legislation in the various states a minor may be an individual of either 21 years of age or 18 years of age. However, most of those states which have adopted the Uniform Gifts to Minors Act have retained the 21 age limit. The Act has been adopted to facilitate gifts to minors. The Act originally grew out of the inability of a minor to contract in his own name. The basic thrust of the law was to make an outright gift to a minor by using certain prescribed words of registration and at the same time reserve management of these gifts to a "custodian" until the minor reached the age of majority. Most registrations under the Act are as follows:

"Mary Doe, as custodian for James Doe, a minor under the New Jersey Uniform Gifts to Minors Act"

There are several parties to any gift under the Act. There is the donor, or maker of the gift, the donee, the minor child receiving the gift, and the custodian, the person who holds or manages the gift until the minor reaches the age of majority.

The consequence of the gift to the donor is that he has removed from his taxable estate the value of the gift forever because the gift is irrevocable. There is no limitation on the size of the gift under the Uniform Act statutes. The only limitations are posed by the Federal Gift Tax or the State Gift Tax if the state in question levies such a tax. Under the Act the donor must make the gift individually and it must be made during the donor's lifetime and not under his Will. The gift also may only be made by an adult since under the Act, minors lack capacity to make a gift.

Once the gift is made to the minor he holds it irrevocably. If the minor dies the custodianship ends and the custodial property must be paid over to the estate of the minor.

Among the responsibilities of the custodian is the necessity of holding the subject of the gift for the minor's benefit only. One example that comes to mind is the attempt by one custodian to secure a personal loan with stocks, which were registered in his name as custodian for the benefit of his minor son. Although strictly prohibited by the Act, I have personal knowledge of the fact that he was able to convince the bank loan officer that it was not a problem. Most states provide that the custodian of the gift may be the donor, an adult member of the minor's family, the guardian of the minor or a banking institution. However, one is cautioned to check the laws of his particular state before embarking on a gift to a minor.

The custodian under the Act is empowered to collect, hold, manage, invest and reinvest the custodial property making sure that the minor benefits from any interest or dividends derived from the investments. The support, maintenance and education of the minor are also legal reasons for the use of custodial property for the benefit of the minor.

At the minor's attaining majority the custodian must turn over the property held. The custodian is also duty bound during the administration of the property to properly register it as custodian, segregate the property from any other personal property of the custodian and to keep records of investment changes and income derived from the investments. With respect to the types of investment the custodian is saddled with the somewhat less than satisfactory "prudent man rule" which says that he must invest the custodial property as would a prudent man of discretion and intelligence who is seeking a reasonable income and the preservation of his capital (Section 4 of the Uniform Gifts to Minors Act). Although no set fees are listed in the Uniform Act, a custodian is entitled to a reasonable fee for his services but unlike an executor who has not been exculpated from the requirement, a custodian is not required to furnish a bond for the faithful performance of his duties. Should a custodian pass away during his administration, the guardian of the minor may become the successor custodian.

Besides the obvious estate tax benefits of the custodial gift, such a gift also allows the donor to shift income from his presumably high income tax bracket to the lower brackets of the minor. The parents of minors who receive income from a custodial gift continue to receive a tax exemption for each child regardless of the amount of custodial gift income as long as the parents can demonstrate that they contribute more than one half the child's support and he is under 19 years of age or a full-time student. However, the Internal Revenue Service has said that to the extent a custodian uses income to discharge a legal obligation to maintain a minor, the income will be taxable to the person who has the legal obligation.

It is important to remember in the case of a gift under the Uniform Gifts to Minors Act that in order to insure non-inclusion of the gift in the donor's estate he should not serve as custodian. Internal Revenue has reasoned that if the donor and custodian are one and the same person, he would be in a position to exercise an inordinate amount of control over the gift. Therefore, the Internal Revenue Service has ruled that the value of property transferred by a donor to himself as custodian for a minor under the Uniform Gift to Minors Act is includable in the donor's gross estate for Federal Estate Tax purposes in the event of the donor's death before the donee reaches majority.

If one lesson can be learned from the explanation of the gift tax and its exclusions, it is that gifts, if made, should be just part of a total unified program of estate planning and not made on impulse or in a vacuum.

DO'S AND DON'TS ON GIFTING

DO'S

—DO take advantage of a gift giving program to reduce Federal Estate taxes.

—DO remember that the gift tax is payable by the person making the gift, not the one receiving it.

—DO remember that any gift made within three years of one's date of death is automatically included in the decedent's estate for Estate Tax purposes, except a gift of $3,000 or less.

—DO remember that a unified phased in credit of $47,000 is available against gift taxes.

DON'TS

—DON'T make a gift unless you can afford it.

—DON'T forget that the $3,000 annual exclusion applies to anyone, not just family members.

—DON'T forget that gifts are made with after income tax dollars.

—DON'T make a gift in a vacuum; make sure the gift is part of an overall financial plan.

Chapter III

WHEN SHOULD YOU HAVE A TRUST?

Before being able to decide when to enter into a trust arrangement, one should have some idea of what a trust is all about. There are libraries full of books attempting to define a trust. However, I believe a short concise definition will be more helpful for our purposes. A trust is an arrangement whereby something of value is held by a person or persons for the benefit of another person or persons.

It is a trust when someone gives something of value to someone else and says, "take care of this for me." If this something of value produces an income the person "taking care of" this something of value is obligated to pay or distribute this income to the person who set up the trust.

The person who set up the trust is called the settlor or grantor and, more infrequently, the trustor. The settlor is the person who owns the "something of value." When he sets up a trust he turns over this "something of value" to the "trustee," the person who is charged with "taking care of" the something of value. When the "settlor" receives the income from the "trustee" he now has a new name, that of "beneficiary" of the trust.

Having assigned the proper labels to the components of the trust, let's proceed with the trust's functions. The settlor-beneficiary will receive the income during his lifetime; in anticipation of his death he may designate a new beneficiary under the terms of the trust to receive the income for this new beneficiary's life or for some stated period of years. Or the trust may provide that it terminates on the beneficiary's death and is to be distributed to various other people known as the "remaindermen."

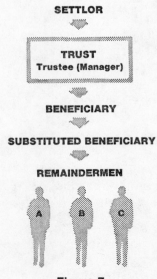

Figure 7

29

The trust that I have just explained is only one of several kinds of trusts. There are at least 21 different kinds of trusts and multitudinous variations on these basic categories. Before describing specifically some of these trusts, there are some basic general categories to explain. Trusts fall into one of two classes. They are either inter-vivos trusts, or so-called "living trusts," or they are testamentary trusts.

Living trusts, as the name implies, are entered into during the settlor's lifetime and are usually, although not always, for the settlor's benefit. During the settlor's lifetime he takes some portion of his assets, be they stocks, bonds, real estate, savings accounts, or any other thing of value, and establishes a trust. In order to establish such a trust, a document or agreement must be drawn by an attorney setting forth the various rights and obligations of the parties to the trust agreement. The agreement will appear fairly complex but only because the layman has little familiarity with this type of document

It will first state by whom the trust is being established and the date upon which it is being established. It will next describe the nature of the assets to be placed in trust or, in the alternative, refer to an annexed schedule to the trust agreement upon which the assets will be listed. The assets in the trust are variously described as the trust principal or the trust corpus. Following the description of assets instructions are given as to which person or persons are to receive the income produced by the trust assets. This paragraph also sets forth how frequently the income is to be paid, that is to say, monthly or quarterly. It is usually more convenient for the income beneficiary to receive the payments on a monthly basis; however since most trusts are funded by stocks and dividends are usually paid quarterly, it is easier for the trustee to distribute the income on a quarterly basis

Following the direction to the trustee regarding income, the trustee is usually given the power to invade the principal or corpus of the trust for the benefit of the beneficiary according to some standard. The usual wording used is "such amounts of principal as the trustee may deem advisable to provide adequately for support, maintenance, and welfare."

The trust then usually provides that the settlor has the power to add property to it. But this addition cannot usually be made without the trustee's approval, since the trustee may find that his obligations as trustee would increase if certain kinds of assets were to be added to the trust corpus. For example, addition of a multi-family dwelling requiring collection of rents, maintenance and insurance would increase the duties of the trustee. In addition this paragraph will also give the settlor the right to withdraw corpus.

The next paragraph will provide for the event or time when the trust will terminate and spell out who the ultimate beneficiaries (remainderman) will be. In some cases there will be partial distributions of trust principal as each beneficiary reaches a certain age. For example, one-third of the trust principal distributed as each beneficiary or remainderman reaches age 25, one-half the balance at age 30 and the balance at age 35.

The remainder of the trust agreement will deal with the powers that the trustee may exercise with respect to the administration of the trust. These powers will include the power over the investments made by the trust. State law will usually provide certain limitations over the investment powers of a trustee in order to insure a conservative investment approach. However, most corporate trustees will request that they be relieved from these restrictions on the theory that the corporate trustee is more experienced than an individual trustee and therefore should be given greater flexibility insofar as investments are concerned. The layman will note that many of the powers set forth are not specifically applicable to his situation. This should not be a matter of concern, rather it should be recognized as a further insurance against some event occurring during the administration of the trust, which is not covered by the powers granted to the trustee.

Many times these miscellaneous powers will include powers to vote proxies, to exercise or sell any rights of subscription to stock or to take any action regarding any reorganization, merger, consolidation, bankruptcy or any other proceeding affecting any stock held by the trustee.

Another power almost always given to the trustee is to hold investments "in the name of a nominee." This term often causes great confusion and only applies to a situation where the trustee is a corporate trustee. Nominee registration is the use of a fictitious partnership used to register securities held by a bank trust department. It is basically a method to facilitate bookkeeping in a trust department. For example, suppose the regular quarterly dividend is to be paid on a particular stock and suppose further that this stock is held by 50 different trusts in the trust department. Rather than having 50 different checks coming to the department for distribution to the various trusts, the use of a nominee will cause the corporation to issue one check in the nominee's name; then the trust department will in turn divide the proceeds of this dividend check among the 50 trusts holding that particular stock.

Somewhere in the trust agreement the fees of the trustee will be spelled out. This is accomplished either by referring to the particular state statute covering trustee's fees or by spelling out specifically the trustee's fees or by referring to a separate agreement under which the fees will be spelled out.

The trust will usually also provide for a paragraph covering revocation and amendment of the trust and spell out a specific procedure in order to accomplish either. With respect to an amendment to a trust, it must usually be accomplished with the same formalities with which the trust was originally executed, that is, signatures by the settlor and trustee and the signatures of witnesses of these signatures.

A provision is also set forth under which the trustee is allowed to resign. This must usually be done in writing and a period of time between the notice and effective date of the resignation is also usually provided. Naturally, provisions are also included for the appointment of a successor trustee in the event the trustee resigns. One should be aware of the fact that in the event a corporate trustee is named in a trust agreement that the courts will usually require that only another corporate trustee may take its place. Also, whenever a trustee is removed or resigns an accounting must be prepared. The accounting must be approved by all the interested parties or sometimes the court in a formal proceeding.

The trustee is also accountable to the settlor of the trust by way of some kind of periodic accounting, either informally or by a formal accounting with court approval. There is also a statement within the body of the trust agreement as to which state laws will govern the construction and administration of the trust. The trust is then signed by the settlor and the trustee and their signatures witnessed. In some states a more formal execution including the execution of an acknowledgment by a notary public is required, usually when the trust holds real property, in order that the instrument might be recorded.

The foregoing is the anatomy of an average trust agreement of the living trust variety.

Testamentary trusts on the other hand, as the name implies, are part of a person's Last Will and testament. They therefore do not become operable until such time as the settlor passes away. An individual may provide that at his demise, after the payment of his debts, expenses of the administration of his estate and Federal Estate Taxes and State Inheritance Taxes, the remainder of his estate be placed in a testamentary trust. The same basic ingredients insofar as the selection of clauses in the trust will be used as in the living trust example just described. Naturally the settlor will not receive any income from the trust since his death will be the event which establishes the trust. The testamentary trust allows the settlor to continue to deal with his property during his lifetime without restriction. The mere fact that the trust has been set up under his Will in no way affects his management of the assets during his lifetime.

I have found that one of the major reasons some people fear trusts is that the attorney or trust officer has failed to adequately explain to the client what the nature of a trust is and how it will help the client to reach his specific objective. Another major factor has been the establishment in years past of very inflexible trusts which the trustees were powerless to change. One such trust that comes to mind is one in which the settlor specifically instructed that his holdings in Pennsylvania Railroad stock not be sold under any circumstances. Under this direction the trustee could do nothing except watch in horror as the stock plummeted downward. Other mistakes have included limiting a particular beneficiary to the income alone of the trust. This mistake occurred because the settlor had little appreciation of our inflationary economy and believed that the income from the trust would always be sufficient for the beneficiary's needs when, in fact, a time came when it was not. This unfortunate situation could have been eliminated by simply giving the trustee the discretionary power to invade the principal of the trust if needed.

REVOCABLE AND IRREVOCABLE TRUSTS

Thus far I have discussed two major categories of trusts, namely living trusts and testamentary trusts. Another major division among trusts is the irrevocable trust versus the revocable trust.

The revocable trust is really the kind previously explained in detail. It allows the settlor to set up the trust and later revoke it either partially or totally as he sees fit. A partial revocation of a trust occurs whenever any portion of the principal or corpus of the trust is withdrawn from the trustee's control. A revocable trust is usually set up because the settlor either wishes to be relieved of the responsibility of managing his assets or because he believes that his judgment has been poor in managing his assets and wishes to seek expert advice in the form of a bank's trust department or investment counsellor to manage his funds. A living trust has also gained much favor in retirement communities where individuals not only wish to be relieved of

There are differences in the tax treatment of revocable and irrevocable trusts.

their investment and management responsibilities but also wish to take care of the contingency that they might become incapable of managing their own affairs as a result of ill health, either physical or mental.

A variation of a revocable trust is the so-called convertible trust or stand-by trust which has been used most effectively by senior citizens. This trust works in the following manner. The trust, like any other trust, is initiated by an attorney preparing a legal document setting forth the provisions of the trust. The trust assets are delivered to the trustee, but the settlor reserves the power to handle the investments himself. The trustee's major function at this point is one of bookkeeping. He collects the dividends and periodically sends the income to the income beneficiary. In the event the settlor wishes the trustee to assume more control, he may exercise his right to do this by notifying the trustee that he is relinquishing his investment power.

The trust will also contain clauses setting up a committee to be made up of the settlor's physician, attorney and a close friend to act as a body to determine whether the settlor is in good mental health and capable of continuing to control the investments of the trust. If their decision is that the settlor is not, the committee will turn over the investment powers to the trustee. This committee's decision is not by any means a legal adjudication of the settlor's mental competence; however, under circumstances where the settlor may be mentally incompetent, it does obviate the necessity and attendant cost of a judicial proceeding to remove the investment control from the settlor.

Although at first blush this kind of trust may appear to solve a multitide of problems, its application as a practical matter is not that easy. First of all many people would be reluctant to serve on such a committee considering the awesome power they would have and also the criticism that they might open themselves to if the settlor or his friends disagreed with their decision. Secondly, the unanimous agreement of the three committee members, which is the usual requisite for this type of committee, may be difficult or impossible to obtain.

Revocable trusts are any trusts which the settlor has the power to alter, amend or discontinue totally.

The irrevocable trust is one where the settlor relinquishes all incidents of ownership over the principal of the trust and its management. What is incidents of ownership? Well, in the eyes of the Internal Revenue Service it is a reservation of any power over the asset retained by the person placing the asset in the irrevocable trust, no matter how slight. Every irrevocable trust involves a gift. Whether or not the gift is taxable will depend on the amount of the gift and also the recipient of the gift. As previously discussed in the chapter on gifts, a gift may be an outright transfer or it may be made in trust. Both of these types of gifts are subject to the $3,000 annual exclusion and, if applicable, the gift tax marital deduction. If the gift is made to charity, however, there would be no taxable gift since there is a specific provision under the gift tax law which provides such gifts are exempt from the gift tax.

One of the primary motives for the establishment of an irrevocable trust under Federal Estate Tax Law before December 31, 1976 was savings in Federal Estate Tax. This is no longer true since a transfer of assets either by gift or will is taxed at the same unified tax rate. Another reason, however, which still holds true under the Tax Reform Act of 1976 is that the donor is afforded some measure of control over the beneficiary's use of the gift.

Perhaps the situation is best illustrated by the following example: A father, age 50, has a substantial estate and would like to gift a portion of it to his son. He is, however, concerned as to whether his son is capable of handling an outright gift of a substantial amount. He has reached this conclusion because his son has demonstrated, at least in the father's judgment, a certain instability in the management of his personal finances. The father is also concerned about what he believes to be his daughter-in-law's spendthrift nature and her apparent control over his son's finances. Notwithstanding these circumstances, he wishes to make a substantial gift.

Through the use of an irrevocable trust he can accomplish his objective of providing a good measure of control over the gift by empowering the trustee of this irrevocable trust to pay only the income to his son and allow invasions into the principal of the trust in the sole discretion of the trustee in accordance with a well-defined standard spelled out in the trust agreement. You may ask what kind of standard. Well, how about a specified percentage over his yearly income? Or for emergency medical expenses or college expenses of any grandchildren?

There are innumerable very sound and well-defined standards which could be applied by the trustee to prevent the total dissipation by the son of the gift. The trust could provide that over a period of time all or portion of the trust assets be turned over to him by the trustee like slices of apple pie. Or the trust could remain in existence for the entire life of the son, terminate at his death and be divided among his grandchildren. The irrevocable trust offers a multitude of choices.

CLIFFORD TRUST

Unlike the revocable trust, the settlor may not continue to receive the income from the trust when the beneficiary is a non-charitable organization. There have been innumerable individuals who have come to me all prepared to enter into an irrevocable trust to gain the previously-mentioned tax benefits. However, they were shocked when they discovered they could not receive the income from the trust, unless the beneficiary is a charitable organization.

The kinds of trusts which have been discussed thus far have either provided money management or Federal Estate Tax savings or both. There is one kind of trust, however, whose primary objective is income tax savings. This kind of trust has been variously named a Clifford Trust, a short-term trust, or a ten-year terminable trust. Its primary objective is income tax savings. It works something like this. An individual in a high income tax bracket has more income than required for his personal needs. However, he does have a large expense coming soon in the form of college expense for his two children. The solution to his problem lies in setting up a trust funded with some income producing property. The income from the trust will be directed to be paid to his two children for a period of ten years and one day. The children are taxable on this income at their income tax levels which are presumably much lower than their father. Any sales of stock in the trust resulting in capital gains are taxable to the father who established the trust, or if the father dies during the term of the trust, the capital gains are taxable to the father's estate.

NOTES

A highly technical area which should be approached with caution.

There are some gift tax consequences regarding this type of trust but they are limited to the commuted value of the income from the trust for the trust term. "Commuted value" merely means a projected or estimated income for the trust during its term. At the end of the ten-year period the trust terminates and its entire principal is returned to the father. Furthermore, in the event the father passes away during the trust term the value of the reversion is included in his estate for Federal Estate Tax purposes. The "reversion" is defined as the value of the trust's assets less the actuarial value of the income interest yet to be paid for the duration of the trust at the father's death.

The children use the income from this trust to discharge the expense of their college education thereby saving their father considerable cash outlay. For the entire ten-year period the father has not paid income tax on the trust income. However, at the end of the term the assets of the trust return to him at a time when presumably his income tax bracket may be lower than when the trust was established. He has succeeded in paying for his children's education using dollars out of which much less was taken in tax rather than dollars of his income which were paying a high rate of tax.

It should be understood that the ten years is a minimum number of years for the trust to be in existence. If one wishes to establish the trust for a longer period of time this may be done without any problem. However, the entire amount to be placed in trust must be done at one time because each time any additions are made to the trust this is tantamount to the creation of a new short-term trust which much meet the ten-year requirement in order to receive the favorable income tax benefits.

OTHER TYPES OF TRUST

There are many other trusts and variations of basic types all designed to meet the specific objectives of the grantor and beneficiaries. Some of those are as follows:

1. A father wishes to give a substantial gift to his son but is not totally convinced that his son has demonstrated the necessary maturity to handle such a gift. Therefore, the father establishes a trust irrevocably with the income payable to his son and distribution of the principal of the trust in the following manner: one-third of the principal when the son attains 21 years of age, one-half the balance at age 25 years and the balance of the trust at age 30 years. If the son passes away before the trust terminates, the trust provides that the assets are divided among his children.

The father as grantor has retained certain powers over the trust in order to make it more flexible. He has reserved the right to direct the trustee to withhold any income payments to the son until he reaches 21 years of age and also controls any invasion of the principal of the trust during its term. The income in this trust is taxable to the son. A gift of the principal has been made by the father and a gift tax would be assessed after deducting any applicable gift tax deductions.

2. An alumnus of Fandango University wishes to remember his school with a charitable gift. After talking to the school alumnae gift-giving chairman, the following plan is devised. Mr. X will establish a trust into which he will place common stocks which have a very low cost basis because they were

Provides income and estate tax savings.

purchased by him many years ago, but which are worth substantially more now. The income from these stocks in the trust will continue to be paid to Mr. X during his lifetime. At Mr. X's death the trust will terminate and the principal will be paid over to Fandango University.

In order to receive maximum income and gift tax benefits, the trust will provide that the income from the trust will equal a minimum of 5% of the net fair market value of the trust's assets as redetermined each year on a set valuation date. Or, in the alternative, the trust could provide an income of 5% on the amount initially placed in trust. The former is a uni-trust and the latter is an annuity trust.

In either event the donor of the charitable gift will be entitled to an income tax deduction for the gift.

By establishing this type of trust Mr. X accomplished three objectives. First, he benefited his alma mater. Second, he reduced income taxes. And third, he reduced estate taxes to the extent of the value of the charitable remainder.

3. As a result of a divorce and in lieu of monthly alimony payments or a lump sum settlement, an alimony trust may be used. It is created by the husband for the benefit of his divorced spouse. All of the income from the trust is payable to the former wife. The trust will provide that the payments are not to be less than a fixed sum, usually a percentage of the fair market value of the initial amount placed in trust. If the income does not produce this fixed payment, provision is made to invade the principal of the trust to make up the difference.

This type of trust is most advantageous from the wife's standpoint in two ways. First of all the husband's obligation to pay alimony usually ends at his death and secondly, the wife does not have to rely or be subject to the vagaries of her former husband's employment income or business or professional income.

One objection to the use of trusts is the fact that their complexity requires that they be prepared by an attorney, with the consequent legal fees payable for their establishment. One of the viable alternatives to the establishment of a trust, at least in the area of gifts to minors, is the use of the Uniform Gifts to Minors Act. A great majority of the states have adopted this uniform piece of legislation which allows the gifting of assets to a minor in a form similar to a trust but without the necessity of a formal agreement or the cost involved for the preparation of the agreement. Under the Uniform Gifts to Minors Act a type of trust is established by merely opening a savings account with the following registration: Fred Frame as Custodian for Jane Frame under the State Uniform Gifts to Minors Act.

This is not the only way to establish a gift. The Uniform Act sets forth the several kinds of assets which can be the subject of Uniform Gifts Act. Among these are stocks, bonds and life insurance, in some states. While a formal trust arrangement may specify the date of the termination of the trust, the Minors Act uniformly terminates the so-called trust at the age of majority. This, however, has been less clear since some states have lowered the age of majority from age 21 to age 18. Most states, like New Jersey, have retained age 21 for the termination of a gift under the Uniform Gifts to Minors Act although the general age of majority has been lowered to age 18 by recent legislation.

Another method of establishing a trust-like arrangement but limited to savings accounts is the establishment of the so-called "in trust for" savings account. This type of account is also sometimes referred to as a Totten Trust. The arrangement is established merely by opening an account in a savings bank, savings institution or commercial bank with the following registration: Fred Frame In Trust For Jane Frame. The consequences of this registration are as follows: first, a trust without benefit of a formal trust agreement has been established. The settlor, the person establishing the account has set up a revocable trust. Therefore, he has the ability to withdraw any or all the assets in the trust at will. By the same token any additions may be made to the trust account by a simple deposit. During the lifetime of the settlor the beneficiary may not, nor does he have the legal right, to invade the principal of the trust account or to receive any of the income or interest paid on the savings trust account. The interest of the beneficiary does not bear fruition until such time as the settlor passes away. During the settlor's lifetime the income from the trust account is taxable to the settlor on the theory that he has complete control over the account during his lifetime and the beneficiary has no vested interest in the account. Further, since he does exercise this total control the trust would be taxable as part of the settlor's estate at his death.

To review, trusts fall into two major categories—Living or Inter-Vivos and Testamentary. There are two other important divisions, that of Revocable and Irrevocable. Trusts can be as flexible as one desires. The objectives served by trusts are either money management or tax savings or both. There are beside these general objectives some special purpose trusts such as charitable trusts and alimony trusts. The alternative to formal trusts are the Uniform Gifts to Minors Act accounts and the "in trust for" or so-called Totten Trust accounts.

NOTES

Note the difference between a Uniform Gift Account and an "in trust for" account.

Chapter IV

TYPES OF ASSET OWNERSHIP AND TAX CONSEQUENCES

The taxability or non-taxability of any asset for Federal Estate Tax purposes or State Inheritance Tax depends upon ownership. If an asset is held in a person's individual name at the time of his death it clearly is taxable as part of his estate. It is interesting to note that the great majority of assets held by people in the United States is not in individual names.

If you reviewed your assets from the standpoint of ownership you would find a very small percentage standing in individual ownership. Your home, for example, is probably owned jointly with your wife. This can be easily checked by referring to the deed which you received when you bought the property. If both your names appear on the deed chances are you own it jointly. The great majority of Saving Accounts are probably jointly held as well. In my experience, the only asset which more often than not is found under individual ownership is one's automobile.

INDIVIDUAL OWNERSHIP

What constitutes individual ownership? As the label implies, it is ownership by one person without any conditions or interests held by other parties. For purposes of the Federal Estate Tax all assets which are held individually are taxable at their fair market value as of the person's date of death or alternatively the fair market value computed six months from the date of death. The executor has the option to select whichever value is lower, for purposes of computing the Federal Estate Tax.

Viewing the asset from an income tax point of view, all the income derived from the asset is taxed solely to the person in whose name the asset is registered.

JOINT OWNERSHIP

There are various types of joint ownership. Before discussing the various types why not first ask the question, "Why joint ownership?" There's not much question that joint ownership is the most popular form of ownership between husband and wife; but why? It is unquestionably the easiest method of transferring the ownership of an asset from one person to another at the time of the death of one of the joint owners. Because of this ease of transfer, joint ownership gained much popularity. Furthermore, the maze of the probate practice which has been criticized as being both complicated and expensive, encourages people to hold assets in joint registration. In many situations people have used the joint ownership vehicle as a substitute for a will, sometimes a very poor substitute. Relying on joint ownership usually creates more problems than it solves. Take the following example:

A husband and wife own the great majority of their property in joint names with the right of survivorship. While driving home from a party one evening they are involved in a car accident killing both of them instantly. Neither of them had bothered to make a will. Their property, therefore, passed to their children under the laws of intestacy of the state in which they died residents. Since the children were minors and no guardians had been appointed by their deceased parents under a will, the court was obligated to appoint a guardian to manage the children's inherited estate until they reached their majority. A guardian in most states will be severely restricted as to the kinds of investments he may make, which can sometimes work a hardship on the children. Furthermore, any major invasion of these funds for the children's benefit will probably require a court order and the consequent legal expenses involved in obtaining the order. Remember, all these expenses come out of the children's share in the estate.

Furthermore, and in some cases more importantly, joint ownership can be very expensive from a Federal Estate Tax standpoint. Under prior law, the Government took the position that the first joint owner to die was taxed on the total value of the jointly-held asset. The law now provides that for estates of decedent's dying after December 31, 1976, where property is owned jointly by husband and wife with rights of survivorship and this joint ownership was created by a transfer subject to gift tax, after December 31, 1976 only 50% of the jointly-held property will be taxed in the decedent's estate.

There are other circumstances in which joint ownership may completely negate a person's intention as to who shall receive his estate. Assume the following set of facts:

"C" and "D" are married and have no children. All their assets were held in joint name. They had agreed that at the death of the survivor of them that "C's" relative would receive their entire estate because he was in the greatest need of assistance. While on a trip to the Caribbean their plane crashed. "D" was the sole survivor of the crash but passed away in the ambulance on the way to the hospital. Technically she had survived her husband, "C," and therefore received his entire estate. Unfortunately, although she had agreed to change her Will to leave her estate to "C's" relative, she had never gotten around to changing it and under her present Will she left her entire estate to her relatives.

This example illustrates the problem that the heirs of the first joint owner to die can be cut off from sharing any of the assets in his estate. However, where the deaths are simultaneous, some states have adopted a Uniform Simultaneous Death Act which provides that where it is impossible to determine who died first, half the jointly held assets are divided among the husband's heirs and the other half to the wife's heirs.

Perhaps the most common form of investment is the savings account. Yet the lack of understanding regarding the significance of how a savings account is registered is unparalleled. Unfortunately, this ignorance is shared not only by banking customers but also by the bank employees. This reference to banking employees is not limited to the teller or platform assistants. In some cases I have noted senior officers who lack any understanding regarding the significance of a savings account registration.

Revenue Act of 1978 provides that there is no necessity to destroy and then recreate a joint tenancy in order to receive the benefits of the qualified "joint interest rule". You need only to file an appropriate gift tax return covering the gift made in 1979.

Most individuals, including bank employees, are aware of the various registrations available for savings accounts. Few, however, understand the legal, Federal Estate Tax, Federal Income Tax and sometimes State Inheritance Tax consequences of a given registration.

The most common registration is the "joint account with the right of survivorship." Most of these accounts are opened by husband and wife on the theory that such an account will afford either of them easy access to the account in time of emergency, such as sickness or incapacity on the part of one of them. This is true, but the problem created is that upon the death of one of the joint owners, the Federal Estate Tax will be applied to the total account unless the account was created by a transfer subject to the gift tax Under these circumstances only 50% of the account will be taxed in the estate of the first joint owner to die where the account was created after December 31, 1976. Few people realize that it would probably be better for a husband and wife to have separate individual accounts, rather than a joint one.

One might argue that this would destroy the advantage of easy access to the entire amounts in both accounts by one of the spouses. This is not true, because by the simple measure of each spouse executing a power of attorney over the other's account, the problem of easy access is solved. What is a power of attorney? Well, it is merely a statement signed by the person in whose name the savings account is registered allowing or authorizing another person to withdraw funds from the account. This power to withdraw may be merely for convenience or it can be looking ahead to a time when the person in whose name the account is registered is ill, incompetent or incapacitated in some way so as to make it impossible for him or her to withdraw funds from the account.

I find that in reviewing people's estate plans and questioning them as to their motive for opening or maintaining a joint account that nine times out of ten their reason has been the convenience of either having access to the account. With this as their only reason, it seems unnecessary to get en-tangled with the Federal Estate Tax problems of a joint account. Two individual accounts, each with a power of attorney over the other, will offer the same convenience. The power of attorney will usually be in the form of one sheet of paper or perhaps a card will be furnished to you by your banking institution on request. In some states the power of attorney is negated by either of two events, (1) the incompetence or (2) the death of the person in whose name the account is registered. Recognizing the real importance of the existence of the power of attorney during an individual's incompetence many states have deleted incompetency as an event which revokes a power of attorney. It should be recognized that the so-called savings account power of attorney is not to be confused with a general power of attorney. A general power of attorney should be drawn by an attorney and contain language which will allow the grantee (the person getting power) control over many other functions such as transferring and purchase of real property, purchase and sale of stocks and bonds, execution of contracts, etc.

In my judgment more than one-half of the joint savings accounts now in force should not have been opened. The blame for this is probably not all to be laid at the feet of the banking fraternity. The reason is more basic. Although wills have been around a long time, people recognized that the easiest way to transfer property at time of death was through joint ownership. No one was overly concerned with Federal Estate or State Inheritance Tax consequences.

Now, however, because of our affluent society and inflation, many more people should be aware of the drawbacks of joint ownership.

There are additional examples of the problems created by joint accounts. Some states have allowed inroads to be made on the otherwise general rule that a Will may not change the survivorship terms of a joint savings account. In a relatively recent decision New Jersey's highest court stated that if the depositor of the joint account contributed all the money to the account, he may dispose of it by an explicit provision of his last Will and testament, even though the joint account registration provided that the surviving joint owner would receive the proceeds of the account. In essence this decision allows an individual to change a non-probate asset into a probate asset.

Apparently others besides myself found this situation somewhat inconsistent and although the bill has not yet passed the New Jersey Legislature, a bill is pending which would provide the right of the surviving depositor named in a joint deposit account to become the sole beneficial owner of the balance in the account on the death of the deceased co-depositor, and that his interest would not be affected by a contrary disposition of the account by the Will of the deceased depositor.

More problems with joint accounts have also been discussed by the New Jersey courts. In a more recent decision, again from the state's highest court, the court criticized banks for their loose handling of joint accounts with the right of survivorship. The facts of the case were as follows: Mrs. Baron maintained a bank account in her name and in the name of her daughter, Mrs. Williams, as "joint tenants with right of survivorship and not as tenants in common." Literally minutes before Mrs. Baron died, Mrs. Williams withdrew the balance in the account, and claimed the entire amount, i.e., $45,000, to the exclusion of Mrs. Baron's other children. It appeared at the trial that Mrs. Baron was a woman of very limited education and could not read or write beyond signing her name. She understood English and spoke it rather brokenly. Mrs. Williams made it clear that Mrs. Baron did not tell the bank officer that she, Mrs. Baron, wanted Mrs. Williams to have the money for herself on Mrs. Baron's death. The bank officer's testimony as to what took place when the account was opened was characterized by the court as "ambiguous and not helpful." The court stated that the officer "could give no satisfactory explanation for the use of the joint tenancy-survivorship language (which certainly could not have been suggested by Mrs. Baron or Mrs. Williams) and was very unclear as to whether its meaning was explained or even whether the survivorship aspect was discussed at all."

Based on these facts, the Supreme Court of New Jersey held that the funds withdrawn by Mrs. Williams should be paid to the administrator of Mrs. Baron's estate for distribution to next of kin, and that Mrs. Williams had no right to retain the funds for herself.

In the course of its opinion, the court digressed from the central issue and made the following interesting appraisal of joint bank accounts and bank employees:

> **"What shines through in this case, as in so many of the welter of decisions in the books concerning joint bank accounts, is the matter of inaccuracy or mistake by lay bank employees in utilizing designations for such accounts by rote and in the routine use by banks of signature cards containing language legally inappropriate**

to the depositor's actual intent. We are convinced such is really the situation in the instant case. These errors arise because of failure to inquire sufficiently as to that intent or of lack of knowledge of how properly to implement it. A bank, now completely protected by statute as to payment of joint accounts after death, has an obligation to its customers, who so frequently rely solely upon it, to make sure their intent is appropriately evidenced. There is no reason in law or policy why a depositor, desiring only a convenience account during his lifetime, should not be able to have that purpose, and no more, carried out. When the intention is truly to make a "poor man's will," that desire ought to be unmistakably expressed. Intelligent inquiry of the depositor as to desire and purpose must be made in every case. We suggest that when the intent is only to have a lifetime convenience account, a power of attorney, rather than an account designation, is the suitable method. When the desire is for a convenience purpose during life and payment to another of the amount remaining on deposit at the depositor's death, as the former's sole and entire property, a power of attorney plus the account designation "A, payable on death of B" is the most appropriate means. If the depositor desires only survivorship, without convenience aspects during his lifetime, the same designation should be used. Language of joint tenancy, the meaning of which the average depositor and indeed most bank employees do not understand, is to be avoided in such situations. Its use will only be justified when the actual intent is to give the other party named on the account an irrevocable beneficial interest therein from inception. Designations which include "or the survivor" or similar expressions are also undesirable because of the problem of interest in the account during lifetime possibly raised thereby when that is not the depositor's intention."

As the foregoing opinion indicates there are several alternatives to joint account registrations. Another type of joint account is the tenancy in common. Under this type of registration there is no survivorship; the interest of each party is presumed to be equal unless otherwise stated. At the death of one party, his interest in the account becomes part of his estate and is administered in accordance with his Will. The other surviving tenant may withdraw his interest from the account at the co-tenant's death or for that matter, at any time. The so-called "in trust for account" is commonly used by individuals who wish to set up savings accounts for their children. They often mistakenly believe that because the bank employee will accept the child's social security number on the account that the income earned on the account is taxable to the child. This is incorrect. The income from an "in trust for account" or so-called "Totten Trust" is taxable to the trustee. Furthermore, the assets in the account are taxable as part of the trustee's assets at the time of his death under the Federal Estate Tax law and sometimes under the State Inheritance Tax law. The reason in both cases is that the donor-trustee has complete control over the account, he may add to the account or withdraw from it without anyone's consent. Since he exercises this total control it is taxable to him both from an income and estate tax standpoint. At the death of the trustee, the beneficiary, assuming he has reached his majority, would receive the assets in the account as part of the non-probate estate of the decedent. If the beneficiary had not reached his majority, a guardian would have to be appointed to receive the assets from the trust account.

The so-called "Totten Trust" is contrasted with an account opened under the Uniform Gifts to Minors Act. This act grew out of a minor's inability to contract in his own name. The basic thrust of the law which has been adopted by most states with slight variations, was to make an outright gift to a minor by using certain prescribed words of registration and at the same time reserve management of these gifts to a "custodian" until the minor reached age 21. For example, the New Jersey Uniform Gift to Minors Act registration reads as follows:

"Mary Doe, as Custodian for James Doe, a minor, under P. L. 1955, Chapter 139 of the laws of N.J."

The parties to a gift under the Act are the *donor*, or maker of the gift, the donee, or minor child receiving the gift, and the *custodian*, the person who holds or manages the gift until the minor reaches the age of majority. In most states majority means 21 years of age, however, lately many states have reduced the age of majority to 18 years of age but retained the 21 year limitation for gifts made under the Act. With respect to the donor, a gift by him removes the asset from his taxable federal estate because he is making an irrevocable gift when he sets up the account. The Uniform Act does not limit the size of the gift that can be made and the only real limitation is the one placed by the Federal Gift Tax. The Act also provides that the donor may make a gift to a minor individually and not jointly. Furthermore, the gift must be made during the donor's lifetime, because an attempted distribution under a Will is ineffective. Adults may only make a gift under the Act. One of the requests often made of banks is to allow the donor to pledge securities which he holds as custodian for a minor for a personal loan to him. Banks should not make such a loan for obvious reasons, but I would be none too surprised to find more than a few such loans in existence. No joint custodians may be used but provisions for a substitute or successor custodian can be made. The custodian under the Uniform Act may set up a savings account or make any reasonable investments. He has the power to collect, hold, manage, invest and reinvest the custodial property. In addition the custodian is authorized to pay over to the minor or expend for his benefit any or all of the custodial property as the custodian deems advisable. This includes monies for support, maintenance and education of the minor. When the minor reaches twenty-one years of age the custodian is obligated to turn over all the assets he holds for the benefit of the minor.

There is no prohibition on the custodian against changing the nature of the custodial property as long as his action is reasonable and intended for the benefit of the minor. For example, if the custodian sells stock and places the proceeds in a savings account under the same Uniform Gift registration this is permissible, as long as the sale of the stock was a prudent exercise of his powers of investment. The custodian's guiding rule is to invest the custodial property as would a prudent man of discretion and intelligence who is seeking a reasonable income and the preservation of his capital.

Although most custodians serve without fee, they are entitled to compensation. When the custodian predeceases the minor for whom he is custodian, the natural guardian of the minor becomes successor custodian. As in the case of all fiduciaries, the custodian is required to keep records of all the transactions he makes for the minor's account.

Custodial gifts are often made by grandparents to their grandchildren. Their motivation sometimes is that there is an income tax savings for them in such a transfer. Unlike the "Totten Trust" account the Uniform Act is based on a complete and total relinquishment of control by the donor. Therefore, the prime benefit is that the donor may shift income from his high taxable bracket to the lower income tax bracket of the minor children. Under these circumstances the minor has taxable income coming to him and should acquire a social security number for the account. It should be noted that the parents of the minors who receive income from the custodial gifts are still in a position of claiming the minors as dependents and not losing their taxable exemption regardless of the amount of custodial income received. The test is as long as the parents contribute more than half of the minor's support and the child is under 19 or if the child is a fulltime student, they may still gain the income tax exemption. The Internal Revenue Service has said, however, that to the extent a custodian uses income to discharge a legal obligation to maintain a minor, the income will be taxable to the person who has the legal obligation.

As indicated in the chapter on gifts, all gifts including gifts made to minors under the Uniform Act, are subject to the Federal Gift Tax. However, as a practical matter, most custodial gifts are usually well below the exemptions and exclusions available under the gift tax law.

From a Federal Estate Tax viewpoint, the donor does remove the asset from taxability in his estate when he makes the custodial gift. However, the Internal Revenue Service has ruled that the value of property transferred by a donor to himself as custodian for a minor under the Uniform Gift to Minors Act is includible in the donor's gross estate for Federal Estate Tax purposes in the event of the donor's death before the minor reaches the age of 21 years. This problem would seem to be easily avoided by having someone other than the donor named custodian, either the parent not making the gift, another relative or perhaps a bank.

The taxability or non-taxability of the gift under the Uniform Act from a State Income or Inheritance Tax standpoint will hinge on local law.

JOINTLY HELD REAL ESTATE

With respect to real estate there are three types of joint ownership which may be listed on a deed. They are (1) a joint tenancy with the right of survivorship, (2) tenancy by the entirety or (3) tenancy in common.

Tax consequences differ.

A joint tenancy with the right of survivorship indicates that the individuals own the property jointly during their lives; however, that at the death of the first, the property will thereafter be owned by the surviving joint owner, notwithstanding any statement in the decedent's will to the contrary.

The tenancy in common implies separate and distinct interests in each party to the ownership; although we most often think of joint ownership involving only two people owning something equally and jointly this is not the case. The tenancy in common may involve several joint owners with unequal interests in the asset owned.

Check your deed. How is your real estate owned?

The tenancy by the entireties is a special joint ownership which basically has the same qualities as joint ownership with the right of survivorship. It differs in the fact that it is a joint ownership between husband and wife, and under certain state laws enjoys immunity from state inheritance tax, but the federal rule of "the first to die owned the whole amount" still applies.

However, let's take a look at a variation of ownership by husband and wife as tenants by the entirety and examine the Federal Estate Tax consequences:

"A" and "B," husband and wife, own a certain piece of real estate as tenants by the entirety. When it was purchased it cost $80,000. "A" paid $70,000 toward the purchase and "B" contributed $10,000. Whatever the value of the property at the husband's death, the wife should be able to trace her proportionate share of the purchase price to the market value at her husband's death. This value should then be deducted from the husband's estate and escape taxation.

SIGNIFICANCE OF REGISTRATIONS OF PROPERTY

We have spent a substantial amount of time discussing why jointly owned assets can be a problem. There are other problem areas. I have seen and reviewed excellently tax-planned Wills, which have been completely nullified by joint ownership assets. If you have a Will which provides for marital and non-marital trusts, this document presumes that the great majority of your assets are in your individual name and will be controlled by the Will. Any time you change this individual registration on your assets to "joint with the right of survivorship" you do irreparable damage to your estate plan, and will cost your heirs thousands of dollars in unnecessary taxes.

We have demonstrated the problem of jointly-held assets. How do we solve it? How do we change joint ownership without incurring other problems, specifically payment of gift taxes? In most cases the simplest method would be to re-register the asset, one-half in the name of the husband and the other half in the wife's name. There is no gift tax under these circumstances because the value of the one-half undivided interest each held under the joint tenancy has been evenly exchanged for an equal amount now held individually. By making this change in ownership the Federal Estate Tax has also been reduced because now only one-half the asset will be included in the estate of the first spouse to die.

Another way of destroying joint ownership would be to register the asset as tenants in common. This is most commonly done with real estate owned by husband and wife as joint tenants. Great care should be taken, however, in dealing with realty held jointly by husband and wife because since January 1, 1955, the creation of a joint tenancy or a tenancy by the entireties by a married couple in real property is not treated as a gift, unless the spouse whose money is used to purchase the real estate elects to make it a gift and files an appropriate gift tax return. In other words, check to see when the real estate was purchased and make this known to your attorney, if you are planning to sever any joint tenancies in real estate.

Another and perhaps somewhat more complicated method of severing a joint ownership would be to have the parties transfer their interests to a trust, reserving the income of the trust to themselves during their lifetime. The trust would be divided into two equal shares at the death of the first spouse, the one trust could be withdrawn by the surviving spouse and the other would be irrevocable. At the death of the surviving spouse, the irrevocable trust would

not be included in her estate and thereby creating a substantial savings in
Federal Estate Tax.

Under the Revenue Act of 1978 the government has finally begun to
recognize the wife's participation in her husband's business although she
is not on the payroll. Under the new law if a wife can demonstrate that she
has "materially participated" in the conduct of a farm or closely-held
business owned jointly with her husband, she may elect to exclude a
portion of the property's value from her deceased husband's estate.
Generally the amount of exclusion is 2% of the property's value for each
year she materially participated in the business. The maximum exclusion,
however, will be 50% of the property's value. The real problem here will be
in proving material participation to the government's satisfaction.

Although the problems of joint ownership are many, one should not conclude
that it is never a good idea to own some assets jointly. Examine each case
and the circumstances surrounding it and then consult your attorney.
Certainly in modest estates jointly held assets will reduce probate and estate
settlement costs. Since taxes are not a major consideration in smaller estates
the savings in these other areas are important. The main points to remember
are that joint ownership may cause problems and you should be aware of the
legal significance of all the registrations of your assets and how they fit into
your overall estate plan.

Chapter V

"MY LAST WILL AND TESTAMENT"

NOTES

Perhaps the following chapter should have been placed at the beginning of this book since the Will is a basic document in all estate planning. Many times in dealing with individuals I have heard them say, "My estate is too small, I don't need an estate plan." They were *dead* wrong (pardon the pun). Everyone has an estate plan, many of them are authored by the laws of descent and distribution of the state you die in, because you haven't taken any active steps to prepare one of your own.

The term "last Will and testament" has no modern day significance since the term "Will" effectively covers the functions of distribution of an estate. In ancient times there was a marked distinction between real and personal property. In recognition of this distinction the term "Will" was used regarding the disposition of real property and "testament" covered the disposition of personal property.

Under the heading of real property is land, and buildings; personal property includes bank accounts, stocks, bonds, certificates of deposit, automobiles, furniture, clothing, cash, jewelry and personal effects.

Everyone has the right to distribute his property to whomever he wishes, subject to certain rights one's respective spouse has to elect a percentage of the decedent's estate. One of the methods of distributing property is through a Will; however, it is not the only means. We've already mentioned that absent a Will, a person's estate will be distributed in accordance with the laws of the state he dies a resident of. Another method is by leaving property in joint name, in order that the surviving joint owner receive the whole amount. The problem with this last method (as indicated earlier), is that from a tax standpoint it can be very costly.

This is true in most estates.

Most states provide that an individual who has reached his majority may make a Last Will and Testament. Although the age of 21 has been the age of majority for many years, many states have reduced the age to 18 years recently. Besides sufficient age, all state laws provide that a person must possess sufficient mental capacity. A person is said to possess sufficient mental capacity according to one state court if he is capable of comprehending the property he is about to dispose of, knows the natural objects of his bounty and understands the Will.

The lack of a properly drawn and executed Will has caused many problems for even the most modest estate. I am reminded of the individual who decided that he would draw his own Will by copying some of the portions of a relative's Will which had been drawn by an attorney. Under the terms of that Will everything was left to the wife. However, in copying this Will the do-it-yourselfer failed to provide for a beneficiary in the event his wife predeceased him. Well, the inevitable happened. His wife died some five years before him. Whether he just neglected to change the Will during this time or whether he was unaware of this problem is not clear. In any event, he passed away with the Will leaving everything to his wife and naming his wife as executrix under the Will with no provision for a substituted or contingent executor. The heirs' first inclination was not to probate the Will since the total estate amounted to less than $25,000. However, their attorney advised that under the laws of the state involved it was mandatory to probate the Will under the factual situation. In looking for the witnesses, it was found that one had passed away some time ago and the other who was 92 years of age lived some 250 miles from the probate court where the witness would have to appear personally in order that the Will be probated. This was accomplished with minimum difficulty. However, the point was that the Will in question, since it was improperly drawn, provided no more aid in the administration of the estate than if the individual had died without a Will. In fact, all the expense incurred in probating the Will and posting a bond for the executor made the probate of this improperly drawn Will more expensive.

A Will, no matter what size the estate, is an important measure in the orderly distribution of a person's property. Any Will should be responsive to one's personal objectives, yet it does not require that you make an itemized list of your assets or a specific direction as to the distribution or recipient of each asset. (Your attorney can assist you in offering advice as to the methods of distributing your assets.) You should realize that your Will may be changed at any time, either by having a totally new one drawn or by amending the provisions through the use of a codicil.

It is extremely important that you give your attorney all the facts regarding your estate. All too often people think that a Will controls the distribution of the entire estate. They forget that in reality everyone has *two* estates. One of these estates passes under your Will. The other estate, the one we rarely understand, is not controlled by a Will. This is life insurance, jointly owned property and possibly other assets. A failure to coordinate the assets of your dual estates could destroy your testamentary objectives and be costly in terms of administration expenses and taxes.

Take the following situation: Mr. Jones left a Will under which he left all of his stock to his son, Peter, and other assets of equal value to his son, Paul. When he died, Paul received his share of the estate, but upon checking the registration of the stock, it was found to be in joint name with Mr. Jones' brother, John. Despite the clause in Mr. Jones' Will, the stock, by virtue of the joint registration, became the legal property of John.

Needless to say John refused to give the stock to Peter and an irreparable family dispute occurred.

This problem could have been avoided had Mr. Jones recognized the need for coordinating his *dual* estates. The use of jointly owned property has become so widespread that I feel quite certain that if you were to examine your estate you would find that between jointly owned property and life insurance a majority of your estate is not controlled by your present Will.

One should also recognize that although there are provisions in some states for recording of your Will prior to your death, no one needs to know of its contents, including the witnesses to your signature. Furthermore, though you make disposition of your property under your Will, either specifically or generally, the existence of these provisions does not prevent you from selling or giving away your property during your lifetime.

As a beginning to the preparation of a Will you should make a complete list of all your assets and liabilities. Forms for this are provided in the Appendix. You then are in a position to decide what assets, either specifically or generally, you wish to dispose of under your Will and to which beneficiaries. It is most important in making your list that you include how the assets are registered. By this I mean individually, jointly, in trust for, etc.

There are a few items which very commonly are overlooked. They are:

A. *Jointly Owned Property*
Under this heading is included jointly owned real estate which is a very common form of ownership between husband and wife. This kind of asset cannot be controlled by a Will, but passes automatically, by operation of law, to the surviving joint owner.

B. *Life Insurance Proceeds*
Unless the life insurance policy has been made payable to the estate of the decedent it usually constitutes the largest single asset outside of the Will. When thinking of life insurance as an asset, include not only your own insurance but also insurance provided by your employer under his group insurance plan.

Now let's talk about a "simple Will." First of all, the so-called "simple Will" does not exist. Simplification in a Will is rarely possible. During the next few pages, we'll try to dissect and label the important parts of a Will, taking some of the mystery out of the legal language. It has been my personal experience that much of the suspicion the layman has toward the attorney is really caused by one of two problems. The layman's lack of understanding or the attorney's inability to communicate legal concepts in layman's language. With this in mind let's attempt to shed some light on this problem.

A Will, like anything else, must have a definite pattern. It begins by identifying the testator, the testator being the individual whose Will it is. It then gives his address in order to establish his domicile. The domicile is important in establishing the jurisdiction under which the estate will be taxed. The first clause also declares the instrument as the person's last Will. For a Will to be valid, it is required in most states that the person making the Will declare that it is his Will. It also states that this new Will revokes any previous Wills or codicils.

There are various ways of revoking a Will, perhaps the most clear cut being its destruction by tearing or burning all copies. However, a statement in the Exordium clause as to the revocation of previous Wills resolves all doubt.

The next paragraph usually found in the Will directs the payment of debts, funeral expenses and the costs of the administration of the estate. Many times people include elaborate instructions regarding funeral arrangements. This very often proves to be the wrong place for such instructions. The Will may not even have been found or reviewed until after interment. (Directions regarding burial are usually best listed in a letter of instructions to the family in order to insure against this possibility.)

This general payment of debts clause usually does not include the payment of the entire balance of any outstanding real estate mortgage. The obligation to pay any such mortgage usually falls on the person to whom the real estate has been given, unless the Will specifically provides otherwise. Furthermore, whether the mortgage should be paid, no matter whose obligation it is, will depend on a variety of factors which can only be determined at the time of the testator's death.

The next clause often deals with the payment of taxes. One of its main functions is to set forth the source for payment of whatever death taxes are due and owing by reason of specific and general bequests and devises, residuary bequests, life insurance, jointly owned property, and inter vivos trusts. The source of the payment of taxes will also depend on the size of the estate and the impact of the Federal Estate Tax. If one's objective is to give the surviving spouse a maximum deduction there should be a specific provision to have all taxes paid out of property willed to beneficiaries other than the surviving spouse.

With respect to the use of United States Treasury bonds for the payment of taxes it should be noted that these so-called "flower bonds" are eligible for payment of Federal Estate Taxes at par. They will be valued at par regardless of the market value, at least to the extent that such bonds are used for the payment of the Federal Estate Taxes owed.

The three clauses dealt with so far concerned themselves with the administrative functions of the Will. The next few sections of most Wills are referred to as the dispositive provisions because they spell out the distribution. The first of these is the disposition of tangible personal property. Under this clause, the Will defines and segregates tangible personal property, names the beneficiaries who are to receive the property and then provides a system for an alternate disposition of the property in the event the primary beneficiaries have not survived the testator. Tangible personal property usually includes clothing, jewelry, household goods, personal effects, automobiles, boats, etc.

It is always wise to have a specific disposition of tangible personal property. The reason is that otherwise the executor may be compelled for tax purposes to have a professional appraisal made and then have to sell numerous items of nominal value. It is also sometimes advisable to provide specifically either that the articles of personal property will be delivered to the legatee at the expense of the estate or that the legatee (the person receiving the tangible asset) must bear the expense of transporting the personal property. This clears up any misunderstanding that might otherwise arise during the administration of the estate.

The problem of establishing ownership between husband and wife with respect to household effects is an age-old one. There is no real or effective method of establishing ownership because normally there are no legal papers of title or sale transferred between husband and wife. At least one method of establishing ownership is the inclusion in the Will of a clause which confirms that the household effects are owned by one of the spouses. The trick perhaps is to confirm the ownership to the spouse who will be the last to die.

The usual tangible personal property clause reads something like the following:

"I give all my tangible personal property to my wife, Annabelle, including all clothing, jewelry, household effects and personal effects. If she does not survive me I leave the above-described property to my children, who survive me, to be divided equally

Should "flower bonds" be part of your investment portfolio?

among them. I further direct that any expenses incurred in either the safekeeping or delivery of the above-described assets to be paid out of my estate as an expense of general administration."

Following the disposition of tangible property the Will usually deals with other bequests. The words "bequeath" and "bequest" refer to the transfer of personal property in a Will as compared to the word "devise" referring to the transfer of real property. All of these terms are steeped in legal traditions; however, they have lost their "magic" in most jurisdictions. By this I mean that if the attorney used the word "bequest" rather than "devise" describing the transfer, the transfer will still be an effective one.

The purpose of this clause is to make two kinds of bequests: specific bequests, i.e., the transfer of specific assets to specific people, or a general bequest, i.e., a transfer of assets out of a general fund and not out of specific property. This clause also attempts to cover the ademption or lapse of any bequest. Simply stated "ademption" means if someone leaves something under his will but sells, loses, gives away or destroys the article before he dies, the bequest is said to have been adeemed. Usually the problem is avoided by adding a clause after any specific bequest such as the following: "if owned by me at the time of my death." The word "lapse" on the other hand is used when the testator leaves something specific to someone but provides that if the legatee dies before the testator the legatee's estate or his heirs will receive the benefit of the bequest. The bequest becomes part of the general estate of the testator.

Many times the Will at this point will also provide for charitable bequests. It is important in making these bequests that the appropriate name and address of the charity is known and included in the Will in order to avoid confusion and possible misdirection of the charitable gift. Sometimes a general gift to the charity is made without specifying any particular use within the charity. If one wishes, however, that the bequest be put to a specific use, it is well to inquire of the charity as to the exact language which should be used in order to insure this objective. Also, in order to insure the deductibility of the charitable bequest for Federal Estate Tax purposes, you should ask your attorney to check the Internal Revenue Code to make sure the object of your charitable bequest is a qualified organization under the code.

Also you may wish to include perpetual care of a cemetery plot or provision for the saying of masses or other forms of worship. With respect to both these objectives, it would be well to review the requirements of the particular cemetery and religious orders before making provisions under the Will.

Now that all personal property has been disposed of the next order of business is for the Will to provide for the distribution of real property. As in the case of personal property it is important to clearly identify the real property with respect to location and exact address. It is also necessary to be specific in describing the beneficiaries who are to receive the real property.

A typical clause in a Will would read something like the following:

"I give and devise my real estate located at 3 Bellemont Road, Nicetown, Wonderful County, New Jersey, to my nephew, Charles Nelson Reilly."

You will note that the description of the location includes the street address, town, county and state. Also, the relationship between the testator and beneficiary is set forth as ''nephew.''

Sometimes attorneys will go one step further in describing real estate by including a ''metes and bounds'' description which is found on the deed to the real estate.

With the devise of all real property in the estate there exists now only the need to cover any lapsed legacies or personal property and real estate not specifically bequeathed or devised. This is taken care of by a so-called residuary clause which usually takes the following form:

''All the rest, residue and remainder of my estate both real property and personal property I give, devise and bequeath to . . .''

This catch-all clause insures that no property will be in the estate which has not been effectively distributed by the Will.

In the event that the Will in question was to be used by a husband survived by a wife and minor children provision would be made for a contingent trust. This contingent trust would only arise if both the husband and wife were killed in a common disaster.

Assume first of all that the Will provided that upon the husband's death he left all of his property both real and personal to his wife, if she survived him. If she does not survive him he leaves his estate to be divided equally among his three children. If all the children have reached their majority, the estate is merely divided equally among them. If, however, they have not reached their majority the contingent trust would come into being and the trustee would manage the property until the last minor child reached his majority. The trustee of this trust would pay the income of the trust to the guardian of the children named under the Will and in addition would invade the principal of the trust for any emergency or extraordinary expenses incurred by the minor children. Upon the youngest child reaching his or her majority the trust would end and whatever assets were in the trust at that time would be divided equally among the children.

There are many variations regarding distributions among children.

One of the most important considerations covered by a Will is the selection of a guardian of the minor children of the testator. It is important because in a real sense you are selecting ''substitute parents'' by naming a guardian. In many situations you are also saving many dollars in bond premiums when you appoint the guardian without requiring him to post bond for the faithful performance of his duties. These bond premiums are a percentage of the estate and are payable on an annual basis out of the minor's estate until he reaches the age of majority.

Check the age of majority in your state.

There are several other important administrative positions which must be filled in order that the Will function properly at the demise of the testator. Among these are the executor and trustee.

The purpose of naming an executor is to name the corporation or individual which will carry out the administrative functions of the estate. When appointing an executor he is usually clothed with certain powers to deal with the decedent's estate under the laws of the jurisdiction where the testator died a resident. However, it is usually preferable to set out at length broad powers under which the executor may function. These powers attempt to place the executor in the same shoes of the decedent with respect to dealing with the property in the estate.

We have now concluded the main body of the Will. The only part that remains is the concluding portion. This is called the "Testimonium." This clause attempts to establish that the testator signed the Will with the full knowledge of its importance and contents, and ends by having his signature at the conclusion, showing the place and date of execution. One form of testimonium clause is as follows:

"**IN WITNESS WHEREOF, I subscribe my name this** *19th* **day of** *April 1975* **at** *Mountainville, New York.*

———————————————
(Signature of Testator)"

The formalities required in executing a Will will depend on local law and none of the foregoing illustrations should be considered any more than examples of parts of a Will.

The number of witnesses to a Will will again depend on the local state law. Some states only require two witnesses; others require more. Your attorney can advise you as to the number. Let me suggest, however, that your witnesses be younger than yourself so that they are likely to outlive you and be around to prove the authenticity of your Will. Many states require that at least one of the witnesses physically present himself at the probate or surrogate's court to testify as to the authenticity of the Will.

Also it is always wiser, I think, to have married women witness your Will. The main and only reason is simple—they are much less likely to change their names than single women. This, of course, becomes important when you are trying to locate one of the witnesses in order to probate the Will. Under the new Uniform Probate Code this problem has been obviated. The Code provides that at the time the Will is signed a statement may be signed by the two witnesses which in effect "pre-probates" the Will and makes their presence at the time of the probate of the Will unnecessary.

All too often after a Will is drawn the great majority of people put it in a drawer or maybe a safe deposit box and never look at it again. A Will should be reviewed periodically. The frequency with which a Will is reviewed will depend on how complicated and susceptible to change is the estate the individual possesses. In any event, it has been my personal recommendation that a Will be reviewed at least every two years with the following considerations in mind:

A. **Changes in personal circumstances.**
B. **Changes in the economic conditions.**
C. **Changes in the tax laws, both federal and state.**

Any of these changes could conceivably affect the provisions of a Will. You will also want to be concerned with whether you still own some of the articles of property you have specifically bequeathed under your Will, and whether there have been changes in the family, marriages, divorces, or the birth of children. A review as to your executor and trustee is also important

In addition to your Will there is another helpful but less formal document which you should consider drafting, perhaps even in your own hand. This document is sometimes referred to as a Letter of Instructions. Its purpose is to provide the executor of the estate and the beneficiaries some additional and more personal information about the testator's estate. It usually includes the following information:

1. A statement as to the location of the Will.

2. Burial instructions, name of cemetery and location of plot, information regarding the location of the cemetery plot deed. If the testator's desire is to be cremated, instructions as to the care and placement or disbursement of the ashes. If you are a veteran you may wish to take advantage of the opportunity to be buried in a national cemetery.

3. A list, including the address of all the people who should be notified of your death and the family relationship of these people to you. This will be helpful also in probating the Will because the court will usually require a listing of all immediate family members.

4. The location of all important legal documents, including social security and medicare cards, title papers to automobiles, deeds to real property, armed services discharge papers, marriage or divorce papers, copies of separation or settlement agreements, birth certificate or baptismal certificate and any other papers of a legal nature.

5. Whether you are a member of any society or lodge which has as part of its membership some death benefit or insurance coverage at the death of a member, and any information regarding the procedure for collecting this benefit and the location of the certificate of insurance.

6. The location and listing of all your life insurance policies, including the name of the company, policy number, beneficiary designation and the amount of coverage. You should also include any policies and their location regarding casualty and home owner's insurance and also insurance policies on which you have been paying the premiums but are insuring other members of the family.

7. The name of the bank and account number of all savings and checking accounts in your name individually or in your name and another jointly. Also information concerning the location of all checking accounts and passbooks or certificates of deposit.

8. A list of all U.S. Savings Bonds, in whose name they are registered, also including their denominations and serial numbers.

9. A list of all stocks, bonds and their location.

10. The location of any safe deposit box or boxes, in whose name they are registered and the location of the key or keys.

11. A listing of any pension or profit sharing plans of which you are a participant including the location of any explanatory booklets.

12. Location of recent income tax returns, both state and federal.

13. A statement regarding the disposition of any tangible personal property having sentimental value and an explanation of the reasons for any unusual distribution made under the Will.

During the course of this chapter I have attempted to point out some of the highlights and prerequisites for having a proper Will drawn by your attorney. Perhaps the following list of Do's and Don'ts will best summarize the approach to proper Will-drafting.

DO'S

—DO have your Will drawn by an attorney.

—DO make a complete list of your assets, including the fair market value, and how the asset is registered, i.e., individual, joint, in trust for, etc.

—DO select guardians, executors and trustees carefully, remembering what each of their responsibilities are in the administration of an estate.

—DO prepare a Letter of Instructions to your executor and beneficiaries.

—DO outline carefully in your mind the objectives which you wish to accomplish in the distribution of your estate.

—DO try and determine your Federal Estate Tax and State Inheritance Tax, if any.

—DO review your Will periodically in the light of changing personal circumstances, changes in the economic conditions and changes in the tax laws which may affect it.

DON'TS

—DON'T sign a Will unless you understand it. Despite the use of legal language your attorney can explain the various sections of the Will.

—DON'T think that your estate is too small to need a Will. Often the smaller the estate, the more important the Will.

—DON'T forget about coordinating your dual estates, i.e. probate assets, assets in your individual name; non-probate assets, assets in joint name and life insurance.

—DON'T list your assets in your Will. You may dispose of them during your lifetime—give fractions or percentages to your various beneficiaries so that no matter what the size of the estate they will be treated equally if the estate increases or diminishes.

—DON'T leave your original Will in an unsafe place. Leave it in a bank safe deposit box or with your attorney.

Chapter VI

HOW TO SELECT YOUR FINANCIAL PLANNING ADVISORS

Many a would-be subject for estate planning is confused before he starts because he really is not sure which advisor he should first consult in the preparation of his estate plan. Most often, as indicated before, he is contacted by the insurance agent but if he (the prospective estate plannee) is the initiator of the project he is confused as to where to begin. Actually, in my judgment, it matters little as to which advisor—attorney, trust officer, accountant or insurance agent—is consulted first; the important thing is to begin, because sooner or later all of them will be necessary in formulating the final program.

For example, let's assume the program is begun by selecting an attorney. A very important part of estate planning is the choice of an attorney to prepare whatever documents are necessary for the estate plan. How does one select the right attorney?

Obviously you will want to choose someone who is experienced in estate planning. Unlike the medical profession, the legal profession generally does not use specific designations like orthopedist and gynecologist, etc., although some states are experimenting with specialization terms. One state (California) requires anyone holding himself out as a specialist, in telephone directories and notices to fellow members of the bar, to undergo formal training in that specialty, successfully pass an examination in his particular specialty and to be rated by his fellow attorneys in that specialty. This state also provides that if an attorney has practiced for ten years he does not require special training or written examination to qualify as long as he can demonstrate a substantial portion of his practice has been in that specialty. It should be noted, however, that this plan is only an experiment and may well require revision after a trial period. Another state (New Mexico) also allows specialization. Under this plan, however, there are really two categories; the "specialist" who devotes sixty-five percent of his practice to the specialty for five years preceding and sixty percent of his time on an on-going basis and the attorney who "limits" his practice to not more than three fields. The second category does not really assure one that the attorney is a specialist but does provide a means for becoming experienced in a given field without formal examination and certification.

In my opinion, there is really a very small percentage of practicing attorneys who are sophisticated in the estate planning field. My experience has been, with respect to all attorneys in the estate planning situations, that they fall into three basic categories. The first is sophisticated in estate planning and is competent to do an estate plan for his client without any other professional assistance. The second has limited knowledge on the subject of estate planning but will allow himself to be guided by other members of the "estate

NOTES

56

planning team," i.e. trust officer, insurance agent and accountant. The third also has limited knowledge on the subject but is so jealous of his position with his client that he will often not listen to the more experienced members of the estate planning team but will prepare what his limited knowledge on the subject allows.

How can the general public be protected from this third class of attorney? The obvious first suggestion is to seek the advice and counsel of the other members of the estate planning team. A second suggestion would be to contact the local county bar association in your state and ask them to give you a list of attorneys who specialize in estate planning and probate work. However, lest I lead you astray, do not assume that an attorney who handles the administration of a decedent's estate is automatically a good estate planner. There is many an old time practitioner who may be an excellent estate administrator but who unfortunately has not kept abreast of the tax laws with regard to estate planning. A third method of selecting an attorney would be by consulting the Lawyers Directory (Martindale Hubbell) which sometimes indicates areas of specialization and rating of attorneys by their peers.

One area of real interest to all potential clients is the legal fee involved in preparing an estate plan. Naturally fees will vary from jurisdiction to jurisdiction. However, the general rule of thumb most preferred by both client and attorney is an hourly fee arrangement. This would appear to be the most equitable method. I have known some attorneys who have charged a percentage of the gross estate or in some cases a percentage of the prospective savings in Federal Estate Taxes and State Inheritance Taxes as a result of the attorney's formulation of an estate plan. This percentage of savings has usually been 10%. Therefore, if $50,000 in taxes were saved through the preparation of the estate plan, the attorney's fee would be $5,000. This percentage arrangement probably is more valid than a percentage of the total estate since the savings in tax was accomplished by the attorney's knowledge and skillful drafting of documents. My personal preference, however, remains an hourly fee arrangement.

Ask your attorney about fees.

Another area regarding attorney's fees is the charging of fees for the administration of one's estate. This again has historically been a percentage fee. However, the general public and attorneys themselves have become increasingly critical of this arrangement. The latest movement in this area has been toward either an agreed set fee determined by an estimate of the work involved in the administration of a given estate or by charging on an hourly fee basis.

Whether you first seek an attorney's advice for the preparation of an estate plan will also depend on how you begin to plan your estate. Most people are motivated by one or two occurrences to do something with their estates. Either some member of their family or close friend passes away leaving their estate poorly planned or they are about to leave on a vacation and want to get their affairs in order before they leave.

A small percentage of people are motivated to begin the job of estate planning after seeing some trust bank advertising. This usually takes the form of a monthly advertising booklet accompanied by a letter offering a meeting with a trust officer to discuss the topic of estate planning without cost or obligation. A person may well start the task of planning an estate by consulting with a trust officer or estate planning officer of a bank. The trust officer will begin by asking you to fill out an asset inventory sheet. There are a great variety of these so-called financial planning questionnaires and example of one appears in the appendix. Take advantage of these offerings; your only investment will be time. The trust department charges no fee to sit down and discuss any problems you may have. This is also a good method for judging the caliber of trust department that you may wish to name as executor and trustee under your estate plan.

Another advertising tool used by many trust departments is the financial planning or estate planning seminar. Experience has shown the banking industry that if the seminar is well planned it can be one of the best and least expensive trust solicitation devices. Those of you who have received invitations to these programs know they are usually held at some central location in the evening. The seminar usually consists of one or more speakers followed by a question-and-answer period. The talks cover Wills and trusts, jointly owned property, the problems of dying without a Will and the cost of trust services. Many times the bank will ask a local attorney, insurance agent or accountant to join the panel so that a cross section of professional opinions can be given. My best advice would be to attend these seminars to gain knowledge and use them as a method for interviewing your prospective "executor" and "trustee."

HOW TO SELECT AN EXECUTOR

At this point you are introduced to another selection process. Who does one name as executor and trustee under one's Will and why? My trust banking experience and professional judgment tell me that the use of a professional executor and trustee is the best road to follow the great majority of the time.

My position has been challenged on modest-sized estates where the limited number of assets would hardly seem to call for the professional management of a bank executor and trustee with the attendant costs for their services. However, I am a firm believer in that hackneyed saying, "You only get what you pay for."

Many times the use of a nonprofessional executor and trustee will cost more money than it will save. The job of executor is a much more complex job than most people realize. I am often confronted with the argument that "I handled my father's estate as executor and there were no problems." This may well be true; at least there were no problems of which anyone was made aware. My point is that probably everything the nonprofessional executor or lay executor had done was completed correctly. The problem was he may have omitted to perform certain of his duties. In other words, he may not have made too many errors of commission, but perhaps there were some costly errors of omission.

To put this job of executor in somewhat more concrete terms a list of some of the executor's more important duties follow:

WILL—　　　　Locate Will ● Offer Will for probate ● Qualify to serve

ASSETS—　　　Identify, collect, inventory and appraise all assets ● Collect debts, compromise claims ● Meet time limit set by court ● File inventory and safeguard

Who have you named as Executor and Trustee?

assets • Arrange funeral • Dispose of perishable assets • Wind up partnership business • Take charge of real property, make repairs, enforce leases, collect rents, maintain insurance

SECURITIES— Collect Dividends, Interest • Exercise Options

BUSINESS— Continue decedent's business under authority of Will or court • Complete contractural obligations

CLAIMS— Payment of claims against estate • Retention of necessary assets • Liquidation of property • Publication of notice • Determine priority of claims • Determine order of liability of assets to meet claims • Protect estate against unjust claims

FILE TAX— RETURNS State Inheritance Tax return • Decedent's final income tax • Estate income tax • Gift Tax return, if necessary • Tax returns in other states • Federal Estate Tax return

ACCOUNTING— Keep all records, and make intermediate and final accountings

DISTRIBUTION— Locate and qualify heirs • Prepare property for distribution • Payment of legacies • Setting up of trusts • Obtaining assent of legatees

DISCHARGE— OF EXECUTOR By receipt and release • By order of court • Obtain final decree

One of the major stumbling blocks in the naming of a corporate executor is the feeling that the cost for its services would be exorbitant. In most cases one will find that corporate executors and individual executors fees are the same. Usually they are couched in terms of a percentage of the fair market value of the estate at the date of the decedent's death. For example, New Jersey speaks in terms of 5% of the first $100,000 of market value of the estate plus 2½% to 3½% of the excess of market value over the first $100,000. In addition the corporate executor receives 6% of all the income received during the administration of the assets in the estate. The fees quoted are set by state law in New Jersey although this is not the case in all states. New Jersey law also provides that where co-executors act, the total executors' commission on the first $100,000 may be increased 1% for each additional executor after the first.

HOW TO SELECT A TRUSTEE

In the more complex estate the use of a trust and the naming of a trustee is an absolute necessity. Like an executor, a trustee of a trust under a Will or a trustee of a living trust is a management function. The basic responsibilities include the management of the assets in the trust. More often than not these assets consist of stocks and bonds. The reason for this is that stocks and bonds are the types of assets most susceptible to management by a trustee. It is unusual to find assets like vacant land and income producing real estate in a trust because they require a more flexible management than is available under a trust. Some large trust departments do possess real property investment divisions who manage real estate in personal trusts but this is the exception among trust departments nationwide.

Many people whose only introduction to the concept of trust is its use as a method of insulating one against excessive probate costs and taxes are prone to want to place all of their assets in a living trust or so-called inter-vivos trust. The fallacy in this is that not all one's assets are the kinds of assets that are susceptible to trust management.

Assuming that there is a need for a trust, how does one select a trustee? The same reasoning process as for the selection of any professional advisor should be used in the selection of a trustee. Experience and investment knowledge are musts. Accurate record keeping is also necessary. Ideally at the time your trustee acts in this capacity, this trustee function should be his only endeavor. The problem with most individual trustees is that they do not have the time to concentrate only on their trust function. They are usually also involved in carrying out the responsibilities of their business or profession.

There are considerable advantages to the use of a corporate trustee, not the least of which is the perpetuality of its existence. Among others is professional investment advice and an organization equipped to handle all the record keeping which trust administration requires. The corporate trustee also has available competent tax advice to deal with any tax problems which might occur during the administration of the trust. For example, every trust must file a tax return, the complexity of which would of course depend on the type of trust involved. If an individual trustee is named, he or she will in all probability have to seek professional tax advice from an accountant to prepare the return whereas a corporate trustee will have this expertise available within its trust department.

The one area in which most trust departments neither wish to serve nor are they competent to serve, is that of trustee of a trust which holds an operating business as one of its assets. The nature of an operating business makes it difficult to manage or closely watch for any long period of time within the structure of a trust. Therefore in these cases if the business must operate in a trust one should give consideration to an individual who possesses in-depth knowledge of the management of the particular business and also the common sense to seek professional help in those areas of trust administration in which he is not expert.

The decision then on whether to use an individual or corporate trustee will depend on the nature of the assets to be held in trust.

THE INSURANCE AGENT

Use the same care in selecting your insurance agent. I have in my experience found very few people who have not been contacted by at least one insurance agent. The insurance agent will call on people as a result of various prospect lists based on recent purchases of real estate, recent births and recent promotions of corporate executives. Some will point toward a one-time sale in attempting to fulfill a present need, such as so-called "mortgage insurance "

The one-time insurance salesman is not your best advisor. I have reviewed insurance portfolios and have seen poor insurance plans evidenced by a hodge podge of whole life and term policies having no total plan in mind. This unfortunately demonstrates the sale of policies by several different agents of several different companies each without consideration of previous purchases. This mistake can be costly and sometimes irretrievable. A good insurance counsellor who recognizes the value of a total program of planning geared to meet your objectives and your pocketbook can be invaluable.

The designation of C.L.U. after the insurance agent's name denotes that he is a Chartered Life Underwriter. He earns this designation through courses of study and by passing several examinations covering estate planning and other insurance related subjects. Looking for this designation for your insurance agent can be helpful. Candidly, however, I have found many insurance men without this designation who demonstrated superior knowledge and dedication in this field. My point is if you are receiving good advice and good service from your agent, don't decide to drop him just because he is not a C.L.U.

The insurance agent can be a valuable member of the estate planning team. His function should be to select those insurance products which will best fit into your estate program.

THE ACCOUNTANT

The next member of the estate planning team is the accountant. The accountant, whether he is a C.P.A. (Certified Public Accountant) or not can be extremely valuable in those estate plans where the individual is involved in his own business or a closely held corporation. This is so because the average businessman is very much concerned with income taxes in the running of his business both corporate and personal. He relies heavily on his accountant who is totally familiar with the problems of the business. I find that the accountant is an excellent recordkeeper, and also is totally familiar with income taxes. The problem sometimes arises when the sophistication in income tax does not carry over into the tax areas which involve estate planning, i.e., Federal Estate Taxes, Gift Tax and State Inheritance Taxes. Many times the client blindly relies on the accountant for all tax advice whether or not the accountant has any real sophistication in the estate planning area.

The accountant can be one of the most effective members of the estate planning team because he probably has a more intimate relationship with the client than any of his other advisors. This is so because he probably visits him on a weekly or monthly basis. In order to capitalize on this relationship he should be imaginative in planning possible gift situations and corporate reorganizations calculated to save tax monies.

Unfortunately, I have found the accountant very jealous of his position with his client and therefore sometimes unreceptive to estate planning suggestions offered by other members of the estate planning team, whether or not they could be beneficial to the client

Lest the accounting profession ban this book, let me say that the accountant remains an important and valuable member of the estate planning team

62

In summary, one should give careful consideration in selecting his attorney, executor and trustee. As a general rule, try to select the attorney who has experience in estate planning. To aid in his selection seek the advice of the trust officer, insurance counselor and accountant. Also consult local bar associations and law directories, if available, listing attorneys' specialties.

With respect to your executor and trustee, look for experience in the areas of investment management, tax knowledge and record keeping. Consider whether your estate would benefit from the use of a corporate executor and trustee.

Choose an insurance agent who is knowledgeable and who regularly calls upon you to review your estate plan. The C.L.U. designation is something to look for but it is not an automatic guarantee that you are receiving the best insurance advice available.

Select an imaginative accountant, one who suggests ways of avoiding problems. Anyone can be a good bookkeeper. Most people who require estate planning require an accountant who will do more than merely file tax returns and "hold your hand" during a tax audit.

Chapter VII

HOW TO BEGIN PLANNING YOUR ESTATE

Any task that one attempts should begin with gathering as many pertinent facts as possible. In the foregoing chapters I have outlined some of the problems and their solutions encountered in estate planning. We are now ready to begin the gathering of those facts which will aid you in your estate plan. (You will at this point want to refer to the Financial Planning Workform in the Appendix.)

We begin with a personal information questionnaire. Naturally, you are aware of this information but probably have never compiled it on one sheet of paper. This data although it may seem extremely simple, will be of great assistance in your attorney's formulation of your estate plan. You will note that the first line requires that you enter your name and age and the name and age of your spouse. Your children's names and respective ages are then listed. It is important in listing your name and those of your wife and children that you list given names as they appear on birth certificates, or, if another name other than that recorded on the birth certificate is normally used, this should be set forth. In preparing the legal documents necessary for the estate plan, the attorney will probably want to list your birth record name and then place after it the initials a/k/a meaning "also known as" in order to avoid any confusion. The ages for the children are important for two reasons, first to determine whether they have reached their majority and secondly to aid in the formulation of any plan of distribution.

The questionnaire also provides for listing grandchildren. Many estate plans for older people may well include educational trusts for grandchildren. The listing of names, addresses and ages will be extremely helpful in helping one to focus upon his objectives and also be helpful to the attorney. The attorney will find this information valuable in preparing the estate plan and in the administration and distribution of your estate among your various beneficiaries. The attorney will place this information in his file and any changes should be reported to him and to your executor and trustee. I have mentioned it before but it bears repeating. It is extremely important to update all your estate planning information on a continual basis.

In addition to grandchildren there is also provision made for listing the names of your parents and those of your spouse. Very often estate programs will include specific bequests to parents. If you are contributing to their support during your lifetime you may well want to include either a specific amount to them at your death or provide a life income from a portion of the income of a trust under your will. In either event listing their names and addresses will be helpful to your attorney and executor.

Conversely, if your parents and those of your spouse have accumulated great wealth a listing of their names should serve to remind you to plan for the expected inheritance you could receive from their estate. A substantial inheritance which has not been taken into account in your estate planning could result in the payment of unnecessary Federal Estate Tax and State Estate or Inheritance tax.

For the same reasons as above, a listing of brothers and sisters is suggested.

In addition to setting down the names and ages of your children, parents, brothers and sisters, the questionnaire also provides for listing your attorney, insurance agent and tax advisor. Let me again caution that in the selection of your attorney that you use not the most convenient one but the one who possesses expertise in the area of estate planning. In my interviewing of clients very few have been unable to come up with the name of at least one insurance agent who has called on them either for the sale of a one-time need policy or for a complete estate plan. Remember to select someone who has demonstrated a total approach to your estate.

By assembling all of this information before meeting with your attorney you will be reducing the amount of time the attorney will need in compiling this information. If your attorney is charging you on a time basis you are saving money.

The next important information is a complete list of assets. The form is divided into five basic areas or types of assets:

A. **Real Estate**
B. **Investments**
C. **Business Interests**
D. **Life Insurance and Employee Benefits**
E. **Miscellaneous Assets**

In completing the first category, real estate, first list the fair market value of the residence. My experience has been that most individuals think of the value of their residence in terms of acquisition value or purchase price rather than market value. For estate planning purposes, market value is the figure with which we must deal. The reason for this is that one is taxed, as you will remember, on the fair market value of all assets at the date of death (unless the alternative valuation is used for Federal Estate Tax purposes). Therefore your advisors, in reviewing the assets in your estate should assume that you passed away "yesterday" and project your taxes on this basis of market value on the date upon which you complete your asset list.

The simplest way of determining the market value of your home is by looking to homes that recently sold in your neighborhood which are comparable to yours, and using this value as an educated estimate. Another method would be by checking the assessed value of your home on the local tax roles and adding to this value some value on a ratio of the purchase price to the assessed value at the time you purchased the home. The best way, but certainly not the least expensive, would be to hire a real estate appraiser, to give you a professional appraisal. Incidentally, this is not only a good idea for estate planning purposes but also a good idea for establishing a solid value for any sale of your home. You will note that the form provides a space next to market value in which to place the amount of current mortgage on the property. This can easily be found by checking the amortization schedule which your mortgage bank has furnished to you or will furnish to you upon request. This mortgage value is then subtracted from your market value and the resulting figure should be placed in the space provided next to the mortgage value. This amount is your net value or so-called equity in your house. It is also the value upon which you will be taxed on your demise. If you have more than one mortgage on your residence this naturally should also be deducted from your market value.

The space provided on the extreme right is for listing how the property is owned, i.e., jointly or individually, or as tenants in common. This is important for both you and your advisor to know. The information will be found on the first page of the deed to the property which you received at time of purchase. If just your name and your spouse's name appears on the deed without any other words of description such as jointly or tenants by the entirety or tenants in common, chances are that you own the property jointly with your spouse. However this will differ according to local state law and your attorney will be able to advise you on this point.

The next type of real estate to be listed is business property. If you are a business owner you should not include any real estate which is owned by your corporation. There should only be listed real estate owned by you individually or jointly or as tenants in common. Again, the fair market value of the property should be listed. A method used for valuing business real estate is a function of the amount of income produced by the investment. As in the value of the residence, the mortgage indebtedness is listed and subtracted from market value to arrive at the net or equity value.

The listing of real estate and its market and equity values should also act as a reminder as to whether you have increased your homeowners and casualty insurance in proportion to the increase in value of your real estate.

The next type of category is becoming much more common in our affluent society, the vacation home or summer home. The summer home or vacation home will usually escape state inheritance tax when it is located outside the jurisdiction. The same approach in valuing it, however, should be used as in the case of your residence and business property.

Vacant land is the next category and as a result of land operators in Florida and the West, it has been more commonplace for people to have this kind of asset in their estate. The accurate valuation of this property is difficult. In many instances the purchase price is close to market, even though the property has been held for more than a few years.

Rental properties such as office buildings, two-family residential dwellings, or any other real estate from which one derives an income, comprise the next category. The same information with regard to this real estate, i.e., market value, mortgage indebtedness, equity value and ownership, should be included. A total should now be made of all the net real estate value and this figure placed in the space provided.

The next major category of assets one should list is investments. The first subheading is stocks. Under this category you should list stock owned in public companies and should not include any stock owned by you in closely-held companies. The form provides for listing closely-held stock under the Business Interest section. Again, the value listed should be the fair market value of the stock and not its purchase price. You should then subtract any loans made with the stock used as collateral. The result of this computation will give you the net value which should be inserted in the space provided. The last column should be used for listing how the securities are held, i.e., individual, joint with the right of survivorship, tenants in common, in trust for or under the Uniform Gifts to Minors Act. If some stock is held individually and other stock in some other form of registration, note this in the margin of the form. The information will be helpful in formulating the estate plan.

More detailed information regarding your stockholdings should be included on a supplemental property list. At this location you should list the name of the stock, the number of shares owned, the approximate market value, and the cost basis or acquisition value of the stock.

Mutual funds should be listed at market and also make a notation for yourself as to whether you have elected a dividend reinvestment program. It is probably simpler to keep track of mutual funds by keeping the slips issued by the company showing the number of full shares owned and fractional shares. The same information with regard to any loans against the mutual funds, the net value and how they are owned should be inserted in the space provided.

The category entitled bonds means corporate bonds. Their market value like the stocks and mutual funds may be ascertained by checking the latest quotations in the Wall Street Journal. Bonds also may be used as collateral for loans and any loans against the bonds should be listed in order to arrive at the net value. With respect to how the bonds are registered, you should be aware that certain bonds are not registered at all, that is they have no owner's name listed on their face. These bonds are so-called bearer bonds. Insofar as their ownership for estate planning purposes is concerned, they are technically owned by the person or persons who provided the funds with which they were purchased. Therefore, you should be careful if you place bearer bonds in someone else's safe deposit box that you place them in a sealed envelope and denote on the outside of the envelope their true ownership. This is especially important where the state inheritance tax department seals and then inventories the safe deposit box as part of its taxing procedure. This will aid in identifying true ownership of the bonds for tax purposes.

The next category is U.S. Savings Bonds. Many times they are purchased through a payroll deduction plan. These bonds are easily valued by checking with your local bank which maintains a booklet furnished by the federal government giving the value of a bond down to the nearest month. You will find that even if the bond has matured, it has still been paying interest. My description thus far has been of the Series E Savings Bond, which is the most commonly purchased savings bond. There are enough special qualities about U.S. Savings Bonds that I believe it worthwhile to digress a moment from the listing of assets to discuss these special qualities at length.

The Series E Savings Bond is the one with which all of us are most familiar. We buy bonds in $25, $50, $75 and $100 denominations and sometimes even larger amounts. However, the purchase price is less than these amounts. The difference between the two figures is considered interest and payable upon redemption. Even if the bond is not redeemed as of its date of maturity, it continues to pay interest at the specified rate. With respect to reporting the

Check your broker for quotations on unlisted securities.

interest on an annual basis, there is no such requirement if you are on a cash-accounting basis, which is true of the vast majority of people. The interest would only be taxed at the time the bonds are cashed.

On the other hand, on Series H bonds interest is received every six months by check from the federal government. As a result of its actual receipt it must be reported as income in the year in which it was received.

When bonds are purchased in joint name the income tax liability is upon the person whose money purchased the bond. If both owners pay equally, then each bears an equal share of the interest income. This is also true if the bond was the subject of a gift to them from a third party. While on the topic of gifts of bonds it is extremely important to remember that when a gift of a Series E bond is made, any accrued interest which has not been reported must be included in the donor's reportable income in the year the gift is made. Any interest paid on the bond after the transfer would be paid by the new owner.

Savings bonds are usually registered in individual name, two people in joint names or two people, one as owner and the other as beneficiary or the so-called p.o.d. (payable on death). Example:

1. **John Jones**

2. **John Jones or Fred Jones**

3. **John Jones payable on death Fred Jones**

At the death of a person, any bonds in his individual name become part of his estate for Federal Estate Tax purposes. The executor will, in accordance with the provisions of the will, either redeem the bonds and use these monies for administration expenses or see to it that the bonds are re-issued in the names of the beneficiaries under the will.

If a bond is owned jointly, either of the named owners may redeem it during their lifetimes without permission of the other. When one of the co-owners dies, the bond is totally or partially taxable in the estate of the decedent but the survivor becomes the sole owner. The survivor then has the option of either redeeming the bond or having it reissued in his sole name.

Whenever the "payable on death" registration is used, the death of the owner causes the beneficiary to become the sole owner of the bond. It is taxable under the Federal Estate Tax to the decedent. The beneficiary may redeem the bond or have it reissued in his name; however, either act would require evidence of the owner's death, i.e., death certificate.

Most people who reach the next subsection of mortgages are ready to list their outstanding mortgages. This is not for this purpose. This mortgage category is for mortgages owed to you or to your spouse jointly, or to you and anyone else. If you hold such a mortgage its present value can be readily ascertained by checking an amortization schedule giving the nearest month's valuation.

The next asset category entitled "Loans" is one which people often do not wish to include. The reason for this is that most loans are made to relatives and close friends. In both cases the lender has little hope of recouping them unless he institutes legal action, which he usually would not want to do for various reasons. However, it should be pointed out that if these loans are

check the registration on your bonds.

68

properly documented, by a promissory note, they may be collectible by the executor of your estate.

This concludes the investment section of the property list. An addition of all the net values of the investment assets should be made and the total amount inserted in the space provided.

The next section of the property list will not be used if you are employed by a corporation in which you hold no stock interest and have no other business interests outside of your employment. This section of the property list is for a person owning all or a portion of a closely-held corporation, or one who is involved in conducting a business or profession as a partner, or one who conducts business as an individual proprietor. The federal government has defined a closely-held corporation as one whose shares of stock are owned by a relatively limited number of stockholders, there is no trading in the stock and the stock has no established market.

Let us first deal with the valuation of the closely-held corporation. This is without a doubt one of the most difficult problems in estate planning. The problem in evaluation features a triangle of forces.

First the business owner who wishes to take the position that his business without his guidance and knowledge has no value at his death and therefore should not be a taxable asset in his estate. Next are the federal estate taxing authorities who are attempting to arrive at a value of the business by using a variety of formulae which all seem to be calculated to arrive at the highest possible value of the business. In this attempt the government is placing value on earning capacity, good will, inventory value, etc. At the third position is the estate planner who is trying to convince the business owner that his business does have some value as a taxable asset in his estate and that he should take a more realistic approach in valuing his business. At the same time, the estate planner is attempting to marshal arguments which will be useful in reducing the government's position on valuation.

The next major category in this property list is the section entitled "Life Insurance and Employee Benefits." Most corporations and public service employment provide group life insurance programs. This coverage ranges from a flat nominal amount to as much as 3½ times the individual's salary. Some of these programs also provide that the employee may purchase additional group insurance at a nominal cost. In any event, the common misconception in the area of life insurance is that it is not a taxable asset in your estate. Wrong! Life insurance, if owned by you, is includable in your federal taxable estate at its face value, in the same manner as any other asset in your estate. At one time there was a relatively small amount of life insurance which escaped federal estate tax but this has not been the case for many years.

The taxability or non-taxability of life insurance proceeds under state inheritance tax law will depend on the laws of the various states. New Jersey for example, exempts from tax any and all life insurance proceeds which are paid to a named beneficiary. New York, on the other hand, sets forth a specific dollar amount which it exempts from tax.

Group life insurance should be listed and considered as a taxable asset even though most group plans reduce drastically at time of retirement. The usual program will decrease at the rate of 10% per year after retirement until the coverage is reduced to 50% of the face value, where it remains. Many corporations will also provide accidental death insurance which is a taxable asset. But since the probability of accidental death is remote in most instances, it should not be included for computing the estimated tax on one's estate. Your beneficiary should be listed in the space provided. The "owner" space provided is really not relevant with respect to group life insurance since, although the corporation is really the true owner, the individual will have the proceeds taxable in his estate as if he were the owner.

In addition to group insurance, you should also set forth your total personal life insurance coverage. A supplemental property list should be used for more specific information on the insurance policies. This provides for listing in addition to the face value, the life insurance company, the type, i.e. whole life, term, endowment, etc., and the policy number. So-called "G.I." or "National Service Life Insurance" should also be listed.

Many times people transfer the ownership of their life insurance to a spouse or children in an attempt to avoid taxes. However, as cautioned before, unless this transfer is made as part of an overall estate plan, it should probably be avoided. In any event, note the beneficiary or beneficiaries of the insurance and the owner of the policy in the spaces provided.

Profit sharing, pension and stock options are fringe benefits sometimes provided by corporations. Completing this property list should prompt you to inquire of your personnel department for details about your fringe benefit program. This usually includes group life insurance, medical insurance plans, pension and profit sharing plans. Large corporations provide extensive booklets regarding their programs but it has been my experience that few people bother to read or study these booklets. In attempting to plan one's estate it is necessary to know what the distribution of assets is under these programs in order to decide whether they should remain as is or be changed.

As under the other categories, the various values under this section should be added and their total placed in the space provided.

The next and final grouping of assets under the title "Miscellaneous" includes savings accounts, cash (checking accounts, etc.), works of art and jewelry, furniture, automobiles and personal effects.

All savings accounts listed in your name individually and those in joint name with your spouse should be listed. In addition any accounts which list you as the trustee in trust for another, probably your child or children, should be included. This type of account is includable in your estate. You should also list any Uniform Gifts to Minors Act account where you are named custodian and you have also been the source of the funds in the account for the reasons given earlier. Under the "cash" section should be listed cash which you may have in your safe deposit box (although I would strongly warn against leaving cash any place).

With respect to the categories of "works of art" and "jewelry," it can usually be presumed that the works of art have been gifted to the wife during the husband's lifetime and therefore if the husband dies first (which actuarily occurs more often than not) are not includable in his estate for Federal Estate Tax purposes. With respect to jewelry, the usual case is that the husband does not have a great deal of jewelry and therefore those items purchased for his wife during his lifetime will not be includable in his estate.

The listing of furniture, assuming your wife has not predeceased you, falls into the same category. It can be presumed to have been a gift to your wife during your lifetime and therefore not includable in your federal taxable estate.

The market value of works of art, jewelry and furniture should be fixed by appraisal. If they are not of great value, a "Guesstimate" can be made. However, if these assets include antiques and expensive jewelry, it would probably be worthwhile to have them appraised professionally. Professionals will necessarily be used at the time of the administration of your estate.

Automobiles may be very easily valued by calling your local auto dealer or bank who will give you its market value, which is based on the so-called NADA Book (National Automobile Dealers Association). If two automobiles are owned it is probably a good idea to have one in your name and the other in your wife's name. This suggestion is not to save on federal or state taxes, but rather to avoid any inconvenience caused by operating a motor vehicle registered in the decedent's name or any problems with insurance coverage on the motor vehicle in the decedent's name. These problems, if any, will depend on local state law.

Personal effects, as ridiculous as it might sound, are a taxable asset from the Federal Estate Tax standpoint as well as in most states. Usually an estimate of their value is sufficient, but I have seen detailed lists and appraisals of personal effects in estates where these items were substantial.

The market values of all these miscellaneous assets should be totalled and placed in the space provided. Now you should add all the subtotals and come up with the grand total.

Besides using this figure for computing any taxes, either Federal Estate or State Inheritance, some other information can be derived. You will recall that I have earlier emphasized the importance of recognizing the difference between probate and non-probate assets. With a detailed property list, we can also compile lists showing probate assets and non-probate assets.

The same property list can be used to separate liquid from non-liquid assets. Liquid assets are cash or securities which can be quickly converted into cash. A savings account is one example.

Such a listing is important because the executor will need to know how much in the way of liquid assets is available for taxes and administration expenses of the estate.

In summary, in gathering information for your estate plan you should:

1. List personal information—name, address, telephone number, age, including similar information for all beneficiaries.

2. List advisors, their names, addresses and telephone numbers.

3. Make a complete list of all your assets giving market value, loans against assets, and how the assets are owned.

4. Make a list of probate and non-probate assets.

5. Determine the dollar amount of the liquid assets in your estate.

In whose name are your cars registered?

Chapter VIII

LIVING ESTATE PLANS

During the course of this next chapter I would like to share with you some living estate plans of the following people:

    I.   **Edward A. Executive, an executive of a large corporation.**
   II.   **Barney Businessman, a business man who is a majority stockholder in a closely held corporation.**
  III.   **Sally Single, an executive secretary and career woman with a large corporation.**
  IV.   **Ronald Retired, a retired man living with his wife in Rossbrook, a retirement community.**
   V.   **Dan Divorced, a young junior executive recently divorced.**
  VI.   **Al Average, a married man just beginning his working career.**

Each of these cases present special problems in estate planning. Perhaps you can relate to one or more of these examples and gain a better perspective for your own estate program.

I.   EDWARD A. EXECUTIVE

Ed is 43 years of age, married to Anne, age 41 and is the father of two children, Joseph 17 years old and Michael 15 years old. A few years ago Ed had read something about taxes and estate planning, but never quite got around to doing anything about an estate program for himself. One day Ed, who is employed as a plant manager for a large manufacturing firm, found that it was necessary for him to leave on a business trip to Europe for several weeks. He remembered that he didn't have a Will, so he contacted an attorney who prepared a Will with all the necessary clauses relating to tax plans. Unfortunately, since time was short, no extensive inventory of Ed's assets was either requested by the attorney nor did Ed volunteer one.

Fortunately, Ed returned from his trip several weeks later safe and sound. Subsequent to his return. Ed was approached by his insurance agent regarding estate planning. During the course of the discussion the agen. raised some questions concerning the effectiveness of Ed's Will as it applied to his insurance program.

The agent suggested that Ed sit down with an attorney experienced in estate planning for a complete review of his situation. The attorney began by taking a complete inventory of Ed's assets. (See Ed's Property List).

The attorney also had an opportunity to review Ed's present Will. He noted that the present Will was not doing a great deal for him in the way of tax savings, mainly because so much of his assets were payable outright to his wife

PROPERTY LIST

Real Estate

	Market Value	Mortgage	Equity	Owner (Indiv. or Jt.)
Residence	$ *50,000*	$ *8,000*	$ *42,000*	*Jt. with wife*
Business Property	$	$	$	
Summer Cottage-Farm	$ *35,000*	$ *20,000*	$ *15,000*	*Jt. with wife*
Rental	$	$	$	

TOTAL EQUITY $ *57,000*

Investments

	Market Value	Loans	Net Value	Owner (Indiv. or Jt.)
Stocks	$ -	$	$	
Mutual Funds	$ -	$	$	
Bonds	$ -	$	$	
U.S. Bonds	$ -	$	$	
Mortgages	$ -	$	$	
Loans	$ -	$	$	

TOTAL $

Business Interests

	Total Market Value	Percentage of Interest	Value of Interest
Close Corporation	-		
Partnership	-		
Proprietorship	-		

TOTAL $

Life Insurance and Employee Benefits

	Market Value	Beneficiary	Owner
Group Insurance	$ *50,000*	*wife*	*husband*
Personal Insurance	$ *130,000*	*wife*	*husband*
Fraternal Assoc. Ins.	$		
Profit Sharing - *Thrift Plan*	$ *23,000*	*wife*	*husband*
Pension Benefits	$ *23,000*	*wife*	*husband*
Stock Options	$ *13,000*	*wife*	*husband*

TOTAL $ *239,000*

Miscellaneous

	Market Value	Owned (Indiv. or Joint)
Savings Accounts	$ *10,000*	*jt. with wife*
	$	
Cash (checking account, etc.)	$ *500*	*jt. with wife*
Works of Art/Jewelry	$	
Furniture	$ *5,000*	*indiv.*
Automobiles	$ *8,500 (2)*	*indiv.*
Personal Effects	$	

TOTAL $ *24,000*

GRAND TOTAL $ *320,000*

This situation would cause the marital deduction trust under his present Will to have little if any assets in it. There were also some problems with respect to the common disaster clause since it presumed that his wife predeceased him in a common accident, thereby destroying the marital deduction. In a review of the powers of the trustees, one of whom was Anne, it was noted that the trustees were empowered to invade the principal of the trusts in their absolute discretion. In essence, this would allow Anne, as a trustee, to invade the trust for her own benefit, as a beneficiary. The attorney pointed out to Ed that this invasionary power would negate the tax savings on the non-marital trust for which the Will had been designed. Furthermore, the attorney noted that a great majority of Ed's assets were in personal and group life insurance and a corporate thrift plan, all made payable to his wife. Therefore, Ed's Will was not controlling these assets.

The attorney told Ed he wanted to review his assets and make some calculations regarding Federal taxes, State Inheritance taxes and estate settlement costs.

He also asked Ed about his estate planning objectives. Ed said that he was naturally interested in saving as much taxes as was legally possible, but was somewhat concerned about his wife's ability to manage money. He felt that if something happened to him, that his sons might take advantage of their mother's good nature and the monies in the estate might possibly be squandered.

Another meeting was scheduled in order that the attorney might formulate some suggestions and prepare tax and estate settlement calculations. The attorney suggested that Anne attend their next meeting.

At this second meeting, the attorney presented Ed and Anne with a flow chart, demonstrating his tax and estate settlement cost liabilities without any estate planning. (See Figure 8.)

He also presented him with a copy of his calculations, assuming a tax planned program. (See Figure 9.)

The attorney pointed out the substantial savings, but cautioned that a person should not be tempted to torture his objectives merely to save taxes. The saving of taxes should be limited to those which allow you to reach your objectives.

The attorney then told Ed that given his objectives he would suggest that a life insurance trust and pour-over will be drafted. Under this arrangement, all Ed's life insurance policies, both personal and group, would be payable to a living trust. The trust would be a so-called "dry trust" because it would never have any assets in it until Ed passed away and the proceeds of the policies were payable to the trustee. The attorney also suggested that any company benefit having a beneficiary designation on it be made payable to the trust.

At the same time the trust was drawn, the attorney suggested that he prepare a pour-over Will. The Will, in broad strokes, would say, "Pay my debts, pay my expenses and then pour-over all my estate assets into the life insurance trust." The attorney explained to Ed that this method would co-ordinate all of his estate into one vehicle of distribution, his life insurance trust.

With respect to Ed's concern over the management of the assets by his wife, the attorney suggested the use of a corporate trustee to manage the assets in

OUTRIGHT DISTRIBUTION

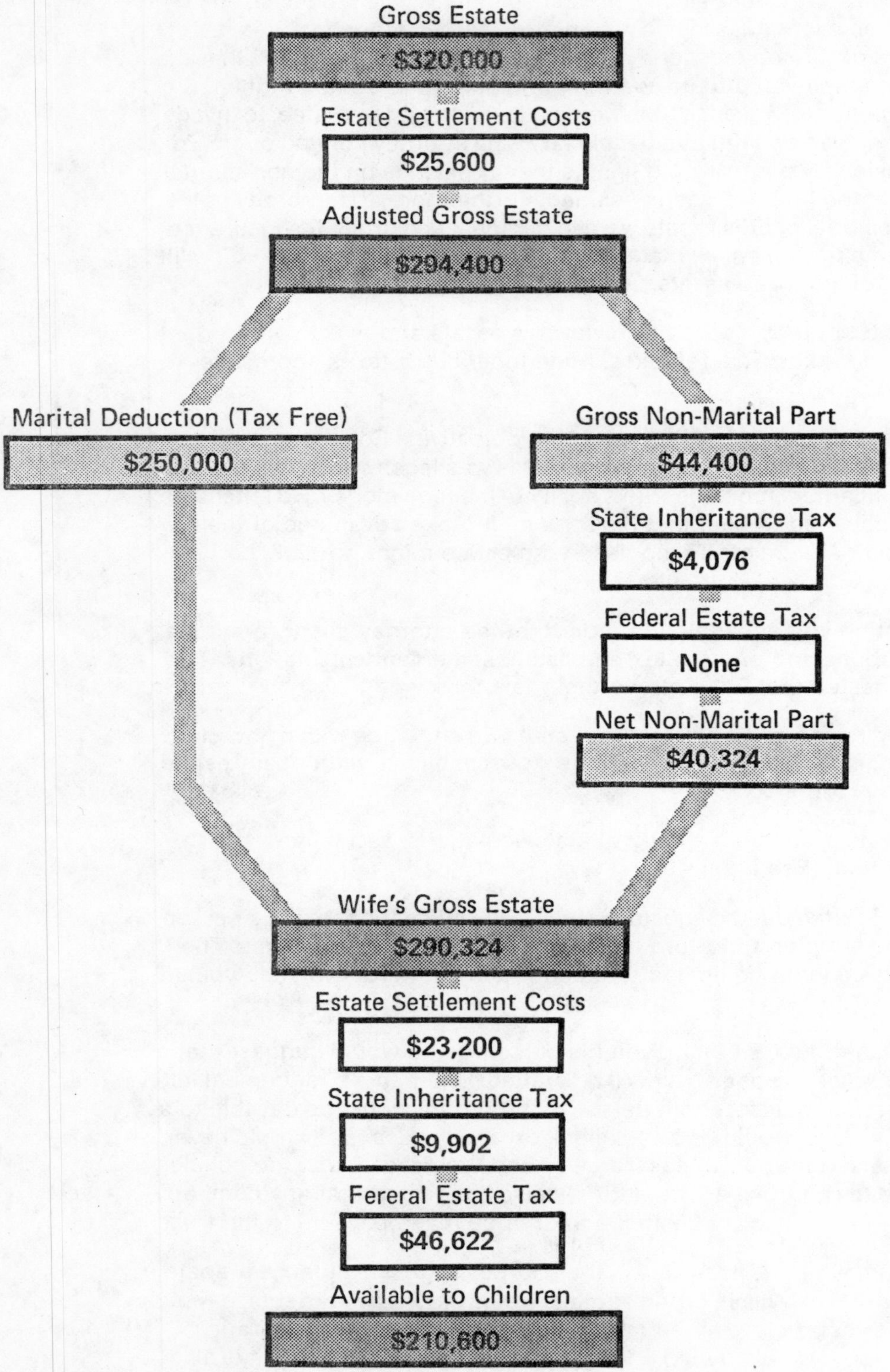

Gross Estate

$320,000

Estate Settlement Costs

$25,600

Adjusted Gross Estate

$294,400

Marital Deduction (Tax Free)

$250,000

Gross Non-Marital Part

$44,400

State Inheritance Tax

$4,076

Federal Estate Tax

None

Net Non-Marital Part

$40,324

Wife's Gross Estate

$290,324

Estate Settlement Costs

$23,200

State Inheritance Tax

$9,902

Fereral Estate Tax

$46,622

Available to Children

$210,600

Figure 8

PLANNED DISTRIBUTION

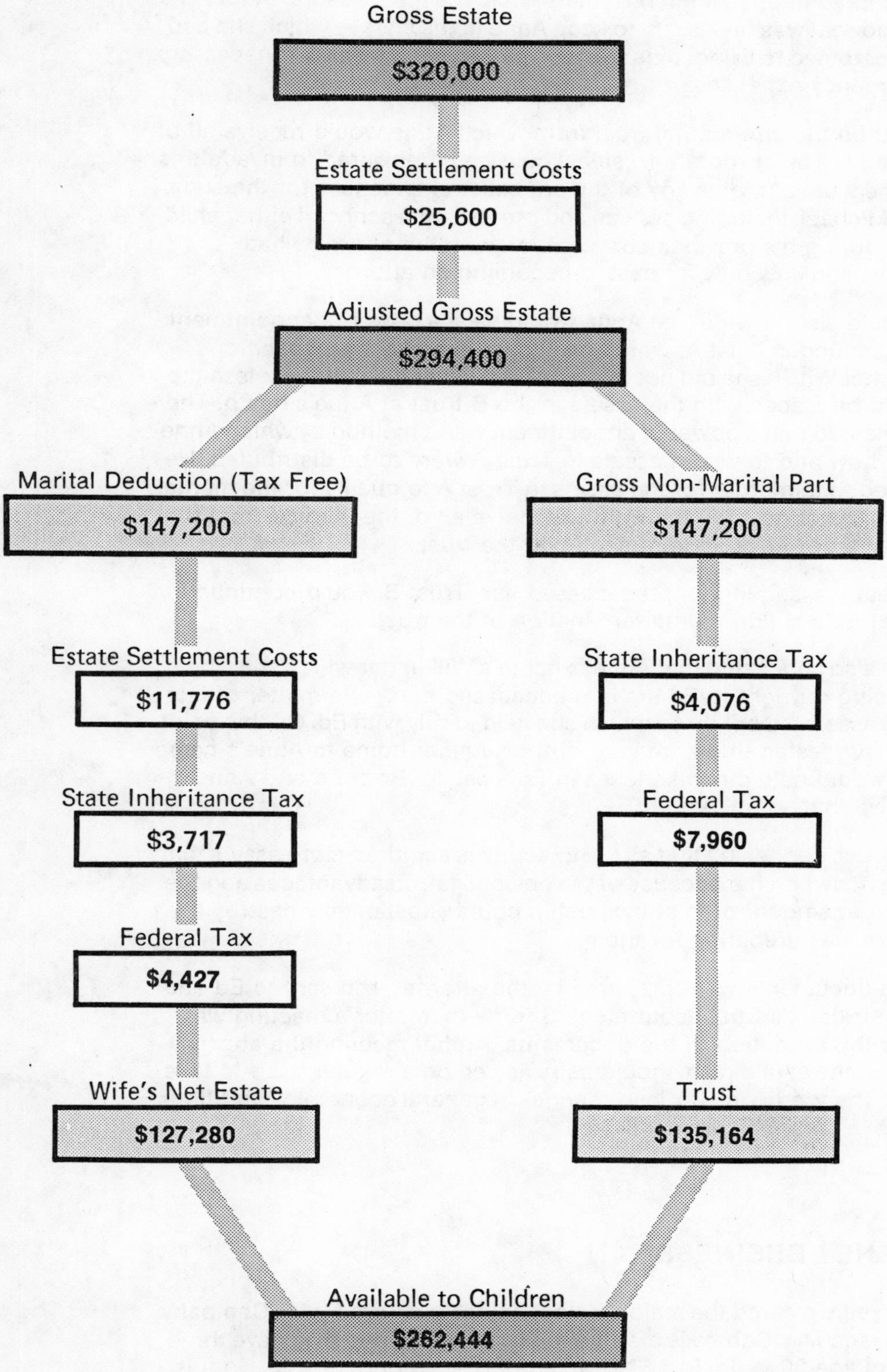

Gross Estate

$320,000

Estate Settlement Costs

$25,600

Adjusted Gross Estate

$294,400

Marital Deduction (Tax Free)

$147,200

Gross Non-Marital Part

$147,200

Estate Settlement Costs

$11,776

State Inheritance Tax

$4,076

State Inheritance Tax

$3,717

Federal Tax

$7,960

Federal Tax

$4,427

Wife's Net Estate

$127,280

Trust

$135,164

Available to Children

$262,444

Figure 9

Ed's estate. The trust would be divided in two parts, the attorney suggested. Part A would be the marital trust from which Anne would receive all of the income, and in addition, as much of the principal as the trustee, in its discretion, thought was necessary to keep Anne in the style to which she had become accustomed to living, plus so much of the principal as was necessary for any emergency expenses.

Part B would be the non-marital trust from which Anne would receive all of the income also. The corporate trustee would be empowered to invade this trust for Anne's benefit, plus any of the educational expenses for the sons, Joseph and Michael, including college and professional school if either child desired. Ed, during his previous conversation with the attorney, had mentioned his son Joseph's interest in becoming an attorney.

The trust would also provide that Anne would have a power of appointment over the assets under Trust A, which she could exercise by a specific statement in her Will. If she did not exercise this power all of the assets in the A trust would be placed with the assets in the B trust at Anne's death. The attorney explained that a power of appointment was a method by which Anne could direct how and to whom assets in Trust A were to be distributed. He also explained that in order for the assets in Trust A to qualify for the marital deduction Anne had to have the right to receive all of the income from the trust and also a power of appointment over the trust.

At Anne's death, assuming he predeceased her, Trust B would continue for the benefit of Ed's children until termination of the trust.

The attorney also suggested that Anne execute a Will under which she would leave everything outright to Ed if she predeceased him. As a matter of fact, Anne had no assets except those which she held jointly with Ed. On this point the attorney suggested that a transfer of the summer home to Anne's name individually would help diminish taxes in Ed's estate. Both Ed and Anne wanted to give that some thought.

The attorney also suggested that as the Executives acquired more assets that they avoid joint ownership because of the obvious tax disadvantages and the fact that a great amount of joint ownership could substantially destroy the estate plan he was preparing for them.

Drafts of the documents were prepared by the attorney and sent to Ed and Anne and their bank's trust department. Shortly thereafter a meeting was arranged for the execution of the documents. At that meeting the attorney cautioned that the estate plan should be reviewed on a regular basis to take into account changes in the tax law, changes in general economic conditions and changes in personal circumstances.

II.   BARNEY BUSINESSMAN

Barney is 59 years old and the majority stockholder in a Ford Motor Company automobile franchise. Barney is married to Mary, age 58, and they have three children. Tom age 30, a doctor; Sharon, age 27, and John, age 23. Tom is married and has two children. Sharon is also married with no children. John is single and works in the automobile business with his father.

Barney is concerned about a variety of estate planning problems. At the present time he has an outdated Will which provides only a simple plan of distribution. He recognizes its shortcomings and has been meaning to do something but he has been very busy in the automobile business.

His major concern is to provide adequately for his wife in the event of his demise. He would like to save taxes, but would want his wife to have the utmost flexibility to enjoy and use the assets of his estate should he pass away first.

The automobile business has been good to him and he would like to "keep the business going" if possible after his death. Unlike many small businessmen who lack successor management, Barney feels that with a little more experience his son John will be an excellent general manager for the business. He has already given much consideration to gifting a portion of Barney Ford (his corporation) to his son in order to reduce the size of his estate and at the same time encourage his son to stay with the business.

Barney's other problem is how to leave a portion of his estate to his other two children. He has already concluded that to leave them stock in Barney Ford would not really benefit them unless the corporation was to pay dividends. His accountant has indicated that it wasn't a good idea to pay dividends. He would like to give them other assets, but the majority of his assets are in Barney Ford and real estate which he holds jointly with Mary, his wife.

His asset picture is shown on the following page.

Beset with these problems, Barney decided to see his attorney. Barney related his concerns to his attorney and gave the attorney a complete list of his assets. After reviewing Barney's asset picture and objectives, the attorney demonstrated the tremendous losses Barney would incur with his present Will. The unplanned flow chart shows what the attorney told Barney about the losses he would incur as a result of a simple Will. (Figure 10)

The attorney then went about trying to offer Barney some solutions to his problem. His first observation was that Barney avoid leaving any of the stock in Barney Ford to his wife. Barney admitted that Mary had no knowledge about or interest in the automobile business. The attorney then suggested that Barney gift a one-third interest in the business to his son John and that the appropriate tax return and tax be paid. Also, that Barney enter into an agreement which would provide that Barney sell and John buy additional shares in the business either during the lifetime of both or at Barney's death. The objectives of the agreement would be to make certain John's continuation of the business, and to insure that John would be properly rewarded for helping to build the business. At Barney's death the payment by John for the remaining two-thirds of the stock could be used to satisfy the liquidity requirements of the estate and also to provide funds for specific bequests to his brother and sister out of his father's estate.

The attorney also suggested that to the extent there was any unequal distribution of Barney's estate among his three children at his death, his wife could remedy this by leaving more under her Will to Tom and Sharon than to John.

The thrust of the entire program would be to leave a maximum marital deduction to Mary under Barney's Will. The remainder, after paying taxes,

PROPERTY LIST

Real Estate	Market Value	Mortgage	Equity	Owner (Indiv. or Jt.)
Residence	$ 80,000	$ 30,000	$ 50,000	jt. with wife
Business Property	$	$	$	
Summer Cottage-Farm	$ 80,000	$ 57,000	$ 23,000	jt. with wife
Rental	$	$	$	
		TOTAL EQUITY $	73,000	

Investments	Market Value	Loans	Net Value	Owner (Indiv. or Jt.)
Stocks	$ 6,250	$ -	$ 6,250	indiv.
Mutual Funds	$	$	$	
Bonds	$	$	$	
U.S. Bonds	$	$	$	
Mortgages	$	$	$	
Loans	$	$	$	
		TOTAL $	6,250	

Business Interests	Total Market Value	Percentage of Interest	Value of Interest
Close Corporation Barney Ford, Inc.	170,000	100%	170,000
Partnership			
Proprietorship			
	TOTAL $	170,000	

Life Insurance and Employee Benefits	Market Value	Beneficiary	Owner
Group Insurance	$ 150,000	wife	husband
Personal Insurance	$ 75,000	wife	husband
Fraternal Assoc. Ins.	$		
Profit Sharing	$		
Pension Benefits	$		
Stock Options	$		
	TOTAL $	225,000	

Miscellaneous		Owned (Indiv. or Joint)
Savings Accounts	$ 30,000	indiv.
	$	
Cash (checking account, etc.)	$ minimal	
Works of Art/Jewelry	$	
Furniture	$	
Automobiles	$	
Personal Effects	$ 20,000	indiv.
	TOTAL $ 50,000	
	GRAND TOTAL $ 524,250	

OUTRIGHT DISTRIBUTION

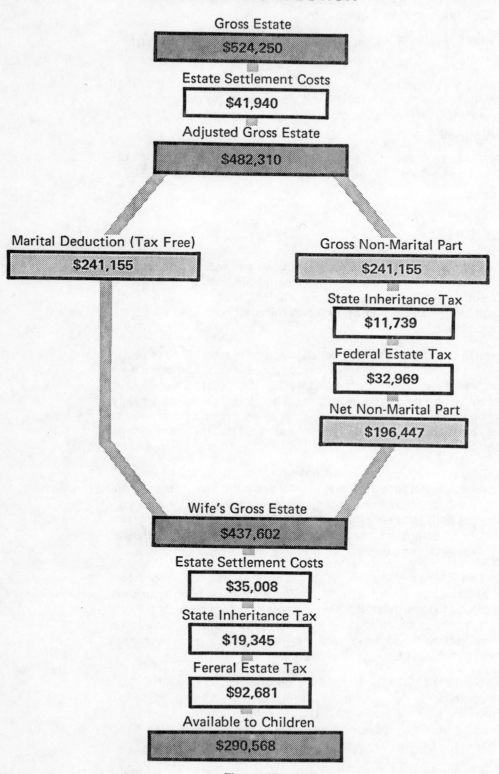

Gross Estate
$524,250

Estate Settlement Costs
$41,940

Adjusted Gross Estate
$482,310

Marital Deduction (Tax Free)
$241,155

Gross Non-Marital Part
$241,155

State Inheritance Tax
$11,739

Federal Estate Tax
$32,969

Net Non-Marital Part
$196,447

Wife's Gross Estate
$437,602

Estate Settlement Costs
$35,008

State Inheritance Tax
$19,345

Fereral Estate Tax
$92,681

Available to Children
$290,568

Figure 10

would be divided equally among the three children, except that John would have deducted from his share the value of the gift of one-third the shares in Barney Ford which his father had given him.

The tax effect of this distribution can be seen in the planned flow chart. (Figure 11)

Barney wasn't totally satisfied with the solution because he was concerned about John's ability to pay for the stock, even on a long term basis. He could fund the purchase with life insurance on his life, but was concerned with the premium cost at his age.

Barney still hasn't made a decision yet. Sometimes estate plans cannot be 100% effective but the old adage "something is better than nothing" still applies.

III.   SALLY SINGLE

Sally is a business woman. She has held an executive secretarial position in a large corporation for many years. Through investments and an inheritance from an uncle, Sally's estate is in excess of $300,000. Sally has read extensively on estate planning and attended seminars sponsored by banks and investment companies.

However, neither the reading material nor the seminars ever discuss the single person's estate plan. Everything written or discussed at seminars, says Sally, presumes that everyone is married. Unfortunately, what Sally says is true, but it's not by design her attorney told her. The plain truth is there really are not a great many ways for single people to save on Federal Estate Taxes. The only way is to reduce your estate before you die. That means making irrevocable gifts during your lifetime.

The first thing Sally's attorney did was to have her list the kinds of assets which comprised her estate. He noted that most were good quality stocks and bonds. Further investigation by the attorney discovered that Sally had a very substantial fringe benefit program through her employment. This program would guarantee her a suitable pension, even at early retirement. Sally was now 57 years of age and has been considering retiring at 62.

Sally had shown an interest in helping with the education of some of her talented nieces and nephews, who would also be the ultimate beneficiaries of her estate. With this in mind, her attorney suggested establishing an educational trust for these children. The trust would be funded by an initial gift and additional gifts would be made to the trust as Sally became more aware of her exact living expenses during retirement.

The attorney also pointed out that since Sally had not made any gifts that a substantial one could be made to the trust without incurring any gift tax. This could be accomplished by making a $3,000 gift under the annual gift tax exclusion to each of her ten nieces and nephews. This would reduce her estate and also the state inheritance tax payable at her death.

The difference in Federal Estate Tax on her present estate as compared to the proposed plan by her attorney is shown in the following examples:

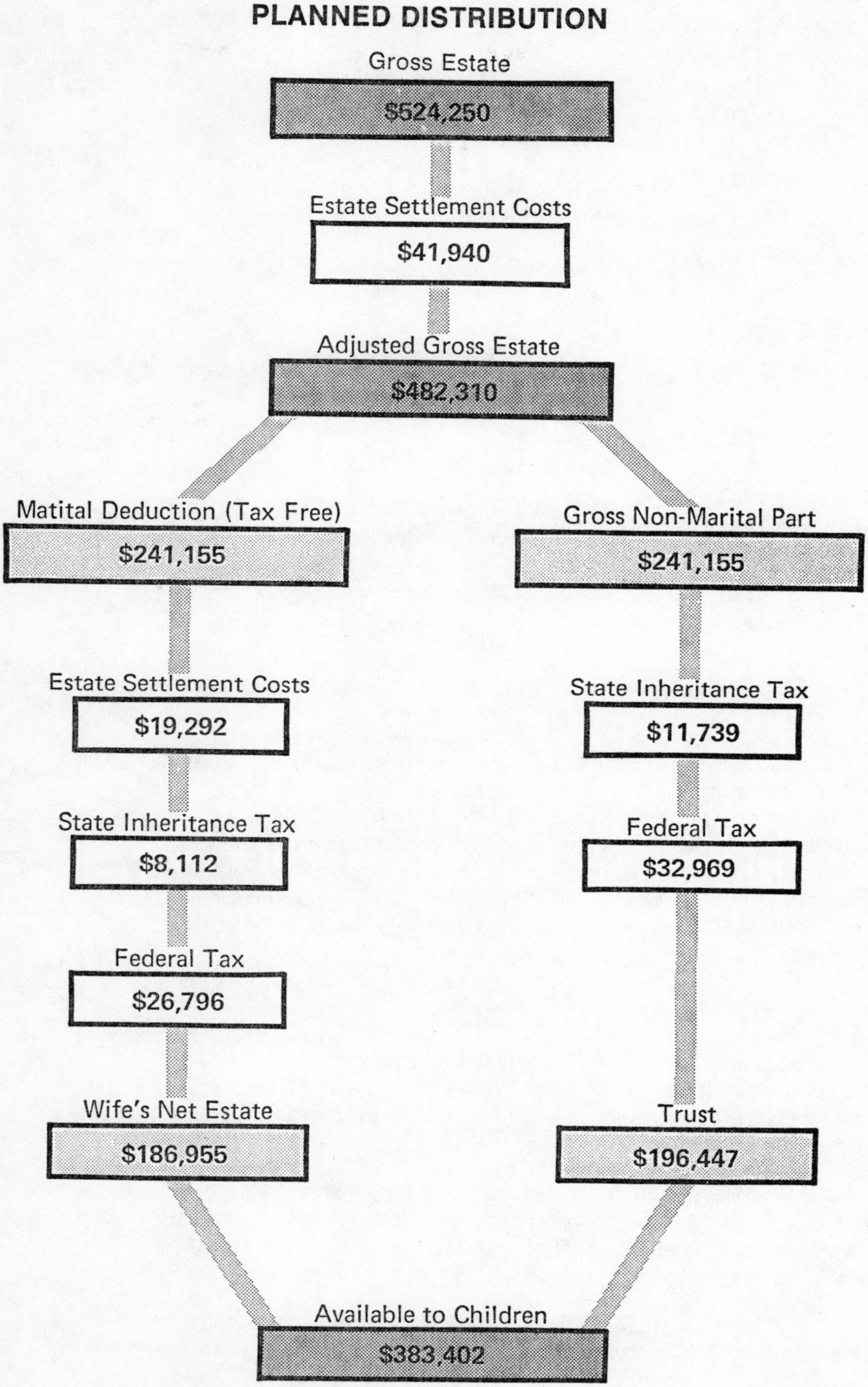

PLANNED DISTRIBUTION

Gross Estate

$524,250

Estate Settlement Costs

$41,940

Adjusted Gross Estate

$482,310

Matital Deduction (Tax Free)	Gross Non-Marital Part
$241,155	**$241,155**
Estate Settlement Costs	State Inheritance Tax
$19,292	$11,739
State Inheritance Tax	Federal Tax
$8,112	$32,969
Federal Tax	
$26,796	
Wife's Net Estate	Trust
$186,955	**$196,447**

Available to Children

$383,402

Figure 11

Before Educational Trust

$300,000	Gross Estate
24,000	(Minus) Estate Settlement Costs
$276,000	Adjusted Gross Estate
59,976	(Minus) ($29,616 Federal Estate Tax) ($30,360 State Inheritance Tax)
$216,024	Total Available to Heirs

With Educational Trust

Trust

$30,000

$270,000	Gross Estate
21,600	(Minus) Estate Settlement Costs
$248,400	
48,150	(Minus) ($20,808 Federal Estate Tax ($27,342 State Inheritance Tax
$200,250	
30,000	(Add) Trust $30,000 ←
$230,250	Total Available to Heirs

SAVINGS =$14,226

Sally approved of this program and the attorney prepared the trust, naming the trust department of a local bank as trustee. In addition to the trust, the attorney also prepared a simple Will for Sally which provided that upon her death, the assets in her estate be divided equally among her nieces and nephews. He cautioned her that although the trust was irrevocable, that she would have the opportunity to change her Will at any time. The attorney further advised that the Will be reviewed at least every five years and certainly upon the date of her retirement.

IV.   MR. AND MRS. RONALD RETIRED

Mr. and Mrs. Retired are residents of Rossbrook, a retirement community. Through careful planning the Retireds have avoided registering their assets in joint names. Mr. Retired credits his reading about the problems of jointly held assets in a financial article in the local newspaper.

In any event, the Retireds have never done anything much about estate planning other than avoiding jointly owned property. They have simple Wills which leave everything to the survivor. Their estates are substantial and they have two children, Rodney, age 26 and Alice, age 31, and four grandchildren, two in each family.

Mr. Retired has an estate of $300,000, made up of a condominium, a small amount of insurance and the remainder in stocks and bonds. Mrs. Retired has a similar estate, but her total assets are approximately $275,000.

Mr. Retired was prompted to review his situation after having attended a seminar on the subject of estate planning sponsored by the trust department of the local bank. At the invitation of the trust officer he met with him to discuss his estate. The trust officer listened to Mr. Retired's objectives, which were two in number. First, provide security for his wife in the event of his death, and second, save as much taxes as was consistent with his first objective.

The trust officer offered two possible solutions. The first was the use of reciprocal marital deduction Wills. This would mean that each of the Retireds would have Wills drawn which would provide that after the payment of estate settlement costs, one-half the adjusted gross estate would be payable outright to the survivor. This would pass Federal Estate Tax-free under the marital deduction. The remainder of the estate, after deducting Federal Estate Taxes and State Inheritance taxes, would be placed in a trust. The survivor would receive the income from the trust, plus so much of the principal as was necessary (1) to keep the survivor in the style that he or she was accustomed to living and (2) for emergency expenses, such as nursing home fees, if they were required. The trust officer indicated that this program would save substantial taxes.

The following unplanned and planned flow charts (Figures 12 and 13) demonstrate the Retired's situation under simple Wills as compared to reciprocal marital deduction Wills. In each case it is presumed that Mr. Retired passed away first.

As an alternative to this plan, the trust officer also suggested a so-called equalization of estate plan. Under this plan both Mr. and Mrs. Retired's Wills would be identical also. However, each would provide that after leaving personal property to the survivor, that all the rest, residue and remainder of the estate, exclusive of the amount necessary for the payment of Federal Estate and State Inheritance taxes, would be left in a single trust.

The survivor would receive the income from this trust, plus so much of the principal as was needed for emergencies. At the death of the survivor, the trust set up by the first spouse would not be included in the surviving spouse's estate and thereby save substantial taxes.

The following charts (Figure 14) demonstrate the Retired's tax and estate settlement cost picture under the above-described program.

Through a comparison of this chart with the previous reciprocal marital deduction charts, you will note a slightly greater saving under this program.

In comparing the two plans, the trust officer pointed out two important points. First, the tax savings in both cases were for the benefit of the Retired's children and did not benefit either of them directly. Second, although the second plan saved more tax, there was more tax paid at the death of the first spouse because no assets qualified for the marital deduction.

The trust officer suggested that the Retireds consult with an attorney to get his view on the programs. After doing so the Retireds decided on the reciprocal marital deduction program.

OUTRIGHT DISTRIBUTION

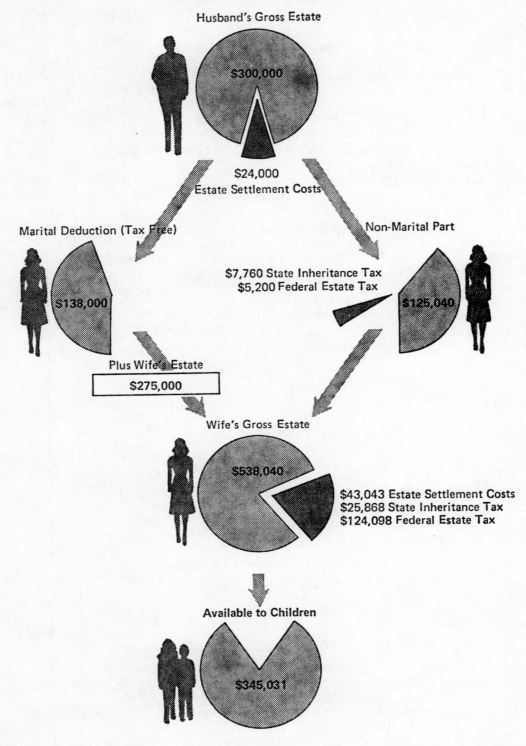

Husband's Gross Estate

$300,000

$24,000
Estate Settlement Costs

Marital Deduction (Tax Free)

$138,000

Non-Marital Part

$7,760 State Inheritance Tax
$5,200 Federal Estate Tax

$125,040

Plus Wife's Estate

$275,000

Wife's Gross Estate

$538,040

$43,043 Estate Settlement Costs
$25,868 State Inheritance Tax
$124,098 Federal Estate Tax

Available to Children

$345,031

Figure 12

PLANNED DISTRIBUTION

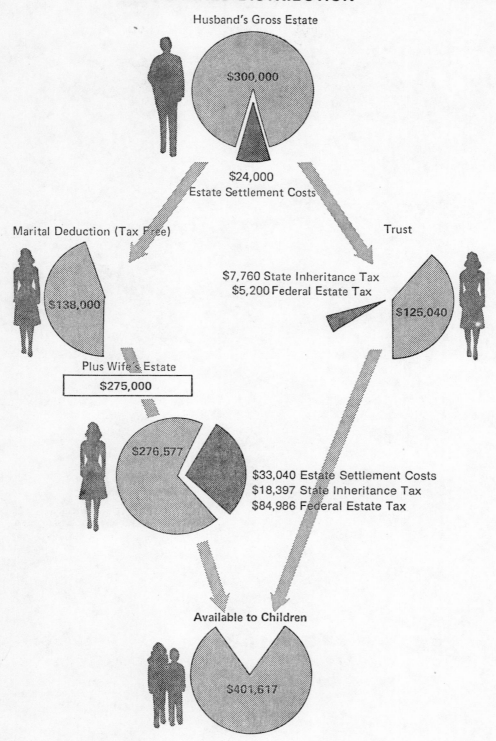

Husband's Gross Estate

$300,000

$24,000
Estate Settlement Costs

Marital Deduction (Tax Free)

Trust

$138,000

$7,760 State Inheritance Tax
$5,200 Federal Estate Tax

$125,040

Plus Wife's Estate

$275,000

$276,577

$33,040 Estate Settlement Costs
$18,397 State Inheritance Tax
$84,986 Federal Estate Tax

Available to Children

$401,617

Figure 13

EQUALIZATION OF ESTATE PLAN

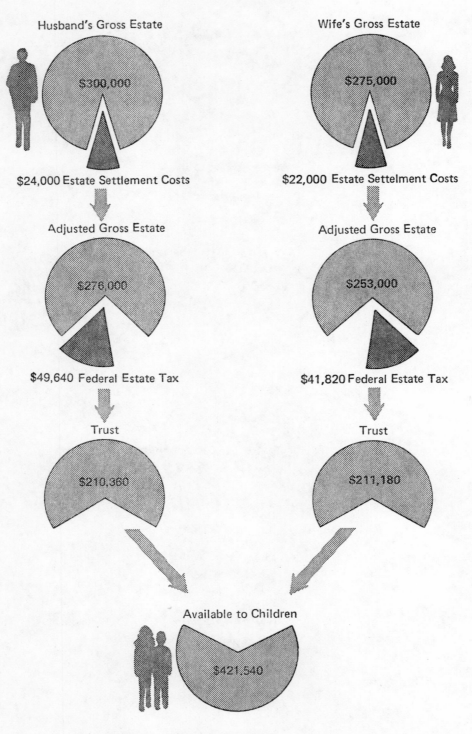

Husband's Gross Estate

$300,000

$24,000 Estate Settlement Costs

Adjusted Gross Estate

$276,000

$49,640 Federal Estate Tax

Trust

$210,360

Wife's Gross Estate

$275,000

$22,000 Estate Settelment Costs

Adjusted Gross Estate

$253,000

$41,820 Federal Estate Tax

Trust

$211,180

Available to Children

$421,540

Figure 14

V.   DAN DIVORCED

Dan Divorced had been married for five years before his divorce and is the father of a son, age three and a half years. Dan has had several jobs, all in the sales and marketing field and has consistently earned a good income. Previous to his divorce, Dan and his wife had executed simple Wills in which they left everything in their respective estates each to the other. These Wills had been executed before the birth of their son, Sammy.

In accordance with the terms of the divorce decree, Dan is obligated to keep $100,000 in life insurance in an irrevocable trust for the benefit of his son, Sammy, and also contribute to his support. The divorce did not provide for any payment of alimony since Dan's wife had instituted the divorce proceeding, under a revised divorce law which does not require any specific grounds other than the parties no longer wish to live as husband and wife and that they can prove to the court's satisfaction that they have been separated and living in separate households for the statutory period required under the law. She also made no claim for any alimony payments. Prior to the divorce a property settlement had been entered into by both parties which each thought was fair and equitable.

Dan asked his attorney about the details of setting up such a trust, and the tax consequences regarding its establishment. The attorney explained that since Dan already had $40,000 of whole life insurance that he should probably keep this in force and merely add the required $60,000 by way of an additional purchase. He advised, however, that he check with his insurance agent as to the kind of insurance he should purchase and what were the advantages and disadvantages of cashing in his $40,000 whole life policy if it was decided that whole life was the wrong kind of insurance to use in his situation.

The agent suggested that Dan retain the $40,000 whole life policy. However, in order to keep down immediate costs, which was a concern of Dan's, the additional $60,000 insurance would take the form of a term policy, which was at a considerably lower premium than $60,000 of whole life.

The attorney next explained the mechanics of setting up the irrevocable life insurance trust. The attorney suggested that under the circumstances he would strongly urge the use of a corporate trustee to insure impartiality in the administration of the trust and professional investment management at the time the trust was funded.

The attorney pointed out that according to the settlement agreement, the obligation to keep this trust in force extended only to the date upon which Sammy reached his majority. He also advised that in the event of Sammy's predeceasing Dan, an alternate beneficiary could and should be provided.

The attorney further indicated that since the transfer was an irrevocable one, the proceeds of the insurance would probably not be included in Dan's estate for Federal Estate Tax and State Inheritance tax purposes.

In addition to Dan's irrevocable insurance trust, the attorney advised Dan to execute a new Will, providing for whatever beneficiaries he chose. Dan told the attorney that his only heir was his son and he wanted him to have his entire estate. The attorney then suggested the preparation of a pour-over Will. This type of Will would provide for the payment of debts and expenses and then recite that all the remainder of the estate be poured over into the irrevocable life insurance trust at Dan's death.

Dan, who is only 30 years old, was advised by the attorney that there was statistically a good possibility that Dan would remarry. Therefore, his objectives with respect to the disposition of his entire estate could change, especially if he were to begin a new family with his second wife.

VI.   AL AVERAGE

Al Average, who is 25 years old, is married to Theresa, age 23. They have two children, Harry, 3, and Michael, 6 months. Al works for Universal Widgets, in their receiving and stores department. Al has no Will and really hadn't given any thought to getting one if it hadn't been for the untimely death of his best friend, Chuck. Chuck, a construction worker, was killed on a construction site when the cable on a crane snapped and sent the load of steel girders plummeting to the ground. Chuck, like Al, had a wife and two children and no Will. Al doesn't understand all the details, but from what he has been able to learn, the administration of Chuck's estate is causing problems for his wife and children.

Another reason Al never bothered to have a Will drawn was his belief that Wills were only for people with substantial estates. He's now begun to think twice about this after seeing the problem of Chuck's family.

Al and Theresa went to the attorney who had represented him when they purchased their home. The attorney asked Al to make a list of his assets.

The attorney observed that Al had no Federal Estate Tax or any substantial state inheritance tax problems. With respect to the new unified Federal Tax he explained that since Al's total estate was well below the $250,000 marital deduction and the tax credit available that he need not concern himself with any tax problems.

The attorney also pointed out that although there would be a small state inheritance tax at Al's death, there were certain substantial exemptions available. In Al's state of domicile, there were three basic exemptions from the state inheritance tax. First, any life insurance on Al's life, whether it be a group insurance or personal, made payable to any named beneficiary, would not be taxable as part of his estate. This meant that Al's group insurance at the plant, which was made payable to Theresa at his death, would not be taxed under the state inheritance tax. It also meant that his personal insurance made payable to his wife wouldn't be taxed either.

The second exemption under the state inheritance tax law in Al's state of residence provided that any real property held jointly by husband and wife also escaped the levy of any tax. Al remembered that the attorney at the title closing of his house suggested that Al and Theresa put their house in joint names, but he hadn't given it much thought until now.

The third exemption was one which applied only to parents, grandparents, a wife and children, but it provided that the first $5,000 to each of these beneficiaries was received by them tax free.

The attorney then prepared a rough tax calculation on Al's estate, which looked something like the following:

$50,600	Gross Estate
$ 4,048	(Minus) Estate Settlement Costs
$46,552	Adjusted Gross Estate
-0-	(Minus) Federal Estate Tax; State Inheritance Tax
$39,000	(Minus) $24,000 Real Estate; $15,000 Life Insurance
$ 7,552	Taxable Estate
$ 5,000	(Minus) Class 1 $5,000 Exemption
$ 2,552	Net Taxable Estate
$ 25.	Tax

Al and Theresa were pleased to see the tax was so little, but were concerned about any other problems. The attorney told them that each should have a simple Will but that it was important to select certain people to help in the administration of their estates. Specifically, an executor, a trustee, and a guardian. All would be named in the Will. It was suggested by the attorney that Al act as executor under Theresa's Will and Theresa be named under Al's Will. Assuming that either survived the other, there seemed to be no great difficulty in administering their estates.

The real problem would occur if they passed away leaving their children, Harry and Michael, not yet having reached their majority. Some provision should be made for this possibility. The attorney then suggested that each of their Wills include clauses which would establish a "contingent trust" for the benefit of their children. This would cover the situation not only if Al and Theresa passed away in a common accident, but also in the event they passed away at different times but both before the children became adults. The purpose of this trust would be to hold and invest all the assets in Al and Theresa's estate for the benefit of their children.

The usual selection for someone to act as trustee would be a person possessing some investment knowledge or a bank trust department which offers services as trustee. In addition to the trustee, the attorney advised that the selection of a competent guardian for the children would also be necessary. He explained that the guardian's job would be to provide a home for the children at the death of Al and Theresa. The guardian would also receive monies from the trustee for clothing, food and education of the children. The guardian and trustee could be the same person if Al and Theresa were of the opinion that this one person possessed the qualifications for both positions.

Both Al and Theresa liked the program the attorney outlined and told him to proceed with a draft of their Wills, while they gave some thought as to whom to choose as trustee and guardian. The attorney also asked that they consider at what age they would want the trust to terminate and the assets be paid out to the children. Al believed that considering the size of his estate he would just as soon see the trust terminate when the youngest child reached age 21.

Drafts were prepared and the names of a trustee and guardian were decided upon. A short time later the Wills were signed by Al and Theresa. Al remarked at their signing that he was relieved that he had taken this step to protect his wife and family.

Chapter IX

SPECIAL TECHNIQUES AND NEW DEVELOPMENTS

THE PRIVATE ANNUITY

Many of you, I am sure, are familiar with the concept of an annuity, some of you may even have purchased one or more. The basic idea of an annuity is the payment of a certain amount of dollars in exchange for a guaranteed income, either over a period of years or for the life of the purchaser or the purchaser and his wife or other beneficiary. This is called a commercial annuity, as distinguished from a private annuity.

The commercial annuity is purchased from an insurance company. The amount of income received from any given annuity will depend usually on two factors, the amount of dollars paid and the life expectancy of the purchaser.

The private annuity is a transfer of property from one person to another for a promise by the recipient of the property to pay to the original owner a certain income for life. More often than not, private annuities are between family members and the subject of the annuity is real property or an interest in a closely-held business. The amount of income will depend on the value of the transferred property, an interest rate and the life expectancy of the person who transferred the property.

Caution: Consult your attorney.

Why get involved in a private annuity? There are several reasons, most of them tax reasons.

The first thing that occurs is that the person transferring the property has removed a substantial asset from his estate and thereby reduced the payment of Federal Estate Taxes and State Inheritance Taxes at his death. Secondly, because it is presumably an "arm's length transaction" there is no gift tax involved when the transfer is made.

An attack by the Internal Revenue Service can be made on the gift tax aspects of a private annuity when the annuity payment exceeds a figure computed on the basis of the life expectancy tables. For example, if the annuity table provides that a person should receive $15,000 per year considering the age of the transferor and the value of the property transferred but instead he receives $20,000 per year, the extra payment is a taxable gift. Third, there are income tax advantages to the person receiving the annuity payment. The tax law provides that each payment is made up of (a) return of capital, (b) capital gain and (c) ordinary income. The bookkeeping may be a problem but in most cases well worth the time.

As a practical matter, although the private annuity has gained in popularity recently, there are a limited number of estate planning situations to which it can be applied. One of the most significant problems is the ability of the family member to pay the computed annuity, let alone pay an amount in excess of that number. First of all, the person to whom the property has been transferred has to pay income tax on the income produced by the transferred property. Also, in most cases this net income is less than the amount of annuity payment required.

Therefore, unless one can count on the transferee of the property having a substantial amount of income in order to be able to afford the annuity payment, the private annuity will not work.

It has been suggested by many estate planners that a combination gift and private annuity might be the answer. It would work in the following manner:

A father would transfer some property to his son under the private annuity concept. In addition he would also make a gift to the son of other income producing property. The object of the dual transfer would be to have the son use the income from the property transferred under the private annuity plus the income from the gifted property to satisfy the annuity payment.

Again this situation presumes sufficient wealth on the part of the father to be able to afford these transfers and not be concerned regarding guaranteed payment. By guaranteed payment I mean that the annuity payment, to qualify as a private annuity, may not be secured in any way.

We have thus far outlined the advantages to the transferor, the person who gives the property. What advantages are there to the transferee? Since we have already indicated that the great majority of private annuities occur intra-family the obvious advantages is that the estate received by the transferee has escaped federal and state death taxes, to the extent of the annuity and or gift.

Secondly, if the transferor passes away at any time before his life expectancy, the transferee has acquired property for far less than market value. This is true because the obligation to pay the annuity ceases at the transferor's death in our example.

To summarize, the private annuity is an exciting estate planning tool. However, do not be bedazzled by it. Its application is limited and before entering into such an arrangement be sure your attorney and accountant have explained all its pitfalls.

This should be viewed in light of the revisions to the Gift Tax law by virtue of the 1976 Tax Reform Act effective Dec. 31, 1976

THE "SEC. 303 REDEMPTION"

The source and method of payment of Federal Estate Taxes is always of major concern, but especially so in an estate in which the major asset is a closely-held corporation. In many cases the only way to pay the tax is to sell the corporation to gain the necessary tax dollars. Even if a partial sale of stock could be arranged this will often cause the family of the decedent to lose a controlling interest in the corporation.

The Federal Government, in recognition of the acute liquidity problem, offered relief under Section 303 of the Internal Revenue Code in which

changes in the tax law provided some relief.

special tax treatment is afforded to distributions by the corporation in redemption of stock to pay death taxes. This section, as recently amended, provides that if a corporation's stock constitutes more than 50% of the decedent's adjusted gross estate a redemption of stock equal to the total of the Federal Estate Tax, the state inheritance tax and estate settlement costs which are allowable as deductions to the estate will be treated as a distribution in exchange for the stock redeemed. In other circumstances a distribution of this kind might be taxed as a dividend.

This section, then, allows the executor or the administrator of the estate to come up with the necessary liquidity requirements of the estate without incurring income tax. The provisions of Section 303 really allow a dividend to be treated as a sale or exchange.

There is no requirement that the stock redeemed be held by the estate. Any beneficiary may redeem the stock under this provision or anyone who received the stock as a gift in contemplation of death and where the stock was part of the decedent's taxable estate.

It should also be noted that the proceeds of the redemption do not actually have to be used to pay death taxes nor does the estate have to have a liquidity problem to take advantage of a "303 Redemption."

The stock redemption program will only work if the corporation has the money to pay for the stock. Providing these monies is called funding and the two means most commonly used are the corporation's accumulated earnings or the purchase of life insurance. An agreement is usually drawn between the corporation and the stockholder where insurance is used as the funding media. This agreement provides that the corporation agrees to purchase life insurance on the stockholder's life and use the proceeds to purchase the decedent stockholder's shares. The policy is paid for and owned by the corporation. In some instances a combination of the accumulated earnings and insurance proceeds may be used for the purchase.

Excessive accumulated earnings in a corporation will cause a penalty tax to be levied; however, when it can be shown that the accumulation is based on the need to fund a 303 Redemption, the penalty tax will not be assessed.

Caution: check with your attorney.

With respect to the amount of insurance to be purchased, the exact amount cannot be calculated. The reason for this is that the amount of insurance necessary cannot be determined until the decedent's estate tax, state tax and estate settlement costs are finally determined. Therefore, a periodic review of the value of the corporation and hypothetical calculations regarding taxes and estate settlement costs should be made.

The 303 Redemption, although discussed in a vacuum here, should not be applied in a vacuum. It is an estate planning tool or technique which must be considered along with all the other factors of any given estate plan.

PENSION REFORM ACT OF 1974

On September 2, 1974 President Gerald R. Ford signed a bill making sweeping changes in private retirement benefit laws. Its objectives included (1) insuring pensioners of a guaranteed pension benefits by tightening the rules of administration of pension and profit sharing plans, (2) placing self-employed individuals who are covered under HR 10 or Keogh Plan, programs on a more equal plane with corporate pensioners, by allowing a maximum annual deduction equal to 15% of the self-employed individual's earned income with a ceiling of $7,500 per year. This changed the 10% of earned income with a ceiling of $2,500 provisions of the previous HR 10 law. And (3), the new law provided for some type of pension benefit for persons who are not covered by any pension or profit sharing plan at their place of employment. This is through the establishment of an Individual Retirement Account. An IRA is a private pension plan which allows annual contributions, which are tax exempt, of 15% of the person's annual compensation with a ceiling on the contribution of $1,500. The interest or dividends earned on these contributions are not currently taxed; however, at the time of distribution at retirement the ordinary income tax tables will apply.

The most interesting aspect of the pension reform law in my opinion has been the introduction of the IRA. The deduction under this part of the law became available for all years beginning with January 1, 1975. The law provides for the establishment of a retirement account, or an individual annuity or an individual retirement bond, with certain limitations. There is a specific prohibition against any investment in life insurance contracts. The amount of deduction is on a per-person basis and not per-family. Therefore, if husband and wife are both employed and neither of them are covered by a corporate plan, each may deduct up to $1,500 per year toward their respective individual retirement account. The distribution of the plan is made mandatory as each person reaches age 70½.

If the yearly contribution is to be invested in an individual annuity, the law defines annuity as an annuity contract or endowment contract issued by an insurance company which is not transferable. Also, the premium cannot be more than $1,500 per year. The contract must also provide that the entire interest of the purchaser of the annuity is non-forfeitable.

The law provides a third method of investment, that of Retirement Bonds. The special U.S. bonds are issued under the Second Liberty Bond Act and are subject to certain restrictions. First, the interest on the bond is payable only when the bond is redeemed. Also, if the bond is redeemed within twelve months after its date of purchase no interest is paid. Interest on the bond ceases when the purchaser reaches age seventy and one-half. The purchaser of the bond may redeem the bond under three conditions: (1) if he has reached age fifty-nine and one-half, (2) if he is disabled or (3) redeems the bond within one year after he purchased it.

In addition to individuals establishing individual retirement accounts for themselves, employers, self-employed people and unions may establish these accounts for their employees or members. This means that as a substitute for adopting a more formal, more complicated and more costly plan, employers may decide to adopt individual retirement accounts for their employees.

The act had another important feature in that no matter what type of investment is selected initially there is an opportunity to transfer assets in the account from a savings account to a retirement annuity or to a bond investment. Furthermore, it also provides that if you are employed and covered under a qualified plan you may convert to an individual plan when you change employment and your new employer has no qualified plan. All the above transfers may be made without any taxes being paid.

A so-called "defined benefit program" may provide an even greater deduction. Check with your attorney.

New law provides an additional tax deductible $250 contribution for a non-working spouse.

1978 Revenue Act allows this contribution to be eligible for the gift tax annual exclusion.

The value of an annuity purchased for use in an IRA establishment for a husband and non-working wife qualifies for the estate tax exclusion under the 1978 Revenue Act.

One drawback to IRA is that unlike the qualified pension plan, any death benefit paid under the account is taxable as part of your federal taxable estate.

Although the limits of the plan may seem not very substantial when compared with a corporate pension plan or an amended HR 10 plan, my educated guess would be that as HR 10 limits were raised, so will the limits on the contributions allowable under IRA. The real impact of this new law cannot be measured for several years. However, it has gained substantial popularity through advertisements by banks soliciting savings accounts which qualify under the act.

The expanded HR 10 plan also offers to the self-employed substantial tax benefits. When we speak of self-employed, we are talking about doctors, lawyers, accountants and all other professionals in addition to all those individuals who are involved in businesses which are not incorporated.

Contributions may be invested in stocks, bonds, certificates of deposit, life insurance, annuities and also a special series of Government Bonds. An example of an investment of $7,500 contributed each year and invested at an annual rate of 5% interest would provide a total of $136,330 in ten years.

When the distribution is made from this account the payments will be taxed as ordinary income, unless the HR 10 plan was set up prior to the 1974 change in the law. To the extent contributions were made prior to 1974, there will be a portion of the distribution which will qualify for capital gains treatment.

Earlier withdrawal from the plan, which is any withdrawal prior to attaining age fifty-nine and one-half, will be subject to a special 10% tax imposed on the amount of the distribution, in addition to the ordinary income tax on the distribution.

Under the HR 10 plan as under IRA, there is no exemption from the Federal Estate Tax on any death benefit paid as a result of the self-employed's death. However, if the plan covers employees to the extent that the death benefit consists of employer contributions, which are payable to a beneficiary other than the estate of the employee, there is an exemption.

A major change under the qualified retirement plans for corporations is the new minimum vesting standards. Vesting refers to the period of time an individual must be a member of the plan in order to receive benefits when he terminates his employment.

There are three basic alternatives. The first provides that if an employee has ten years of service he has a non-forfeitable right to 100% of his accrued benefit derived from employer contributions. This is the so-called ten-year rule. The second alternative states that a plan will qualify under the new law if an employee who has completed at least five years in the plan has a non-forfeitable right to a percentage of his accrued benefit derived from employer contributions, which percentage is not less than a percentage determined under the following table:

Years of Service	Non-Forfeitable Percentage
5	25
6	30
7	35
8	40
9	45
10	50
11	60
12	70
13	80
14	90
15 or more	100

As you will notice from the table, the minimum number for vesting is five years of service giving the employee a 25% interest in the employer contributions to that date. One hundred percent vesting occurs after 15 years.

The third alternative is the rule of 45. Under this provision an employee must have at least 5 years of service in the plan. The number of years of service is then added to his age and if the sum of these two numbers equals 45 or more, he has a non-forfeitable right to a percentage of the employer contributions under the following table:

If years of service equal or exceed	and sum of age and service equals or exceeds	then the non-forfeitable percentage is
5	45	50
6	47	60
7	49	70
8	51	80
9	53	90
10	55	100

The law also provides that even in light of the rule of 45, the benefits of an employee must be a minimum of 50% for ten years of service plus an additional ten percent for every year over ten years.

Each qualified plan must select one of the above vesting rules.

With respect to corporate qualified retirement plans, one of the most important non-tax oriented benefits under the new law is the requirement that plans which provide a benefit in the form of an annuity use a joint and survivor annuity with 50% or more continuing for the surviving spouse at the death of the first spouse. The spouse covered by the plan does have the option, however, to elect not to take this type and seek a higher benefit under a straight life annuity.

Under the law prior to this change, although most plans provided for the opportunity to receive a reduced benefit for the husband's life in order that the annuity continue for the life of the surviving wife, not all plans provided for this option. Further, some employees were denied the option where they had had medical problems which presumptively would shorten their lives.

All too often you have read or heard about the man who works for a company the better part of his life counting on receiving a pension. However, at retirement it was found that the pension was non-existent or substantially reduced from its original amount. Pension Benefit Guaranty Corporation, whose purpose it is to insure plans against this failure, is a new and very important part of the new law. It is the responsibility of the employer to pay premiums for the insurance covering their plans to the Pension Guaranty Corporation. In most cases the premium in the first year will be one dollar per plan member and in succeeding years the premium will be set by the Guaranty Corporation based on its experience of plan failures. This program removes all possibility of the loss of earned pension benefits.

A significant change in the retirement law has occurred under the Revenue Act of 1978. Now a lump sum distribution from a qualified plan is eligible for the estate tax exclusion provided that the person receiving the distribution elects not to treat it as a lump-sum distribution which would be eligible for favorable income tax treatment.

The changes in the pension laws are many and varied and a close examination of every existing pension or profit sharing plan and HR 10 plan is necessary. The mandatory rules for those who are allowed to participate in a plan, the three alternative methods of achieving vesting for participants, and the most complicated administrative and reporting requirements must be studied carefully. The new opportunities under pension and profit sharing, an expanded HR 10 plan and a totally new IRA now offer employees and employers a wide variety of responsibilities and choices for retirement security.

GLOSSARY

Wills, Estates and Trusts

Abatement—A reduction, a decrease or a diminution of a legacy under a Will.

Ademption—A person disposing that which he bequeathed under his Will so as to make the provision under the Will of no effect, i.e., selling a watch during his lifetime that he had bequeathed under his Will.

Adjusted gross estate—Arrived at by deducting estate settlement costs from the gross estate, also known as the taxable estate.

Admeasurement—Ascertaining at common law either spouses' interest in real property owned by the other.

Administration—The management of a decedent's estate.

Administration expenses—Those necessarily incurred in the administration of the estate, or in the collection of assets, payment of debts and distribution of property; examples include executors' commissions, attorney's fees, costs of funeral and miscellaneous expenses.

Administrative expense—Disbursements or payments made incidental to the management of an estate.

Administrator—The bank or person appointed by court to manage and distribute the personal property of one who dies without a Will; may also handle real property which must be sold in order to pay debts.

Administrator with Will annexed—The bank or individual appointed to manage the estate when the named executor dies, resigns, is removed or refuses to act.

Advancement—Money or property given by a parent to his child, which he had previously decided to bequeath under his Will and now intends to be deducted from that child's share at the ultimate distribution of the estate under his Will.

Agency account—An arrangement whereby a bank or trust company acts on behalf of an individual in handling his property, legal title remaining in the individual.

Ancillary administration—Administration of a decedent's estate in a state where he had property other than the state he resided in at his death.

Annuity—A yearly payment of money for life or a term of years.

Attestation clause—That clause in a Will in which the witnesses certify that the Will has been signed before them and describes how all parties signed the Will.

Beneficiary—One named in a Will to receive a devise or legacy or the use of estate assets.

Bequest—A direction in a Will to pay over or distribute personal property; also called legacy.

Codicil—An amendment of the Will, made in a separate instrument and with the same formalities as the Will itself.

Common disaster—The death of two or more persons at the same time and from the same cause, as in the case of an accident.

Common disaster clause—A clause under the Will which prescribes the order of death as between two or more people who die at the same time.

Corporate fiduciary—A bank or trust company exercising fiduciary powers under statutory authorization.

Corpus—The principal fund, or capital, upon which income is earned. Also called principal.

Curtesy—The estate to which at common law a husband is entitled on the death of wife, generally abolished by a statute permitting him to elect to take under the interstate laws.

Custody account—An account in which the custodian or agent is mainly concerned with the preservation of the property and the performance of ministerial acts in connection therewith; the agent or custodian has no investment responsibilities.

Descent and distribution—The distribution of property to heirs and next of kin, as directed by state laws, constituting the estate of a person who dies without a Will or leaving an invalid Will.

Devise—A testamentary disposition of real property.

Domicile—The legal residence of a person which determines the place of probate of a Will, the tax situs and many other legal relationships.

Donee—The person who receives a gift.

Donor—The person making a gift.

Dower—The statutory provision made for a widow, relating to property of a deceased husband (at common law, a one-third interest in real estate).

Estate tax, federal—A tax on the net value of the estate without regard to distributive shares, based essentially on the right to transfer or transmit.

Exclusion, annual—The continuing right of a donor to make a tax-free gift of up to $3,000 to any number of donees in any year; applies only to gifts of present interests.

Executor—The trust company or individual appointed to carry out the terms of a Will. One responsible for the filing of the Federal Estate Tax Return, State Inheritance Tax Return, decedent's final Income Tax Return and Federal Gift Tax Return, if required. In preparing these returns it would be necessary to compute the fair market value of all assets as of the decedent's date of death.

Fair market value—Price at which a willing seller and a willing buyer will trade.

Fiduciary—A person or institution having a duty created by his position to act primarily for another's benefit.

Foreign Will—Will of a person not a resident within state at the time of his death.

Gift tax, federal—A tax on the donor of inter vivos gifts, based on the right to transfer or transmit, and payable primarily by the donor.

Gift tax marital deduction—A provision under the Federal Gift Tax Law which allows a gift of up to $100,000 from one spouse to the other to pass gift-tax free and one-half the value of any gift over $200,000 to pass gift-tax free.

Goodwill—A reservoir of good relations built up by a business; the probability that customers will continue to do business there. For purposes of valuation of a business or its stock, said to exist where earnings exceed a normal return on the invested capital.

Gross estate—Includes everything in which the decedent owned an interest at his death, embracing life insurance, joint property and transfers made in contemplation of death or intended to take effect at or after death, or where the power to change the enjoyment of property has been retained.

Guardian—One named to manage the person or the property, or both, of a child during minority.

Heirs and next of kin—Those entitled under the laws of descent and distribution to the estate of a person dying without a Will.

In terrorem clause—A clause in a Will attempting to prevent a Will contest which provides that any beneficiary contesting the Will shall forfeit his legacy under the Will.

Incident of ownership—Pertaining to ownership of insurance; the retention of an interest by the decedent of more than 5% of the policy.

Incidents of ownership—A term used to describe that amount of control over an asset which would have that asset included as part of one's Federal taxable estate.

Inheritance tax—A state tax on the value of the share passing to the particular heir, devisee or legatee and based essentially on the right to receive.

Insurance Trust—A trust consisting of life insurance policies or proceeds.

    Funded Insurance Trust—A trust to which other property is also transferred, with the income to be used for the payment of premiums.

    Unfunded Insurance Trust—A trust which contains no fund for payment of premiums.

Inter-vivos transfers—Transfers of property made during one's lifetime as opposed to testamentary disposition made under a person's Will.

Intestate—Death without a valid Will.

Issue—Children, grandchildren and others directly descending from a common ancestor.

Joint and survivor annuity—An annuity from which one spouse receives the income during his life and upon his death the payments continue for the benefit of the surviving spouse.

Jointly owned property—Property owned by two or more persons with the right of ownership in the one or ones who survive; normally unaffected by a Will. In certain states, however, it may be willed under well-defined circumstances.

Lapsed legacy—Occurs when the legatee dies before the testator.

Legacy—A disposition in a Will of personal property.

  Demonstrative—A legacy payable primarily out of a specific fund.

  General—A pecuniary legacy payable out of the general estate.

  Specific—A legacy of a particular article or specified part of the estate.

Letters of administration—Documents issued as proof of authority of bank or individual to act as administrator.

Letters of instruction—An informal writing having no legal standing, which sets forth personal directions and wishes by the testator to his executor and/or beneficiaries.

Letters testamentary—Documents issued as proof of authority of bank or individual to act as executor.

Life estate—An interest in property for life.

Marital deduction—A deduction for Federal Estate Tax purposes from the gross estate of property passing to a surviving spouse in a manner conforming to the law; the deduction is limited to 50% of the adjusted gross estate or $250,000, whichever amount is greater.

Pour-over Will—A Will whereby assets controlled by the Will are directed to be poured-over into a trust.

Power of appointment—The right to direct the disposition of property upon the happening of a certain event, such as the right of an income beneficiary to designate the person to receive the principal upon his death.

  General Power—A power exercisable in favor of the donee, his estate, his creditors, or the creditors of his estate.

  Limited or Non-General Power—A power not exercisable in favor of the donee, his estate, his creditors or the creditors of his estate.

Power of attorney—A document authorizing another person to act as your agent.

Reciprocal Wills—Wills made by two persons in which they each leave everything to the other.

Remainderman—The ones entitled to receive the principal upon termination of the trust. A remainder is vested when payable to a designated beneficiary or class of beneficiaries whether or not living at the termination of the trust. It is contingent when dependent on some occurrence or event to take place in the future.

Residuary clause—A testamentary provision disposing of property remaining in the estate after all other legacies and devises.

Residuary estate—What remains after all devises and bequests have been distributed or paid, and debts and expenses have been paid.

Spendthrift—One who spends money in an unwise manner; one who wastes his estate.

Spendthrift trust—A trust created to provide a fund for the maintenance of a beneficiary, and at the same time protect this fund against the beneficiary's incapacity or improvidence and also against claims of creditors.

Spouse's right of election—A spouse's right to elect a statutory share of the deceased spouse's estate in lieu of what was left under the Will.

Sprinkling or spray trusts—A trust which permits distribution of funds to the beneficiaries in proportion to their needs.

Tenancy—An interest in lands or property.

  Joint Tenancy—See "Jointly Owned Property."

  Tenancy by Entireties—The owning of lands or property by husband and wife, with the survivor taking all, and with interest generally non-separable during life of both.

  Tenancy in Common—The owning of lands or property by several persons, with the share of the one dying passing under his Will or under the intestacy laws to his heirs, and not to the survivors.

Testate—Death leaving a valid Will.

Testator—The person who makes a Will.

Trust—An arrangement whereby property is held by a bank or individual for the benefit of others.

Irrevocable Trust—A trust which cannot be ended by the persons creating it.

Inter Vivos, or Living Trust—A trust set up and becoming effective during the lifetime of the person creating it.

Revocable Trust—A trust which may be ended by the person creating it

Spendthrift Trust—A trust protecting the beneficiary from creditors or his own improvidence.

Testamentary Trust—A trust created by Will.

Trustee—The bank or individual holding the trust property for the benefit of others.

Will—An instrument disposing of property at death.

APPENDICES

FINANCIAL PLANNING WORKFORM

RELATIONSHIP	NAME	AGE	ADDRESS
Principal	_____	_____	_____
	_____	_____	
			Phone _____
Spouse	_____	_____	_____
Sons	_____	_____	_____
	_____	_____	_____
	_____	_____	_____
Daughters	_____	_____	_____
	_____	_____	_____
	_____	_____	_____
Grandchildren	_____	_____	_____
	_____	_____	_____
	_____	_____	_____
	_____	_____	_____
Parents	_____	_____	_____
Brothers and Sisters and other dependents	_____	_____	_____

Attorney Name _____ Address _____

Insurance Counsellor Name _____ Address _____

Tax Advisor Name _____ Address _____

Date _____

FINANCIAL PLANNING WORKFORM

RELATIONSHIP	NAME	AGE	ADDRESS
Principal	_____	_____	_____
	_____		_____
			Phone _____
Spouse	_____	_____	_____
Sons	_____	_____	_____
			_____
	_____	_____	_____
			_____
Daughters	_____	_____	_____
			_____
	_____	_____	_____
			_____
Grandchildren	_____	_____	_____
			_____
	_____	_____	_____
			_____
	_____	_____	_____
Parents	_____	_____	_____
Brothers and Sisters and other dependents	_____	_____	_____

Attorney   Name _____ Address _____

Insurance Counsellor   Name _____ Address _____

Tax Advisor   Name _____ Address _____

Date _____

PROPERTY LIST

Real Estate

	Market Value	Mortgage	Equity	Owner (Indiv. or Jt.)
Residence	$_____	$_____	$_____	_____
Business Property	$_____	$_____	$_____	_____
Summer Cottage-Farm	$_____	$_____	$_____	_____
Rental	$_____	$_____	$_____	_____

TOTAL EQUITY $_____

Investments

	Market Value	Loans	Net Value	Owner (Indiv. or Jt.)
Stocks	$_____	$_____	$_____	_____
Mutual Funds	$_____	$_____	$_____	_____
Bonds	$_____	$_____	$_____	_____
U.S. Bonds	$_____	$_____	$_____	_____
Mortgages	$_____	$_____	$_____	_____
Loans	$_____	$_____	$_____	_____

TOTAL $_____

Business Interests

	Total Market Value	Percentage of Interest	Value of Interest
Close Corporation _____	_____	_____	_____
Partnership _____	_____	_____	_____
Proprietorship _____	_____	_____	_____

TOTAL $_____

Life Insurance and Employee Benefits

	Market Value	Beneficiary	Owner
Group Insurance	$_____	_____	_____
Personal Insurance	$_____	_____	_____
Fraternal Assoc. Ins.	$_____	_____	_____
Profit Sharing	$_____	_____	_____
Pension Benefits	$_____	_____	_____
Stock Options	$_____	_____	_____

TOTAL $_____

Miscellaneous

		Owned (Indiv. or Joint)
Savings Accounts	$_____	_____
	$_____	_____
Cash (checking account, etc.)	$_____	_____
Works of Art/Jewelry	$_____	_____
Furniture	$_____	_____
Automobiles	$_____	_____
Personal Effects	$_____	_____

TOTAL $_____

GRAND TOTAL $_____

PROPERTY LIST

Real Estate	Market Value	Mortgage	Equity	Owner (Indiv. or Jt.)
Residence	$_____	$_____	$_____	_____
Business Property	$_____	$_____	$_____	_____
Summer Cottage-Farm	$_____	$_____	$_____	_____
Rental	$_____	$_____	$_____	_____

TOTAL EQUITY $_____

Investments	Market Value	Loans	Net Value	Owner (Indiv. or Jt.)
Stocks	$_____	$_____	$_____	_____
Mutual Funds	$_____	$_____	$_____	_____
Bonds	$_____	$_____	$_____	_____
U.S. Bonds	$_____	$_____	$_____	_____
Mortgages	$_____	$_____	$_____	_____
Loans	$_____	$_____	$_____	_____

TOTAL $_____

Business Interests	Total Market Value	Percentage of Interest	Value of Interest
Close Corporation			
_____	_____	_____	_____
Partnership			
_____	_____	_____	_____
Proprietorship			
_____	_____	_____	_____

TOTAL $_____

Life Insurance and Employee Benefits	Market Value	Beneficiary	Owner
Group Insurance	$_____	_____	_____
Personal Insurance	$_____	_____	_____
Fraternal Assoc. Ins.	$_____	_____	_____
Profit Sharing	$_____	_____	_____
Pension Benefits	$_____	_____	_____
Stock Options	$_____	_____	_____

TOTAL $_____

Miscellaneous		Owned (Indiv. or Joint)
Savings Accounts	$_____	_____
	$_____	_____
Cash (checking account, etc.)	$_____	_____
Works of Art/Jewelry	$_____	_____
Furniture	$_____	_____
Automobiles	$_____	_____
Personal Effects	$_____	_____

TOTAL $_____

GRAND TOTAL $_____

STOCKS

Name	No. of Shares	Approximate Market Value	Cost Basis
_____	_____	_____	_____
_____	_____	_____	_____
_____	_____	_____	_____
_____	_____	_____	_____
_____	_____	_____	_____

MUTUAL FUNDS

Name	No. of Shares	Approximate Market Value	Cost Basis
_____	_____	_____	_____
_____	_____	_____	_____
_____	_____	_____	_____
_____	_____	_____	_____
_____	_____	_____	_____

BONDS

Name	Face Value	Approximate Market Value	Cost Basis
_____	_____	_____	_____
_____	_____	_____	_____
_____	_____	_____	_____
_____	_____	_____	_____

LIFE INSURANCE

Company	Type	Policy Number
_____	_____	_____
_____	_____	_____
_____	_____	_____
_____	_____	_____

STOCKS

Name	No. of Shares	Approximate Market Value	Cost Basis
_____	_____	_____	_____
_____	_____	_____	_____
_____	_____	_____	_____
_____	_____	_____	_____
_____	_____	_____	_____

MUTUAL FUNDS

Name	No. of Shares	Approximate Market Value	Cost Basis
_____	_____	_____	_____
_____	_____	_____	_____
_____	_____	_____	_____
_____	_____	_____	_____
_____	_____	_____	_____

BONDS

Name	Face Value	Approximate Market Value	Cost Basis
_____	_____	_____	_____
_____	_____	_____	_____
_____	_____	_____	_____
_____	_____	_____	_____

LIFE INSURANCE

Company	Type	Policy Number
_____	_____	_____
_____	_____	_____
_____	_____	_____
_____	_____	_____

113

UNIFIED RATE SCHEDULE FOR ESTATE AND GIFT TAXES
Effective January 1, 1977

In order to estimate your Federal Estate Tax—

FIRST, total your Gross Estate by adding together the market value of everything you own. This will include the proceeds of Life Insurance if payable to your estate or if you, the insured, have any rights of ownership in the policies. You should also include the value of property owned jointly with the right of survivorship, except the portion (if any) paid for by the surviving owner or previously gifted to the surviving owner. The value of other property, although not owned at the time of death, may also have to be included, such as property revocably transferred, gifts made within three years of death or taking effect at death, and property subject to certain general powers of appointment.

SECOND, subtract from the Gross Estate the following deductions:
  a) Funeral Expenses, Debts, and Estate Administration Expenses.
  b) Marital Deduction or Community Property exemption as applicable.

In Common Law States a marital deduction is allowed for the value of property left to or for the benefit of, in some cases, a surviving wife or husband. This cannot exceed one-half the adjusted gross estate.

THIRD, the balance remaining is known as the TAXABLE ESTATE. To determine the tentative tax, consult the table of rates below. (In some cases the tax may be reduced by a credit if the gross estate includes property that was taxed in another estate in recent years.) After computing the tax, apply the phased-in credit of $47,000 as shown on the table following the tax chart.

If the amount with respect to which the tentative tax to be computed is:	The tentative tax is:
Not over $10,000	18 percent of such amount.
Over $10,000 but not over $20,000	$1,800, plus 20 percent of the excess of such amount over $10,000.
Over $20,000 but not over $40,000	$3,800, plus 22 percent of the excess of such amount over $20,000.
Over $40,000 but not over $60,000	$8,200, plus 24 percent of the excess of such amount over $40,000.
Over $60,000 but not over $80,000	$13,000, plus 26 percent of the excess of such amount over $60,000.
Over $80,000 but not over $100,000	$18,200, plus 28 percent of the excess of such amount over $80,000.
Over $100,000 but not over $150,000	$23,800, plus 30 percent of the excess of such amount over $100,000.
Over $150,000 but not over $250,000	$38,800, plus 32 percent of the excess of such amount over $150,000.
Over $250,000 but not over $500,000	$70,800, plus 34 percent of the excess of such amount over $250,000.
Over $500,000 but not over $750,000	$155,800, plus 37 percent of the excess of such amount over $500,000.
Over $750,000 but not over $1,000,000	$248,300, plus 39 percent of the excess of such amount over $750,000.

If the amount with respect to which the tentative tax to be computed is:	The tentative tax is:
Over $1,000,000 but not over $1,250,000..............	$345,800, plus 41 percent of the excess of such amount over $1,000,000.
Over $1,250,000 but not over $1,500,000.......	$448,300, plus 43 percent of the excess of such amount over $1,250,000.
Over $1,500,000 but not over $2,000,000.........	$555,800, plus 45 percent of the excess of such amount over $1,500,000.
Over $2,000,000 but not over $2,500,000..............	$780,800, plus 49 percent of the excess of such amount over $2,000,000.
Over $2,500,000 but not over $3,000,000..............	$1,025,800, plus 53 percent of the excess of such amount over $2,500,000.
Over $3,000,000 but not over $3,500,000..............	$1,290,800, plus 57 percent of the excess of such amount over $3,000,000.
Over $3,500,000 but not over $4,000,000..............	$1,575,800, plus 61 percent of the excess of such amount over $3,500,000.
Over $4,000,000 but not over $4,500,000..............	$1,880,800, plus 65 percent of the excess of such amount over $4,000,000.
Over $4,500,000 but not over $5,000,000..............	$2,205,800, plus 69 percent of the excess of such amount over $4,500,000.
Over $5,000,000	$2,550,800, plus 70 percent of the excess of such amount over $5,000,000.

Phase-In of $47,000 Tax Credit—

In the case of Decedents dying in:	The Following credits shall be allowed to the estate:
1977	$30,000
1978	34,000
1979	38,000
1980	42,500
1981	47,000

STATE INHERITANCE TAX TABLES

Data in this section is based on laws in effect August 1, 1975 except as noted. The tax tables, copyrighted by Kennedy-Sinclaire, Inc., are reproduced with their permission. Laws of the various states are subject to continuous change and it is suggested you consult your State Taxing Authority for regulations in effect.

State Inheritance Tax Tables, revised to include changes through 1979, were not available in time for this printing, so could not be included here. A copy of the table for your state will be sent to you when available if you send your name and address to Dow Jones Books, P.O. Box 300, Princeton, New Jersey 08540.

ALABAMA

Alabama law provides that there shall be assessed as Alabama estate tax an amount exactly equal to the maximum credit allowable under the Federal estate tax law on account of State inheritance or estate tax paid.

Thus, the amount of Alabama tax would be the amount of the State death tax credit indicated in Column 3 of the rate table shown on page 139.

The tax shown in Column 2 of the rate table is the sum of the Alabama and Federal estate taxes. The difference (if any) between the taxes indicated in Columns 2 and 3 is the "net" Federal estate tax.

Suppose, for example, that a person domiciled in Alabama dies leaving property subject to tax which, after the deductions, amounts to $300,000, all consisting of property in Alabama. In that case the estate taxes would be:

Federal estate tax (before deducting Unified Credit)	$84,200
Alabama estate tax	3,600
Total	$87,800

This data based on laws in effect February 1977.

ALASKA

Alaska law provides that there shall be assessed as Alaska estate tax an amount exactly equal to the maximum credit allowable under the Federal estate tax law on account of State inheritance or estate tax paid.

Thus, the amount of Alaska tax would be the amount of the State death tax credit indicated in Column 3 of the rate table shown on page 139.

The tax shown in Column 2 of the rate table is the sum of the Alaska and Federal estate taxes. The difference (if any) between the taxes indicated in Columns 2 and 3 is the "net" Federal estate tax.

Suppose, for example, that a person domiciled in Alaska dies leaving property subject to tax which, after the deductions, amounts to $300,000, all consisting of property in Alaska. In that case the estate taxes would be:

Federal estate tax (before deducting Unified Credit)	$84,200
Alaska estate tax	3,600
Total	$87,800

This data based on laws in effect February 1977.

ARIZONA

The tax applies to the net estate, which is the gross estate less the allowable exemptions and deductions. The property is valued either at date of death or six months later, at the option of the executor.

Only one-half of community property is includible, for tax purposes, in the gross estate of a married person.

Life Insurance Proceeds are includible in the gross estate if they are payable to the estate. Proceeds payable to other beneficiaries are includible in the gross estate in proportion to premiums paid by the insured, or they are includible if the insured possessed at his death any of the incidents of ownership.

Property Owned Jointly With Right of Survivorship. Federal estate tax rule applies.

A Marital Deduction is allowed for the value of separate property passing unconditionally (or in trust, under certain conditions) to the surviving spouse. But the deduction may not exceed the difference between (1) the value of the surviving spouse's separate property, and (2) one-half the total value of the separate property of both spouses. Life insurance can qualify for the deduction, whether payable outright to the spouse or (in some cases) in trust.

Exemption. Property to the value of $100,000 is exempt.

Arizona has an ESTATE TAX to absorb the maximum credit for State tax allowed by the Federal estate tax law.

RATES		
Net Estate (after deducting the $100,000 exemption and other deductions)	Tax	Rate on Next Bracket
$ -0-	$ -0-	$4/5$%
50,000	400	$1^3/5$
100,000	1,200	$2^2/5$
200,000	3,600	$3^1/5$
400,000	10,000	4
600,000	18,000	$4^4/5$
800,000	27,600	$5^3/5$
1,000,000	38,800	$6^2/5$
1,500,000	70,800	$7^1/5$
2,000,000	106,800	8
2,500,000	146,800	$8^4/5$
3,000,000	190,800	$9^3/5$
3,500,000	238,800	$10^2/5$
4,000,000	290,800	$11^1/5$
5,000,000	402,800	12
6,000,000	522,800	$12^4/5$
7,000,000	650,800	$13^3/5$
8,000,000	786,800	$14^2/5$
9,000,000	930,800	$15^1/5$
10,000,000	1,082,800	16

ARKANSAS

Arkansas law provides that there shall be assessed as Arkansas estate tax an amount exactly equal to the maximum credit allowable under the Federal estate tax law on account of State inheritance or estate tax paid.

Thus, the amount of Arkansas tax would be the amount of the State death tax credit indicated in Column 3 of the rate table shown on page 139.

The tax shown in Column 2 of the rate table is the sum of the Arkansas and Federal estate taxes. The difference (if any) between the taxes indicated in Columns 2 and 3 is the "net" Federal estate tax.

Suppose, for example, that a person domiciled in Arkansas died leaving property subject to tax which, after the deductions, amounts to $300,000, all consisting of property in Arkansas. In that case the estate taxes would be:

Federal estate tax (before deducting Unified Credit)	$84,200
Arkansas estate tax	3,600
Total	$87,800

This data based on laws in effect February 1977.

CALIFORNIA

The tax is computed at graduated rates on the value of the share passing to each beneficiary in excess of the applicable exemption. The exemption (including the Marital Exemption) is taken from the lowest bracket or brackets.

Only one-half of community property is includible, for tax purposes, in the estate of a married person. EVEN THIS ONE-HALF IS EXEMPT WHEN LEFT OUTRIGHT TO SURVIVING SPOUSE.

A Marital Exemption, up to one-half the clear market value of the decedent's separate property, is allowed for the value of property passing to a surviving spouse.

Life Insurance Proceeds payable to the estate are taxable. Proceeds payable to the surviving spouse in a single sum are exempt. Proceeds payable to other beneficiaries are taxable (a) if the policy was issued after 6/25/35, or (b) if the policy was issued on or before 6/25/35 and the insured had right to change beneficiary or surrender policy for cash . . . EXCEPT THAT proceeds under (a) and (b) are exempt up to a total of $50,000.

Property Owned Jointly With Right of Survivorship—Rule similar to Federal estate tax rule applies. If the property was converted from community property, it is treated as community property for inheritance tax purposes.

California ESTATE TAX absorbs the maximum credit for State tax allowed by the Federal estate tax law.

RATES

	Share	Tax	Rate on Next Bracket
Class A (spouse*; lineal issue or ancestor; adopted or acknowledged child or issue of such; adopted child of lineal issue or of child mentioned above)	$ -0-	$ -0-	3%
	25,000	750	4
	50,000	1,750	6
	100,000	4,750	8
	200,000	12,750	10
	300,000	22,750	12
	400,000	34,750	14

Exemptions: (1) Each minor child of decedent, $12,000. To give effect, subtract $360 from tax. (2) Others in Class A, $5,000 each. To give effect, subtract $150 from tax. (Similarly, in case of spouse's share, take the Marital Exemption from lowest brackets above $5,000.)
*Community property passing outright to spouse is exempt.

	Share	Tax	Rate on Next Bracket
Class B (brother, sister, or descendant of such; wife or widow of son, husband or widower of daughter)	$ -0-	$ -0-	6%
	25,000	1,500	10
	50,000	4,000	12
	100,000	10,000	14
	200,000	24,000	16
Exemption: $2,000 each.	300,000	40,000	18
To give effect, subtract $120 from tax.	400,000	58,000	20

	Share	Tax	Rate on Next Bracket
Class C (others)	$ -0-	$ -0-	10%
Exemption: $300 each.	25,000	2,500	14
To give effect, subtract $30 from tax.	50,000	6,000	16
	100,000	14,000	18
	200,000	32,000	20
	300,000	52,000	22
	400,000	74,000	24

California GIFT TAX. The rates and exemptions are the same as those under the inheritance tax. The exemptions are allowed only once—not each year; and, like the inheritance tax exemptions, they reduce the first bracket. There is also a $3,000 annual exclusion allowed, generally, for gifts to each donee in each year (except gifts of future interests).

COLORADO

The tax is computed at graduated rates on the value of the share passing to each beneficiary in excess of the applicable exemption. The exemption "comes off the top" of the share.

The tax as so computed is increased by 10%. The additional 10% tax is known as the "Old Age Pension Tax."

Life Insurance Proceeds are taxable if payable to the insured's estate. As for proceeds payable to other beneficiaries and with respect to which the insured possessed any of the incidents of ownership at his death, the first $75,000 is exempt and the excess above $75,000 is taxable.

Property Owned Jointly With Right of Survivorship. General rule: decedent's fractional interest is taxed. But the Federal estate tax rule applies to joint bank accounts and U.S. Savings Bonds.

Colorado ESTATE TAX absorbs the maximum credit for State tax allowed by the Federal estate tax law.

RATES
(Increase tax as computed below by 10%—the Old Age Pension Tax.)

	Share in Excess of Exemption	Tax	Rate on Next Bracket
Class A (parent; spouse; descendant; stepchild; child adopted during minority) *Exemption:* $30,000 for widow or widower, $15,000 for minor child under 16, $10,000 for each other person in the class.	$ -0-	$ -0-	2%
	50,000	1,000	4
	75,000	2,000	5
	100,000	3,250	7
	150,000	6,750	7½
	500,000	33,000	8
Class B (wife or widow of son; husband or widower of daughter; grandparents; brothers & sisters; certain mutually acknowledged children) *Exemption:* $2,000 for each.	$ -0-	$ -0-	3%
	10,000	300	5
	20,000	800	7
	50,000	2,900	8
	100,000	6,900	9
	200,000	15,900	10
Class C (uncles; aunts; nieces; nephews; their descendants) *Exemption:* No tax if transfer does not exceed $500. If it does, there is no exemption.	$ -0-	$ -0-	6%
	2,500	150	7
	5,000	325	8
	10,000	725	9
	15,000	1,175	10
	20,000	1,675	11
	30,000	2,775	12
	40,000	3,975	13
	50,000	5,275	14
	250,000	33,275	15
	500,000	70,775	16
Class D (others) *Exemption:* No tax if transfer does not exceed $500. If it does, there is no exemption.	$ -0-	$ -0-	10%
	2,500	250	11
	5,000	525	12
	10,000	1,125	13
	15,000	1,775	15
	25,000	3,275	17
	500,000	84,025	19

Colorado GIFT TAX. "Annual exclusions" are allowed under the gift tax. (They are $3,000 for Class A donees, $1,500 for Class B, and $1,000 for Class C and D.) The gift tax is NOT increased 10% by an "Old Age Pension Tax."

CONNECTICUT

The tax is computed at graduated rates on the total value of the shares passing to EACH CLASS. One exemption is allowed for each class (not for each share). The exemption is taken from the lowest bracket.

Life Insurance Proceeds payable to the estate or to named beneficiaries are exempt.

Property Owned Jointly With Right of Survivorship. General rule: decedent's fractional interest is taxed. But first $5,000 of aggregate of joint bank accounts, savings and loan accounts, and U.S. Savings Bonds is exempt.

Connecticut ESTATE TAX absorbs the maximum credit for State tax allowed by the Federal estate tax law.

RATES

	Total Value of Property Passing To Class	Tax	Rate on Next Bracket
Class AA (husband, wife) *Exemption:* $50,000 for the class.	$ 50,000	$ -0-	3.9%
	150,000	3,900	5.2
	250,000	9,100	6.5
	400,000	18,850	7.8
	600,000	34,450	9.1
	1,000,000	70,850	10.4
Class A (parents, grandparents, adoptive parent and any natural or adopted descendant) *Exemption:* $10,000 for the class.	$ 10,000	$ -0-	2.6%
	25,000	390	3.9
	150,000	5,265	5.2
	250,000	10,465	6.5
	400,000	20,215	7.8
	600,000	35,815	9.1
	1,000,000	72,215	10.4
Class B (spouse or unremarried widow or widower of any natural or adopted child, step-child, brother or sister by whole or half blood or by adoption, natural or adopted descendant of such brother or sister) *Exemption:* $3,000 for the class.	$ 3,000	$ -0-	5.2%
	25,000	1,144	6.5
	150,000	9,269	7.8
	250,000	17,069	9.1
	400,000	30,719	10.4
	600,000	51,519	11.7
	1,000,000	98,319	13.0
Class C (all others, except certain charities which are wholly exempt) *Exemption:* $500 for the class.	$ 500	$ -0-	10.4%
	25,000	2,548	11.7
	150,000	17,173	13.0
	250,000	30,173	14.3
	400,000	51,623	15.6
	600,000	82,823	16.9
	1,000,000	150,423	18.2

IMPORTANT. Taxes and rates shown above reflect the 30% surtax which became effective June 8, 1961.

DELAWARE

The tax is computed at graduated rates on the value of the share of the estate passing to each beneficiary in excess of the applicable exemption. The exemption is taken from the lowest bracket.

Life Insurance Proceeds payable to the estate are taxable. Proceeds payable to named beneficiaries are exempt.

Property Owned Jointly With Right of Survivorship. Rule similar to the Federal estate tax rule applies.

Delaware ESTATE TAX absorbs the maximum credit for State tax allowed by the Federal estate tax law.

RATES

	Share	Tax	Rate on Next Bracket
Class A (husband, wife) *Exemption.* $20,000.	$ 20,000	$ -0-	1%
	50,000	300	2
	100,000	1,300	3
	200,000	4,300	4

	Share	Tax	Rate
Class B (children. natural or adopted. lineal descendants. parents. grandparents. wife or widow of son. husband or widower of daughter) *Exemption: $3.000 each.*	$ 3.000 25.000 50.000 75.000 100.000 200.000	$ -0- 220 720 1.470 2.470 7.470	1% 2 3 4 5 6
Class C (brothers and sisters of either whole or half blood. their lineal descendants: brothers. sisters of parents. children of such brothers and sisters) *Exemption: $1.000 each.*	$ 1.000 25.000 50.000 100.000 150.000 200.000	$ -0- 1.200 2.700 6.200 10.200 14.700	5% 6 7 8 9 10
Class D (all others) *Exemption: None.*	$ -0- 25.000 50.000 100.000	$ -0- 2.500 5.500 12.500	10% 12 14 16

Delaware GIFT TAX imposes a tax on gifts made by individuals during a calendar quarter. It is patterned after the Federal gift tax law. except there is no $30.000 specific exemption for Delaware gift tax purposes. The gift tax rates range from 1% on taxable gifts up to $25.000. to 6% on the portion of taxable gifts exceeding $200.000.

FLORIDA

Florida law provides that there shall be assessed as Florida estate tax an amount exactly equal to the maximum credit allowable under the Federal estate tax law on account of State inheritance or estate tax paid.

Thus. the amount of Florida tax would be the amount of the State death tax credit indicated in Column 3 of the rate table shown on page 139.

The tax shown in Column 2 of the rate table is the sum of the Florida and Federal estate taxes. The difference (if any) between the taxes indicated in Columns 2 and 3 is the "net" Federal estate tax.

Suppose. for example. that a person domiciled in Florida dies leaving property subject to tax which. after the deductions. amounts to $300.000. all consisting of property in Florida. In that case the estate taxes would be:

Federal estate tax (before
deducting Unified Credit) $84.200
Florida estate tax 3.600

Total $87,800

This data based on laws in effect February 1977.

GEORGIA

Georgia law provides that there shall be assessed as Georgia estate tax an amount exactly equal to the maximum credit allowable under the Federal estate tax law on account of State inheritance or estate tax paid.

Thus. the amount of Georgia tax would be the amount of the State death tax credit indicated in Column 3 of the rate table shown on page 139.

The tax shown in Column 2 of the rate table is the sum of the Georgia and Federal estate taxes. The difference (if any) between the taxes indicated in Columns 2 and 3 is the "net" Federal estate tax.

Suppose. for example. that a person domiciled in Georgia dies leaving property subject to tax which. after the deductions. amounts to $300.000. all consisting of property in Georgia. In that case the estate taxes would be:

Federal estate tax (before
deducting Unified Credit) $84.200
Georgia estate tax 3.600

Total $87.800

This data based on laws in effect February 1977.

HAWAII

The tax is computed at graduated rates on the value of the share passing to each beneficiary in excess of the applicable exemption. The exemption is taken from the lowest bracket.

Life Insurance Proceeds payable to the estate are taxable. Proceeds payable to named beneficiaries are exempt.

Property Owned Jointly With Right of Survivorship. In general. Federal estate tax rule applies: except that where survivor is decedent's spouse. taxable portion under general rule is cut in half.

The Federal Estate Tax is deductible in computing the State inheritance tax.

Hawaii ESTATE TAX absorbs the maximum credit for State tax allowed by the Federal estate tax law.

RATES

	Share	Tax	Rate on Next Bracket
Class 1 (husband. wife) *Exemption: $20,000*	$ 20.000 35.000 50.000 100.000 250.000	$ -0- 300.00 750.00 2.750.00 10,250.00	2% 3 4 5 6
Class 2 (children. grandchildren. parents adopted children) *Exemption: $5,000 each*	$ 5.000 20.000 50.000 100.000 250.000	$ -0- 225.00 1,125.00 3,375.00 12,375.00	1½% 3 4½ 6 7½
Class 3 (others) *Exemption: $500 each*	$ 500 5.000 20.000 50.000 100.000	$ -0- 157.50 1,057.50 3,157.50 7,157.50	3½% 6 7 8 9

IDAHO

The tax is computed at graduated rates on the value of the share passing to each beneficiary in excess of the applicable exemption. The exemption "comes off the top" of the share.

Only one-half of community property is includible. for tax purposes, in the estate of a married person. Community property passing to a surviving spouse is exempt.

Life Insurance Proceeds. There is no statutory provision. Under the rule generally followed. proceeds payable to the estate would be taxable. but proceeds payable to any other beneficiary would be exempt.

Property Owned Jointly With Right of Survivorship. Rule similar to Federal estate tax rule applies.

The Federal Estate Tax is deductible in computing the State inheritance tax.

Idaho ESTATE TAX absorbs the maximum credit for State tax allowed by the Federal estate tax law.

RATES

	Share in Excess of Exemption	Tax	Rate on Next Bracket
Class 1 (a) Widow. minor child	$ -0-	$ -0-	2°₀
	25.000	500	4
Exemption: $10,000 each.	50.000	1,500	6
Also exempt: community	100.000	4,500	8
property passing	200.000	12,500	10
to widow.	500.000	42,500	15
(b) Husband. lineal issue (except minor child). lineal ancestor. adopted or mutually acknowledged child. *Exemption:* $4,000 each. Also exempt: community property passing to husband.			
Class 2 (Sister brother their descendants.	$ -0-	$ -0-	4°₀
husband of daughter.	25.000	1.000	6
wife or widow of son)	50.000	2.500	8
Exemption $1,000 each.	100.000	6.500	12
	200.000	18.500	16
	500.000	66.500	20
Class 3 (Uncles. aunts.	$ -0-	$ -0-	6°₀
their descendants)	25.000	1.500	9
Exemption $500 each.	50.000	3.750	12
	100.000	9.750	15
	200.000	24.750	20
	500.000	84.750	25
Class 4 (Others)	$ -0-	$ -0-	8°₀
Exemption. None	25.000	2.000	14
	50.000	5.500	20
	100.000	15.500	30

ILLINOIS

The tax is computed at graduated rates on the value of the share passing to each beneficiary in excess of the applicable exemption. The exemption comes off the top of the share.

Life Insurance Proceeds payable to the estate are taxable. Proceeds payable to named beneficiaries are exempt

Property Owned Jointly With Right of Survivorship. Decedent's fractional interest is taxed.

Federal Estate Tax is deductible in computing the State inheritance tax.

Illinois ESTATE TAX absorbs the maximum credit for state tax allowed by the Federal estate tax law.

RATES

	Share in Excess of Exemption	Tax	Rate on Next Bracket
Class 1. (a) Father mother. lineal	$ -0-	$ -0-	2°₀
ancestor. husband. wife.	50.000	1 000	4
child. wife or widow of son.	150.000	5.000	6
husband or widower of	250.000	11.000	10
daughter. descendant.	500.000	36.000	14*
mutually acknowledged child. Legal adoption is equivalent to blood relationship. *Exemption:* $20,000 each (b) Brother. sister. *Exemption:* $10,000 each			
Class 2. Uncle. aunt. niece. nephew:	$ -0-	$ -0-	6°₀
lineal descendant of uncle.	20.000	1 200	8
aunt. niece. nephew.	70.000	5.200	12
Exemption. $500 each	170.000	17.200	16
Class 3. Others. except charitable.	$ -0-	$ -0-	10°₀
religious or educational	20.000	2 000	12
institutions wholly	50.000	5 600	16
exempt.	100.000	13.600	20
Exemption $100 each	150.000	23.600	24
	250.000	47 600	30

*If the taxable transfer to a spouse exceeds $5 000 000 the rate on the excess is 6°₀

INDIANA

The tax is computed at graduated rates on the value of the share of the estate passing to each beneficiary in excess of the applicable exemption.

Life Insurance Proceeds payable to the estate are taxable Proceeds payable to named beneficiaries are exempt

Property Owned Jointly With Right of Survivorship. Generally. the Federal estate tax rule applies But real property held by tenants by the entireties is not taxable

Indiana ESTATE TAX absorbs the maximum credit for State tax allowed by the Federal estate tax law

RATES

	Share	Tax	Rate on Next Bracket
Class A (spouse, child under 18, lineal issue or ancestor, acknowledged or adopted child and lineal issue of such child; adoptive parents) *Exemption: Spouse, $15,000. Child under 18, $5,000 each. Others in Class A, $2,000 each.*	$ -0- 25,000 50,000 200,000 300,000 500,000 700,000 1,000,000 1,500,000	$ -0- 250 750 5,250 9,250 19,250 31,250 52,250 92,250	1% 2 3 4 5 6 7 8 10
Class B (brother, sister, or descendant of brother or sister; wife or widow of son, husband or widower of daughter) *Exemption: $500 each.*	$ -0- 100,000 200,000 500,000 1,000,000	$ -0- 5,000 13,000 43,000 103,000	5% 8 10 12 15
Class C (others) *Exemption: $100 each.*	$ -0- 100,000 200,000 500,000 1,000,000	$ -0- 7,000 17,000 53,000 128,000	7% 10 12 15 20

IOWA

The tax is computed on the value of the share passing to each beneficiary. An exemption, where allowable, "comes off the top" of the share.

No tax is payable in an estate not exceeding $1,000 after the payment of debts.

Life Insurance Proceeds payable to the estate are taxable. Proceeds payable to named beneficiaries are exempt.

Property Owned Jointly With Right of Survivorship. In general, Federal estate tax rules apply. But where decedent and surviving spouse are only joint owners, not more than one-half is taxable.

Federal Estate Tax is deductible in computing the State inheritance tax.

Iowa ESTATE TAX absorbs the maximum credit for State tax allowed by the Federal estate tax law.

RATES

	Share in Excess of Exemption	Tax	Rate on Next Bracket
Class 1 (wife, husband) *Exemption: $80,000.* (children) *Exemption: $15,000* for each.	$ -0- 5,000 12,500 25,000 50,000	$ -0- 50 200 575 1,575	1% 2 3 4 5

(other lineal descendants) *Exemption: $5,000 for each.* (father, mother) *Exemption: $10,000 for each.*	75,000 100,000 150,000	2,825 4,325 7,825	6 7 8
Class 2 (brother, sister, son-in-law, daughter-in-law, step-child) *Exemption: None*	$ -0- 12,500 25,000 75,000 100,000 150,000	$ -0- 625 1,375 4,875 6,875 11,375	5% 6 7 8 9 10
Class 3 (any person not included in Class 1 and Class 2) *Exemption: None*	$ -0- 50,000 100,000	$ -0- 5,000 11,000	10% 12 15
Class 4 (societies, institutions, or associations organized under laws of another state or country for charitable, educational, religious, or humane purposes, or resident trustees for uses outside the State)	$ -0-	$ -0-	10%
Class 5 (firms, corporations or societies organized for profit)	$ -0-	$ -0-	15%

KANSAS

The tax is computed at graduated rates on the value of the share passing to each beneficiary in excess of the applicable exemption. The exemption comes "off the top" of the share. Any share valued at less than $200 after the exemption has been subtracted is not taxable.

Life Insurance Proceeds payable to the estate are taxable. Insurance proceeds payable to other designated beneficiaries are exempt.

Property Owned Jointly With Right of Survivorship. Federal estate tax rule applies.

Federal Estate Tax is deductible in computing the State inheritance tax.

Kansas ESTATE TAX absorbs the maximum credit for State tax allowed by the Federal estate tax law.

RATES

	Share in Excess of Exemption	Tax	Rate on Next Bracket
Class A (husband, wife) *Exemption: $75,000.*	$ -0- 25,000 50,000 100,000 500,000	$ -0- 125 375 1,125 9,125	1/2% 1 1 1/2 2 2 1/2
(Lineal ancestor, lineal descendant, adopted child, spouse or surviving spouse or lineal	$ -0- 25,000 50,000 100,000	$ -0- 250 750 2,250	1% 2 3 4

| descendant of adopted child, spouse or surviving spouse of son or daughter) *Exemption: $15.000 each.* | 500,000 | 18,250 | 5 |

Class B (brother, sister) *Exemption: $5,000 each*	$ -0-	$ -0-	3%
	25,000	750	5
	50,000	2,000	7½
	100,000	5,750	10
	500,000	45,750	12½

Class C (others, except charities, etc.) No exemption unless share is less than $200, in which case entire share is exempt.	$ -0-	$ -0-	10%
	100,000	10,000	12
	200,000	22,000	15

Class C (others) *Exemption: $500 each*	$ -0-	$ -0-	6%
	10,000	600	8
	20,000	1,400	10
	30,000	2,400	12
	45,000	4,200	14
	60,000	6,300	16

Estates over $3,000,000. Provisions of the inheritance tax law do not apply to net estates of $3,000,000 or more Such estates are subject to the Kentucky estate tax

KENTUCKY

The tax is imposed at graduated rates on the value of the share passing to each beneficiary in excess of the applicable exemption. The exemption "comes off the top" of the share.

Life Insurance Proceeds payable to the estate are taxable. Proceeds payable to named beneficiaries are exempt.

Property Owned Jointly With Right of Survivorship. General rule: The decedent's fractional interest is taxed. Special rules apply to jointly owned U.S. Government bonds.

The Federal Estate Tax is allowed as a deduction in computing the State inheritance tax.

Kentucky ESTATE TAX absorbs the maximum credit for State tax allowed by the Federal estate tax law.

RATES

	Share in Excess of Exemption	Tax	Rate on Next Bracket
Class A (parent, spouse; child by blood or by adoption during infancy; stepchild; grandchild) *Exemption: Wife, infant child by blood or adoption; child by blood or adoption during infancy who has been declared incompetent—$10,000 each. Others in Class A—$5,000 each.*	$ -0-	$ -0-	2%
	20,000	400	3
	30,000	700	4
	45,000	1,300	5
	60,000	2,050	6
	100,000	4,450	7
	200,000	11,450	8
	500,000	35,450	10
Class B (brother, sister; nephew, niece of whole or half blood; son-in-law, daughter-in-law, aunt, uncle) *Exemption: $1,000 each.*	$ -0-	$ -0-	4%
	10,000	400	5
	20,000	900	6
	30,000	1,500	8
	45,000	2,700	10
	60,000	4,200	12
	100,000	9,000	14
	200,000	23,000	16

LOUISIANA

The tax is computed at graduated rates on the value of the share passing to each beneficiary in excess of the applicable exemption. The exemption is taken from the lower bracket.

Only one-half of community property is includible, for tax purposes, in the estate of a married person.

Life Insurance Proceeds payable to the estate are taxable. Proceeds payable to named beneficiaries are exempt. *Where the premiums were paid from community property and the proceeds were payable to the insured's estate, it has been ruled that only one-half of the proceeds were subject to the inheritance tax.*

Usufruct to Spouse is exempt.

Louisiana ESTATE TAX absorbs the maximum credit for State tax allowed by the Federal estate tax law.

RATES

	Share	Tax	Rate on Next Bracket
Class 1 (husband, wife direct descendant by blood or affinity, ascendant) *Exemption: $5,000 for each. To reflect exemption, subtract $100 from tax.*	$ -0-	$ -0-	2%
	25,000	500	3
Class 2 (collateral relative, including brother or sister by affinity) *Exemption: $1,000 for each. To reflect exemption, subtract $50 from tax.*	$ -0-	$ -0-	5%
	21,000	1,050	7
Class 3 (others) *Exemption: $500 for each. To reflect exemption, subtract $25 from tax.*	$ -0-	$ -0-	5%
	5,500	275	10

Louisiana GIFT TAX imposes a tax on gifts by individuals during life. Gifts to charitable, etc., organizations, are not taxable. The tax is based on the full value of the gift at the time of transfer. In computing the amount of gifts to each donee during a calendar year, an annual exclusion is deducted before rates are applied; thus the annual exclusion, in effect, "comes off the top" of the gift, rather than "out of the first bracket." There is also a lifetime exemption of $30,000.

	Gift After Ann. Exclusion	Tax	Rate on Next Bracket
Annual exclusion: $3,000.	$ -0- 15,000	$ -0- 300	2% 3

MAINE

(Applicable to estates of decedents dying on or after October 1, 1975)

The tax is computed at graduated rates on the value of the share passing to each beneficiary in excess of the applicable exemption. The exemption "comes off the top" of the share.

Life Insurance Proceeds payable to the estate are taxable except for that part of the proceeds which is bequeathed to or descends to the widow, widower, or issue of the decedent. Proceeds payable to named beneficiaries are exempt.

Property Owned Jointly With Right of Survivorship. General rule: The decedent's fractional interest is taxed. (The statute excepts joint bank deposits and joint building and loan shares from this rule; Federal rule will apply.)

Federal Estate Tax is deductible in computing the State inheritance tax.

Maine ESTATE TAX absorbs the maximum cedit for State tax allowed by the Federal estate tax law.

RATES

	Share in Excess of Exemption	Tax	Rate on Next Bracket
Class A (husband, wife) *Exemption.* $50,000. (father, mother, child, adopted child, stepchild, adoptive parent) *Exemption.* $25,000 each. (grandchild who is natural or adopted child of natural or adopted deceased child) *Exemption.* $25,000. If more than one grandchild, their total exemption is, per stirpes, $25,000. (grandparent, lineal ancestor of remoter degree, wife or widow of natural or adopted son, husband or widower of natural or adopted	$ -0- 50,000 100,000 250,000	$ -0- 2,500 5,500 17,500	5% 6 8 10

daughter, grandchild who is natural or adopted child of natural or adopted living child, lineal descendant of remoter degree)
Exemption: $2,000 each.

Class B (brother, half-brother, sister, half-sister, uncle, aunt, nephew, niece, grandnephew, grandniece, cousin) *Exemption:* $1,000 each.	$ -0- 25,000 100,000 250,000	$ -0- 2,000 9,500 27,500	8% 10 12 14
Class C (others, except charities, etc.) *Exemption:* $1,000 each.	$ -0- 75,000 150,000	$ -0- 10,500 22,500	14% 16 18

MARYLAND

The tax is computed at a flat rate on the value of the share passing to each beneficiary.

Life Insurance Proceeds payable to the estate are taxable. Proceeds payable to named beneficiaries are exempt.

Property Owned Jointly With Right of Survivorship. The decedent's fractional interest is taxed, *except where the property passes to a surviving spouse.* (The statute excepts from the imposition of tax "any interest legal or equitable, of any surviving spouse . . . in any property of any nature owned by husband and wife either as joint tenants or as tenants by the entireties passing to such surviving spouse.")

Federal Estate Tax is deductible in computing the State inheritance tax.

Maryland ESTATE TAX absorbs the maximum credit for State tax allowed by the Federal estate tax law.

Maryland has a tax on executors' and administrators' commissions. This tax—based on the value of the gross estate—is added to the inheritance tax. The rates of the tax on commissions are—

1% of first $20,000 of gross estate, and
1/5 of 1% on balance of gross estate,
OR
10% of the total commissions allowed, whichever is greater

RATES

Beneficiaries	Rate of Tax
Class 1 (husband, wife, father, mother, child or other lineal descendant, step-child, step-parent. Also spouse of lineal descendant with respect to single joint savings account with balance under $2,000.) *Exemption* None unless share is $150 or less, in which case entire amount is exempt.	1% on the entire share

Class 2 (all others, except charities, etc.) 10% on the
Exemption: None unless share is $150 entire share
or less, in which case entire amount
is exempt.

MASSACHUSETTS

The tax is computed at graduated rates on the value of the share passing to each beneficiary

Life Insurance Proceeds are taxable except for the first $25,000 payable to the insured's spouse and children.

Property Owned Jointly With Right of Survivorship. The Federal estate tax rule applies. But domicile of husband and wife, owned by them as joint tenants or tenants by entireties, is fully exempt if it is single-family property and is exempt up to $25,000 if it is multiple-family property.

Federal Estate Tax is deductible in computing the State inheritance tax.

NOTE· The tables below incorporate the 14% additional inheritance tax imposed by Chapter 546, Laws of 1969.

Exemptions. There is no tax if share of SPOUSE is $30,000 or less: or if share of ANY OTHER CLASS A BENEFICIARY is $15,000 or less: or if share of ANY OTHER PERSON is $5,000 or less.

If share exceeds the exemption ($30,000 or $15,000 or $5,000 as the case may be), there is no exemption: the entire share is taxed. The tax, however, may not lower the share below the exemption.

Adopted Child is treated as natural born child

Massachusetts ESTATE TAX absorbs the maximum credit for State tax allowed by the Federal estate tax law

RATES (estates of persons dying on or after Jan. 1, 1970)

	Share	Tax	Rate on Next Bracket
Class A (husband,	$ -0-	$ -0-	2.052%
wife, father, mother	10,000	205.20	3,420
child, grandchild)	25,000	718.20	4.902
Exemption: See	50,000	1,943.70	6.270
below	100,000	5,078.70	7.752
	250,000	16,706.70	9.120
	500,000	39,506.70	10.602
	750,000	66,011.70	11.970
	1,000,000	95,936.70	13.452
Class B (lineal	$ -0-	$ -0-	3.420%
ancestor except	10,000	342.00	4.902
parent; lineal de-	25,000	1,077.30	7.752
scendant except	50,000	3,015.30	9.120
child or grandchild;	100,000	7,575.30	10.602
wife or widow of	250,000	23,478.30	11.970
son: husband of	500,000	53,403.30	13.452
daughter)	750,000	87,033.30	14.820
Exemption: See	1,000,000	124,083.30	16.302
below.			

	Share	Tax	Rate on Next Bracket
Class C (brother	$ -0-	$ -0-	6.270%
sister, half brother	10,000	627.00	9.120
half sister, nephew,	25,000	1,995.00	11.970
niece, stepchild,	50,000	4,987.50	14.820
or step-parent)	100,000	12,397.50	16.302
Exemption: See	250,000	36,850.50	17.670
below.	500,000	81,025.50	19.152
	750,000	128,905.50	20.520
	1,000,000	180,205.50	22.002
Class D (others)	$ -0-	$ -0-	9.120%
Exemption· See	10,000	912.00	11.970
below	25,000	2,707.50	13.452
	50,000	6,070.50	14.820
	100,000	13,480.50	16.302
	250,000	37,933.50	17.670
	500,000	82,108.50	19.152
	750,000	129,988.50	20.520
	1,000,000	181,288.50	22.002

MICHIGAN

The tax is computed at graduated rates on the value of the share passing to each beneficiary in excess of the applicable exemption. The exemption is taken from the lowest brackets.

Life Insurance Proceeds payable to the estate are taxable. Proceeds payable to a trustee for named beneficiaries, and proceeds payable direct to a named beneficiary, are exempt

Property Owned Jointly With Right of Survivorship. Not taxable.

Michigan ESTATE TAX absorbs the maximum credit for State tax allowed by the Federal estate tax law.

RATES

	Share	Tax	Rate on Next Bracket
Class 1 (wife)	$ -0-	$ -0-	2%
Exemption: $30,000 plus	50,000	1,000	4
additional $5,000 for each	250,000	9,000	5
minor child to whom no	500,000	21,500	6
property is transferred.	750,000	36,500	8

To give effect to exemptions, subtract $600 from tax computed per table, also $100 for each $5,000 exemption, until exemptions total $50,000. Above $50,000, subtract at rate of 4%.

(husband)
Exemption: $30,000. To give effect to exemption, subtract $600 from tax per table.

(parent, grandparent, child, brother, sister, descendant, wife or widow of son, husband of daughter, adopted child, mutually acknowledged child)

Exemption: $5,000 for each. To give effect to exemption, subtract $100 from tax computed per table.

	Share	Tax	
Class 2 (others, except persons or corporations exempt from real and personal property taxes, charities, etc.)	$ -0-	$ -0-	10%
	50,000	5,000	12
	500,000	59,000	15

Exemption: None, unless share is less than $100, in which case there is no tax.

MINNESOTA

The tax is computed at graduated rates on the value of the share passing to each beneficiary in excess of the applicable exemption. The exemption is taken from the lowest brackets.

Life Insurance Proceeds payable to the estate are taxable. If payable to a beneficiary other than the estate, they are taxable if the insured possessed at his death an incident of ownership; otherwise they are exempt.

Property Owned Jointly With Right of Survivorship. In general, the Federal estate tax rule applies. But where property was acquired prior to 4/29/35 by decedent and spouse as joint tenants, not more than one-half is taxable.

The Federal Estate Tax is deductible in computing the State inheritance tax.

Minnesota ESTATE TAX absorbs the maximum credit for State tax allowed by the Federal estate tax law.

RATES

	Share	Tax	Rate on Next Bracket
Class A (widow; minor or dependent child, either by blood or adoption)	$ -0-	$ -0-	1½%
	25,000	375	2
	50,000	875	3
	100,000	2,375	4
Exemption: (1) Widow, $30,000; (2) child,	150,000	4,375	5
$15,000. To give effect,	200,000	6,875	6
	300,000	12,875	7
subtract $475 from tax in	400,000	19,875	8
case of widow and $225	500,000	27,875	9
in case of child.	1,000,000	72,875	10
Class B (husband; adult child or other lineal descendant; adult adopted child or issue; lineal ancestor; stepchild; mutually acknowledged child or issue)	$ -0-	$ -0-	2%
	25,000	500	4
	50,000	1,500	6
	100,000	4,500	7
	200,000	11,500	8
	400,000	27,500	9
	1,000,000	81,500	10
Exemption: $6,000 each. To give effect, subtract $120 from tax.			

	Share	Tax	
Class C (brother, sister, or their descendant; husband of daughter; wife or widow of son)	$ -0-	$ -0-	6%
	25,000	1,500	8
	50,000	3,500	10
	100,000	8,500	12
Exemption: $1,500 each.	150,000	14,500	14
To give effect, subtract	200,000	21,500	16
$90 from tax.	300,000	37,500	18
	400,000	55,500	20
	500,000	75,500	22
	1,000,000	185,500	25
Class D (others)	$ -0-	$ -0-	8%
Exemptions: $500 each.	25,000	2,000	10
To give effect, subtract	50,000	4,500	12
$40 from tax.	100,000	10,500	14
	150,000	17,500	16
	200,000	25,500	18
	300,000	43,500	20
	400,000	63,500	22
	500,000	85,500	26
	1,000,000	215,500	30

Minnesota GIFT TAX is imposed at rates identical with the inheritance tax rates. Classes of beneficiaries are also the same. A $3,000 annual exclusion is allowed for gifts to each donee each year (except, generally gifts of future interests). SPECIFIC EXEMPTIONS and CREDITS AGAINST THE TAX are allowed.

MISSISSIPPI

The tax is computed at graduated rates on the net estate, which is the gross estate reduced by allowable deductions and exemptions. The estate is valued at date of death or, at the election of the executor, six months later.

Life Insurance Proceeds payable to the estate are included in the gross estate for tax purposes. Proceeds payable to beneficiaries other than the estate, and as to which the insured possessed at his death an incident of ownership, are included in the gross estate to the extent the total proceeds of such insurance exceeds $20,000.

A Specific Exemption of $60,000 may be deducted in computing the net estate.

Property Owned Jointly With Right of Survivorship. Federal estate tax rule applies.

RATES

Net Estate (after deductions and exemptions)	Tax	Rate on Next Bracket
$ -0-	$ -0-	1%
60,000	600	1³/₅
100,000	1,240	2²/₅
200,000	3,640	3¹/₅
400,000	10,040	4
600,000	18,040	4⁴/₅
800,000	27,640	5³/₅
1,000,000	38,840	6²/₅
1,500,000	70,840	7¹/₅
2,000,000	106,840	8

2,500,000	146,840	$8\frac{4}{5}$
3,000,000	190,840	$9\frac{3}{5}$
3,500,000	238,840	$10\frac{2}{5}$
4,000,000	290,840	$11\frac{1}{5}$
5,000,000	402,840	12
6,000,000	522,840	$12\frac{4}{5}$
7,000,000	650,840	$13\frac{3}{5}$
8,000,000	786,840	$14\frac{2}{5}$
9,000,000	930,840	$15\frac{1}{5}$
10,000,000	1,082,840	16

MISSOURI

The tax is computed at graduated rates on the value of the share passing to each beneficiary in excess of the applicable exemption. The exemption comes "off the top" of the share.

Life Insurance Proceeds payable to the estate are taxable. Proceeds payable to named beneficiaries are exempt.

Property Owned Jointly With Right of Survivorship. Not taxable.

Federal Estate Tax is deductible in computing the State inheritance tax.

Missouri ESTATE TAX absorbs the maximum credit for State tax allowed by the Federal estate tax law.

RATES

	Share in Excess of Exemption	Tax	Rate on Next Bracket
Class A spouse, lineal ancestor, lineal descendant, adopted child or its descendant)	$ -0-	$ -0-	1%
	20,000	200	2
Exemptions: (1) Husband	40,000	600	3
or wife, $20,000. IN	80,000	1,800	4
ADDITION, PROPERTY	200,000	6,600	5
PASSING TO SUR-	400,000	16,600	6
VIVING SPOUSE IS			
EXEMPT TO EXTENT			
OF ONE-HALF THE			
CLEAR MARKET VALUE			
OF THE ESTATE IF			
NO LINEAL DESCEN-			
DANTS SURVIVE, OR			
ONE-THIRD THE			
VALUE IF THERE ARE			
SUCH DESCENDANTS.			
(2) Insane, blind, or			
otherwise incapacitated			
lineal descendants,			
$15,000 each.			
(3) Other Class A benefici			
aries, $5,000 each or value			
of homestead allowance to			
such person, whichever			
is greater.			

Class B (brother, sister, or their descendants;	$ -0-	$ -0-	3%
	20,000	600	6
son-in-law, daughter-	40,000	1,800	9
in-law; aunt, uncle, or	80,000	5,400	12
their descendants)	200,000	19,800	15

Exemptions: (1) Brother, sister, their descendants; son-in-law, daughter-in-law; $500 each.   400,000   49,800   18
(2) Aunt, uncle, their descendants; $250 each.

Class C (brother or sister of grandparents;	$ -0-	$ -0-	4%
	20,000	800	8
descendant of such brother	40,000	2,400	12
or sister)	80,000	7,200	16
Exemption: $100 each.	200,000	26,400	20
	400,000	66,400	24

Class D (others)	$ -0-	$ -0-	5%
Exemptions: None, but if	20,000	1,000	10
share less than $100,	40,000	3,000	15
no tax.	80,000	9,000	20
	200,000	33,000	25
	400,000	83,000	30

MONTANA

The tax is computed at graduated rates on the value of the share passing to each beneficiary in excess of the applicable exemption, if any. The exemption is taken from the lowest bracket.

Life Insurance Proceeds. The law provides: "All insurance payable upon the death of any person over and above $50,000 shall be deemed a part of the property and estate passing to the person or persons entitled to receive the same and if payable to more than one person the said $50,000 exemption shall be prorated between such persons in proportion to the amount of insurance payable to each." It has been held that the $50,000 exemption applies even to insurance payable to the executor of the insured's estate.

Property Owned Jointly With Right of Survivorship. Decedent's fractional interest is taxed, as though the property had been owned by tenants in common, "except such part thereof as may be shown to have originally belonged to the survivor . . ."

The Federal Estate Tax is deductible in computing the State inheritance tax.

Montana ESTATE TAX absorbs the maximum credit for State tax allowed by the Federal estate tax law.

RATES

	Share	Tax	Rate on Next Bracket
Class 1 (spouse, lineal issue, lineal ancestor;	$ -0-	$ -0-	2%
	25,000	500	4
adopted or mutually	50,000	1,500	6
acknowledged child	100,000	4,500	8
and lineal issue of			
such child)			
Exemption: (1) Spouse,			
$25,000. To give effect,			
subtract $400 from			
tax computed from table.			

(2) Minor lineal issue; or, in general, any adopted or mutually acknowledged child or issue of such, $5,000. To give effect, subtract $100 from tax computed from table.
(3) Other Class 1 Beneficiaries, $2,000 each. To give effect, subtract $40 from tax computed from table.

Class 2 (brother, sister, or descendant of either; son's wife or widow, husband of daughter) *Exemption:* $500 each. To give effect, subtract $20 from tax computed from table.	Share	Tax	Rate
	$ -0-	$ -0-	4%
	25,000	1,000	8
	50,000	3,000	12
	100,000	9,000	16

Class 3 (uncle, aunt, first cousin) *Exemption:* None			
	$ -0-	$ -0-	6%
	25,000	1,500	12
	50,000	4,500	18
	100,000	13,500	24

Class 4 (others) *Exemption:* None			
	$ -0-	$ -0-	8%
	25,000	2,000	16
	50,000	6,000	24
	100,000	18,000	32

NEBRASKA

The tax is computed—at a flat rate in the case of Class 1 beneficiaries, and at graduated rates in the case of Class 2 and Class 3 beneficiaries—on the value of the share passing to each beneficiary. An exemption is granted for each share. The exemption (in the case of Class 2 and Class 3 beneficiaries) is taken from the lowest bracket.

Life Insurance Proceeds payable to the estate are taxable. Proceeds payable to named beneficiaries are exempt.

Property Owned Jointly With Right of Survivorship. Federal rule applies.

The Federal Estate Tax is allowable as a deduction in computing the State inheritance tax.

Nebraska ESTATE TAX absorbs the maximum credit for State tax allowed by the Federal estate tax law.

RATES

	Share	Tax	Rate on Next Bracket
Class 1 (spouse, parent, child, brother, sister, wife or widow of son, husband of daughter, lineal descendant, adopted or acknowledged children) *Exemption:* $10,000 each. (In addition, in the case of the surviving spouse,	$ 10,000	$ -0-	1%

the homestead right is exempt, and also the value of other property passing to the spouse to the extent of the spouse's right of inheritance)

Class 2 (uncle, aunt, niece, nephew related by blood or legal adoption, or other lineal descendant of aunt or uncle) *Exemption:* $2,000 each.			
	$ 2,000	$ -0-	6%
	60,000	3,480	9

Class 3 (others) *Exemption:* $500 each.			
	$ 500	$ -0-	6%
	5,000	270	9
	10,000	720	12
	20,000	1,920	15
	50,000	6,420	18

NEVADA

THERE IS NO NEVADA INHERITANCE TAX

NEVADA has had no estate tax or inheritance tax since 1925. (In fact, a provision of the Nevada Constitution prohibits enactment of any law imposing an estate or inheritance tax.) The estate of a Nevada resident, therefore, ordinarily pays only the FEDERAL tax.

If a deceased Nevada resident owned real estate or tangible property located in another State (or even intangible personal property in some circumstances), that State may impose a tax on the transfer of such property.

The Federal tax that is payable, where there is no State tax to be paid, is the "gross" tax shown in Column 2 of the table on page 139 of the appendix. For example, if the taxable estate is $300,000, the Federal tax payable is $87,800 (before deducting unified credit).

NEW HAMPSHIRE

The tax is computed at a flat rate on the share of the estate passing to each beneficiary.

Life Insurance Proceeds. There is no statutory provision, but the general rule is followed. Proceeds payable to the estate are taxable. Proceeds payable to named beneficiaries are exempt.

Property Owned Jointly With Right of Survivorship. Rule similar to the Federal estate tax rule applies. (Note, however, that shares going to Class 1 beneficiaries are exempt. See "Rates," below.)

The Federal Estate Tax is deductible in computing the State inheritance tax.

New Hampshire ESTATE TAX absorbs the maximum credit for State tax allowed by the Federal estate tax law.

RATES

Class 1 (Husband, wife, decedent's lineal ascendants and lineal descendants and their spouses, including adopted children in the decedent's line of succession, a person who for 10 consecutive years prior to his 15th birthday was a member of the decedent's household)	Shares going to Class 1 beneficiaries are ENTIRELY EXEMPT.
Class 2 (others) *Exemption:* None	Shares going to Class 2 beneficiaries are taxed at a flat rate of 15%.

NEW JERSEY

The tax is computed at graduated rates on the value of the share passing to each beneficiary. The exemption, if any, is deducted from the lowest bracket.

Life Insurance Proceeds payable to the estate are taxable. Proceeds payable to named beneficiaries are exempt.

Property Owned Jointly With Right of Survivorship. In general the Federal estate tax rule applies. But there is NO TAX on real property held by husband and wife as tenants by the entirety.

New Jersey ESTATE TAX absorbs the maximum credit for State tax allowed by the Federal estate tax law.

RATES

	Share	Tax	Rate on Next Bracket
Class 1 (parent, grandparent, spouse; child or adopted child or his issue; stepchild or mutually acknowledged child) *Exemption:* $5,000 each. To give effect to the exemption, subtract $50 from tax computed from table.	$ -0-	$ -0-	1%
	15,000	150	2
	50,000	850	3
	100,000	2,350	4
	150,000	4,350	5
	200,000	6,850	6
	300,000	12,850	7
	500,000	26,850	8
	700,000	42,850	9
	900,000	60,850	10
	1,100,000	80,850	11
	1,400,000	113,850	12
	1,700,000	149,850	13
	2,200,000	214,850	14
	2,700,000	284,850	15
	3,200,000	359,850	16
Class 2 (brother or sister, husband or widower of daughter, wife or widow of son) *Exemption:* If share is less than $500, no tax; otherwise, no exemption.	$ -0-	$ -0-	11%
	1,100,000	121,000	13
	1,400,000	160,000	14
	1,700,000	202,000	16

	Share	Tax	Rate on Next Bracket
Class 3 (others) *Exemption:* If share is less than $500, no tax; otherwise, no exemption.	$ -0- 700,000	$ -0- 105,000	15% 16

NEW MEXICO

New Mexico law provides that there shall be assessed as New Mexico estate tax an amount exactly equal to the maximum credit allowable under the Federal estate tax law on account of State inheritance or estate tax paid.

Thus, the amount of New Mexico tax would be the amount of the State death tax credit indicated in Column 3 of the rate table shown on page 139.

The tax shown in Column 2 of the rate table is the sum of the New Mexico and Federal estate taxes. The difference (if any) between the taxes indicated in Columns 2 and 3 is the "net" Federal estate tax.

Suppose, for example, that a person domiciled in New Mexico dies leaving property subject to tax which, after the deductions, amounts to $300,000, all consisting of property in New Mexico. In that case the estate taxes would be:

Federal estate tax (before deducting Unified Credit)	$84,200
New Mexico estate tax	3,600
Total	$87,800

This data based on laws in effect February 1977.

NEW YORK

The tax is computed at graduated rates on the N.Y. "taxable estate"—the gross estate less allowable deductions.

Life Insurance Proceeds are includible in the gross estate if payable to the estate or if the insured possessed at his death any of the incidents of ownership.

Property Owned Jointly With Right of Survivorship. Federal estate tax rule applies.

The Marital Deduction. This is granted for the value of the property passing to the surviving spouse, but it may not exceed one-half the adjusted gross estate. The adjusted gross estate (where there is no real or tangible personal property outside the State) is the gross estate reduced by debts and expenses. (The computation is similar to that under the Federal estate tax law.)

Exemptions. Various exemptions are allowed. They do not reduce either the gross estate or the taxable estate. Instead, *percentages* of the total amount of all exemptions (2% of the first $50,000 and 3% of the next $100,000) are credited directly against the tax as computed from the table below.

The total amount of all exemptions is calculated by adding together:

(1) The value of property passing to and indefeasibly vested in the surviving spouse. *However, this exemption may not exceed $20,000 reduced by the marital deduction.*

(2) Up to $5,000 of the value of property passing to EACH of the following: lineal descendant or ancestor; adopted child or stepchild or lineal descendant of such; brother, sister; the wife, widow, husband, or widower of a child of the decedent; mutually acknowledged child, in certain circumstances.

(3) $100,000 of life insurance (included in the gross estate) payable to spouse. *Reduce the $100,000 "ceiling," however, by the total exemptions under (1) and (2) above, plus the marital deduction.* (If insurance made up any part of the marital deduction, do not take an exemption for it here.)

(4) $100,000 of life insurance (included in the gross estate) payable to beneficiaries other than the spouse. Reduce the $100,000 "ceiling," however, by the total exemptions under (1), (2), and (3) above, and also by $20,000 or the marital deduction, whichever is less.

New York estate tax absorbs the maximum credit for State tax allowed by the Federal estate tax law

RATES

Taxable Estate	Tax	Rate on Next Bracket	Taxable Estate	Tax	Rate on Next Bracket
$ -0-	$ -0-	2%	$2,600,000	$212,000	12%
50,000	1,000	3	3,100,000	272,000	13
150,000	4,000	4	3,600,000	337,000	14
300,000	10,000	5	4,100,000	407,000	15
500,000	20,000	6	5,100,000	557,000	16
700,000	32,000	7	6,100,000	717,000	17
900,000	46,000	8	7,100,000	887,000	18
1,100,000	62,000	9	8,100,000	1,067,000	19
1,600,000	107,000	10	9,100,000	1,257,000	20
2,100,000	157,000	11	10,100,000	1,457,000	21

NEW YORK GIFT TAX is patterned after the Federal gift tax (but no $30,000 specific exemption is allowed). The gift tax rates are three-quarters of the New York estate tax rates.

NORTH CAROLINA

The tax is computed at graduated rates on the value of the share passing to each beneficiary in excess of the applicable exemption. The exemption comes "off the top" of the share.

Life Insurance Proceeds are taxable if payable to the estate. If payable to other beneficiaries they are taxable if the insured possessed at his death an incident of ownership; otherwise they are exempt.

However, a total of $20,000 of proceeds, otherwise taxable, is exempt when paid to Class A beneficiaries. Also, a total of $2,000 is exempt when paid to Class B and C beneficiaries, but only if and to the extent the exemption allowed Class A beneficiaries is less than $2,000.

Property Owned Jointly With Right of Survivorship. Federal estate tax rule applies, except that where real property is held by husband and wife as tenants by the entirety, one-half is taxable.

North Carolina ESTATE TAX absorbs the maximum credit for State tax allowed by the Federal estate tax law.

RATES

	Share in Excess of Exemption	Tax	Rate on Next Bracket
Class A (spouse, lineal ancestor, lineal issue, adopted child, stepchild, son- or daughter-in-law) *Exemptions:* Spouse, $10,000. Each child under 18, $5,000. Incapacitated child 18 or over, under certain conditions, $5,000. Others in Class A, $2,000 each.	$ -0-	$ -0-	1%
	10,000	100	2
	25,000	400	3
	50,000	1,150	4
	100,000	3,150	5
	200,000	8,150	6
	500,000	26,150	7
	1,000,000	61,150	8
	1,500,000	101,150	9
	2,000,000	146,150	10
	2,500,000	196,150	11
	3,000,000	251,150	12

NOTE—In some circumstances (a) grandchildren are allowed the single exemption of their parent; (b) a widow, at her option, is allowed an additional $5,000 for each child under 18 or incapacitated (in which case the children are not allowed the exemption).

	Share in Excess of Exemption	Tax	Rate on Next Bracket
Class B (brother, sister, or descendant of brother or sister; uncle or aunt by blood) *Exemption:* None.	$ -0-	$ -0-	4%
	5,000	200	5
	10,000	450	6
	25,000	1,350	7
	50,000	3,100	8
	100,000	7,100	10
	250,000	22,100	11
	500,000	49,600	12
	1,000,000	109,600	13
	1,500,000	174,600	14
	2,000,000	244,600	15
	3,000,000	394,600	16

	Share in Excess of Exemption	Tax	Rate on Next Bracket
Class C (others) *Exemption:* None.	$ -0-	$ -0-	8%
	10,000	800	9
	25,000	2,150	10
	50,000	4,650	11
	100,000	10,150	12
	250,000	28,150	13
	500,000	60,650	14
	1,000,000	130,650	15
	1,500,000	205,650	16
	2,500,000	365,650	17

North Carolina GIFT TAX. The rates and classes are the same as for the inheritance tax. There is an annual exclusion of $3,000 for gifts each year to each donee. There is also an exemption of $30,000, allowed only once, for total gifts to Class A beneficiaries.

NORTH DAKOTA

(Applicable to estates of decedents dying on or after July 1, 1975)

The tax is computed at graduated rates on the value of the TAXABLE ESTATE, which is the gross estate reduced by allowable deductions and exemptions.

Life Insurance Proceeds are includible in the gross estate if they are payable to the estate. Proceeds payable to other named beneficiaries are includible in the gross estate if the insured possessed at his death any of the incidents of ownership.

Property Owned Jointly With Right of Survivorship. Federal estate tax rules apply.

RATES

Taxable Estate (after deductions and exemptions)	Tax	Rate on Next Bracket
$ -0-	$ -0-	2%
30,000	600	4
60,000	1,800	5
100,000	3,800	7
200,000	10,800	9
400,000	28,800	11
600,000	50,800	13
800,000	76,800	15
1,000,000	106,800	17
1,500,000	191,800	20

OHIO

The tax is computed at graduated rates on the value of the TAXABLE ESTATE, which is the gross estate reduced by deductions and exemptions.

Life Insurance Proceeds. If payable to the estate, they are taxable (with a possible exemption of up to $2,000 if payable under an "employer death benefit plan"). Proceeds payable to beneficiaries other than the estate (whether payable directly to such beneficiaries or to a testamentary or inter vivos trust for their benefit) are exempt.

Property Owned Jointly With Right of Survivorship. If joint owners are husband and wife, one-half the value of the property is included in the gross estate of the first to die. In other cases a rule similar to the Federal estate tax rule applies.

Exemptions: (1) $5,000
   plus
(2) interest transferred to surviving spouse......................... $20,000
   plus
(3) interest transferred to each child aged 18 or older at death of decedent........................ $3,000
   and
interest transferred to each child under 18.............................. $7,000

Ohio ESTATE TAX absorbs the maximum credit for State tax allowed by the Federal estate tax law.

RATES

If taxable estate is—	The tax shall be—
Not over $40,000	2%
Over $40,000 but not over $100,000	$800 plus 3% over $40,000
Over $100,000 but not over $200,000	$2,600 plus 4% over $100,000
Over $200,000 but not over $300,000	$6,600 plus 5% over $200,000
Over $300,000 but not over $500,000	$11,600 plus 6% over $300,000
Over $500,000	$23,600 plus 7% over $500,000

OKLAHOMA

Oklahoma imposes an estate tax on a graduated scale on the fair market value at death of the net estate. The net estate is computed by subtracting exemptions, debts, expenses, and other deductions from the gross estate.

Exemptions. Amounts passing to Class 1 beneficiaries are exempt up to a total of $60,000. All property passing to the surviving spouse as beneficial owner is exempt.

Life Insurance Proceeds payable to the estate or to named beneficiaries are taxable, except that with respect to decedents who died during June 1974, up to $20,000 of proceeds payable to named beneficiaries are exempt.

Property Owned Jointly With Right of Survivorship. Federal estate tax rule applies.

Oklahoma estate tax absorbs the maximum credit for State tax allowed by the Federal estate tax law.

RATES

	Net Estate	Tax	Rate on Next Bracket
Class 1 (parent, child, adopted child, or lineal descendant of decedent or of such adopted child) *Exemption:* $60,000 for the class.	$ -0-	$ -0-	1%
	10,000	100	2
	20,000	300	3
	40,000	900	4
	60,000	1,700	5
	100,000	3,700	6
	250,000	12,700	6½
	500,000	28,950	7
	750,000	46,150	7½
	1,000,000	65,200	8
	3,000,000	225,200	8½
	5,000,000	395,200	9
	10,000,000	845,200	10
Class 2 (all others) *Exemption:* None.	$ -0-	$ -0-	2%
	10,000	200	4
	20,000	600	6
	40,000	1,800	8
	60,000	3,400	10
	100,000	7,400	12
	250,000	25,400	13
	500,000	57,900	14
	1,000,000	127,900	15

Oklahoma GIFT TAX imposes a tax on gifts during life. The rates are the same as those levied under the estate tax. There is a $3,000 annual exclusion for gifts to each donee in each calendar year.

Like the Federal gift tax, the Oklahoma gift tax is "cumulative." The tax for any year is found by (1) computing the tax on all taxable net gifts, including those of the taxable year; (2) then computing a tax on all taxable net gifts except those of the taxable year; (3) then subtracting (2) from (1).

OREGON

(Applicable to estates of decedents dying on or after September 13, 1975)

Oregon imposes two taxes at death. Both are called "inheritance" taxes in the law; but one is an estate tax based on the entire net estate in excess of $25,000, while the other is a true inheritance tax that applies to the shares of the estate separately. The estate tax is generally known as the "basic" tax and the inheritance tax as the "additional" tax.

Life Insurance Proceeds payable to the estate are subject to tax. Proceeds of policies issued prior to Jan. 1, 1960, payable to beneficiaries other than the estate are exempt. On policies issued after Dec. 31, 1959, payable to beneficiaries other than the estate, and as to which the insured held at his death an incident of ownership, $75,000 of the total proceeds is exempt and the rest is subject to tax. (These rules apply to both taxes.)

Property Owned Jointly With Right of Survivorship. Federal rule generally applies. But, only one-half of value of real property owned by tenants by the entirety is taxed. Also, with respect to decedent's separately or jointly owned property passing to surviving spouse, Oregon law presumes that surviving spouse contributed at least one-half.

Oregon ESTATE TAX absorbs the maximum credit for State tax allowed by the Federal estate tax law.

RATES

Net Estate	Tax	Rate on Next Bracket
$ 25,000	$ -0-	3%
75,000	1,500	4
100,000	2,500	7
300,000	16,500	9
500,000	34,500	12

NOTE: A credit against the basic tax is allowed for the first $300,000 of property passing to each of the following surviving spouse, and child or stepchild under 18 or incompetent

THE ADDITIONAL TAX RATES

	Share	Tax	Rate on Next Bracket
Class 1 (grandparent, parent, spouse, child, stepchild, lineal descendant)	(This tax does not apply to shares going to Class 1 beneficiaries)		
Class 2 (brother, sister, uncle, aunt, any of their lineal descendants: son-in-law (including widower of daughter), daughter-in-law (including widow of son))	$ 3,000	$ -0-	3%
	5,000	60	6
	10,000	360	10
	30,000	2,360	14
	50,000	5,160	20
Class 3 (others)	$ 500	$ -0-	5%
	1,000	25	7
	2,000	95	10
	4,000	295	13
	10,000	1,075	20
	25,000	4,075	25

Oregon GIFT TAX has two parts: a "basic" tax and an "additional" tax. The total gift tax payable by an individual for any calendar year is the sum of (1) the basic tax on total net gifts and (2) the additional tax on the net gifts to each of the various donees. Gifts to Class (1) donees—spouse, children, etc.—are subject to the basic tax only.

PENNSYLVANIA

The tax is computed on the fair market value of the net estate at the date of death at rates depending upon the class or classes of beneficiaries to whom the property passes.

Life Insurance Proceeds payable to the estate are taxable. Proceeds payable to named beneficiaries are exempt.

Property Owned Jointly With Right of Survivorship. Not taxable if owned by husband and wife. Otherwise, decedent's fractional interest is taxed.

Family Exemption. $2,000 paid to surviving spouse or if there is no surviving spouse, to children who are members of the decedent's household, will qualify as a deduction. (Effective 9/1/63, decedent's parents who are members of his household may claim this exemption if there is no spouse or child.)

Pennsylvania ESTATE TAX absorbs the maximum credit for State tax allowed under the Federal estate tax law.

RATES

Class A Spouse, children, parents, etc. Flat Rate—6% Covers transfers to grandfather, grandmother, father, mother, husband, wife and lineal descendants, wife or widow, and husband or widower of a child, adopted children and their descendants, stepchildren, and illegitimate child inheriting from family of mother or issue of such child

Class B Others .... Flat Rate—15% Includes transfers to brothers, sisters, other collateral relatives and non-related individuals.
Exemption None

RHODE ISLAND

It is 1% of the net estate in excess of a $10,000 exemption

RHODE ISLAND LEGACY (INHERITANCE) TAX

This tax is computed at graduated rates on the value of the share passing to each beneficiary in excess of the applicable exemption. The exemption is taken from the lowest bracket.

Life Insurance in excess of $50,000 with respect to which the insured possessed at his death any of the incidents of ownership is taxable.

Property Owned Jointly With Right of Survivorship. Federal estate tax rule applies.

Rhode Island ESTATE TAX absorbs the maximum credit for State tax allowed by the Federal estate tax law.

RATES

	Share	Tax	Rate on Next Bracket
Class A (grandparents,	$ 10,000	$ -0-	2%
natural or adoptive	25,000	300	3
parents, spouse, children,	50,000	1,050	4
adopted and mutually	100,000	3,050	5
acknowledged children,	250,000	10,550	6
lineal descendants)	500,000	25,550	7
Exemption: $10,000 each.	750,000	43,050	8
	1,000,000	63,050	9
Class B (stepchildren,	$ 5,000	$ -0-	3%
stepparents, brothers,	25,000	600	4
sisters, wife or widow of	50,000	1,600	5
son, husband or widower	100,000	4,100	6
of daughter)	250,000	13,100	7
Exemption: $5,000 each.	500,000	30,600	8
	750,000	50,600	9
	1,000,000	73,100	10
Class C (nieces, nephews,	$ 3,000	$ -0-	4%
issue of adopted child,	25,000	880	5
adopted child of child,	50,000	2,130	6
husband or widower of	100,000	5,130	7
adopted daughter, wife or	250,000	15,630	8
widow of adopted son)	500,000	35,630	9
Exemption: $3,000 each.	750,000	58,130	10
	1,000,000	83,130	11
Class D (others)	$ 1,000	$ -0-	8%
Exemption: $1,000 each.	25,000	1,920	9
	50,000	4,170	10
	100,000	9,170	11
	250,000	25,670	12
	500,000	55,670	13
	750,000	88,170	14
	1,000,000	123,170	15

RHODE ISLAND GIFT TAX

Specific, or ' lifetime,' exemption: $25,000. Annual exclusion (allowed for gifts to each donee each year): $3,000 Rates range up to 9%.

SOUTH CAROLINA

The tax is an estate tax on the fair market value of the property at date of death (or six months later, at the option of the executor).

Among the allowable deductions are a $60,000 exemption, a deduction for charitable bequests, and a marital deduction.

Life Insurance Proceeds are includible in the gross estate if payable to the estate. If payable to named beneficiaries, they are includible in the gross estate if the insured possessed at his death any of the incidents of ownership.

Property Owned Jointly With Right of Survivorship. Federal estate tax rule applies.

The Marital Deduction. It is allowed for the value of property passing to the surviving spouse. It is limited, however, to one-half the adjusted gross estate. The adjusted gross estate is the gross estate reduced by funeral and estate-administration expenses, debts and claims, and casualty and theft losses during estate administration. Generally, the same rules with respect to the allowance of a marital deduction for ·terminable interests· applies to the South Carolina tax as apply to the Federal tax.

Life insurance qualifies for the marital deduction if payable outright to the surviving spouse. In addition, certain settlement options qualify for the deduction, as do the proceeds also when payable to an insurance trust under certain conditions.

South Carolina estate tax absorbs the maximum credit for State tax allowed by the Federal estate tax law.

RATES

Taxable Estate (the gross estate reduced by deductions and exemptions)	Tax
$ -0- to $40,000	4%
$40,000 to $100,000	$1,600 plus 5% of the excess over $40,000
$100,000 or over.....................	$4,600 plus 6% of the excess over $100,000

SOUTH CAROLINA GIFT TAX

(Applicable to gifts made on and after Jan. 1, 1969)

The rates are 3/4ths of the South Carolina estate tax rates. There is a $30,000 specific, or 'lifetime,' exemption. Also, there is a $3,000 annual exclusion. (The first $3,000 given to any donee in any year is exempt provided such gifts are not future interests.) One-half the value of gifts to donor's spouse is deductible.

The tax is 'cumulative.' It is the excess of the tax on gifts in all years over the tax on gifts in the current year.

SOUTH DAKOTA

The tax is computed at graduated rates on the value of the share passing to each beneficiary in excess of the applicable exemption.* The exemption is taken from the lowest bracket.

Life Insurance Proceeds payable to the insured's estate (or to the executor or trustee for payment of estate or inheritance taxes) are taxable. Proceeds payable to named beneficiaries are exempt.

Property Owned Jointly With Right of Survivorship. Where owned by husband and wife, one-half is taxable. In other cases, Federal estate tax rule applies.

South Dakota does NOT impose an estate tax to absorb the maximum credit for State tax allowed by the Federal estate tax law.

*Exemption is reduced by value of property outside of state received by beneficiary from decedent. If value of property exceeds exemption no exemption is allowed.

RATES

	Share	Tax	Rate on Next Bracket
Class 1 (spouse; lineal issue; legally adopted child; mutually acknowledged child in some circumstances) *Exemption:* Spouse, $60,000 (subtract $1,725 from tax computed from table). *Others,* $10,000 each (subtract $150 from tax computed from table)	$ -0- 15,000 50,000 100,000	$ -0- 225 1,275 3,525	1½% 3 4½ 6
Class 2 (lineal ancestor) *Exemption:** $3,000 each (subtract $90 from tax per table)	$ -0- 15,000 50,000 100,000	$ -0- 450 2,550 7,050	3% 6 9 12
Class 3 (brother, sister, or their descendant; wife or widow of son, husband of daughter) *Exemption:** $500 each (subtract $20 from tax per table)	$ -0- 15,000 50,000 100,000	$ -0- 600 3,400 9,400	4% 8 12 16
Class 4 (brother or sister of parent; descendant of such brother or sister) *Exemption:** $200 each (subtract $10 from tax per table)	$ -0- 15,000 50,000 100,000	$ -0- 750 4,250 11,750	5% 10 15 20
Class 5 (others) *Exemption:** $100 each (subtract $6 from tax per table)	$ -0- 15,000 50,000 100,000	$ -0- 900 5,100 14,100	6% 12 18 24

TENNESSEE

The tax is computed at graduated rates on the share passing to *each class* of beneficiaries. There is only one exemption to a class; it is applied against the lowest bracket.

Life Insurance Proceeds payable to the insured's estate, or to named beneficiaries, or in such manner as to be subject to claims against the estate, are taxable.

Property Owned Jointly With Right of Survivorship. Portion attributable to decedent's contribution is taxable. If contributions of parties cannot be ascertained, decedent's fractional interest is taxed. Where money or evidences of indebtedness were deposited subject to individual control of decedent, all is taxed unless it can be shown it was not entirely the decedent's property.

Tennessee ESTATE TAX absorbs the maximum credit for State tax allowed by the Federal estate tax law.

RATES

	Value of Property Passing to Class	Tax	Rate on Next Bracket
Class A (husband, wife, son, daughter, lineal ancestor or descendant, adoptive ancestor, legally adopted child and lineal descendant of adopted child) *Exemption:* $60,000 for the class.	$ 60,000 100,000 300,000 500,000	$ -0- 2,200 15,200 30,200	5.5% 6.5 7.5 9.5
Class B (others) *Exemption:* $1,000 for the class	$ 1,000 50,000 100,000 150,000 200,000 250,000	$ -0- 3,185 7,935 13,935 20,685 28,685	6.5% 9.5 12 13.5 16 20

Tennessee GIFT TAX is computed at graduated rates on the total gifts made during the calendar year to each of two classes—the classes being identical with those shown above for inheritance tax purposes.

There is an annual exemption of $10,000 for gifts to persons in Class A. The class is treated as a whole, and there is but one $10,000 exemption for the class. Such an exemption is allowed annually. It is applied against the first bracket.

There is a like exemption for gifts to persons in Class B, except that the amount is $5,000.

TEXAS

The tax is computed at graduated rates on the value of the share passing to each beneficiary in excess of the applicable exemption. The exemption is taken from the lowest bracket.

Only one-half of community property is includible, for tax purposes, in the estate of a married person.

Life Insurance Proceeds. $40,000 of the total proceeds payable to beneficiaries other than the estate is exempt. Any excess above $40,000, and all proceeds payable to the estate, are taxable.

It has been held that, where premiums on policies were paid from community property, only one-half of the proceeds payable to wife-beneficiary were subject to tax, and the entire $40,000 exemption was applied against the taxable portion.

Property Owned Jointly With Right of Survivorship. Federal estate tax rules generally apply. However, Texas law presumes equal contributions by the joint tenants.

Texas ESTATE TAX absorbs the maximum credit for State tax allowed by the Federal estate tax law.

RATES

	Share	Tax	Rate on Next Bracket
Class A (spouse, descendant of spouse, descendant or ascendant of decedent, adopted children or descendant of adopted children, son-in-law, daughter-in-law) *Exemption: $25,000 each.*	$ 25,000 50,000 100,000 200,000 500,000 1,000,000	$ -0- 250 1,250 4,250 16,250 41,250	1% 2 3 4 5 6
Class B (the United States,(tax, rates, and exemptions to be used in Texas are same as for Class A)			
Class C (brothers, sisters or their descendants) *Exemption: $10,000 each.*	$ 10,000 25,000 50,000 100,000 250,000 500,000 750,000 1,000,000	$ -0- 450 1,450 3,950 12,950 30,450 50,450 72,950	3% 4 5 6 7 8 9 10
Class D (uncles, aunts, or their descendants) *Exemption: $1,000 each.*	$ 1,000 10,000 25,000 50,000 100,000 500,000 1,000,000	$ -0- 360 1,110 2,610 6,110 46,110 106,110	4% 5 6 7 10 12 15
Class E (all others) *Exemption: $500 each.*	$ 500 10,000 25,000 50,000 100,000 500,000 1,000,000	$ -0- 475 1,375 3,375 8,375 56,375 131,375	5% 6 8 10 12 15 20

UTAH

Utah law provides that there shall be assessed as Utah estate tax an amount exactly equal to the maximum credit allowable under the Federal estate tax law on account of State inheritance or estate tax paid.

Thus, the amount of Utah tax would be the amount of the State death tax credit indicated in Column 3 of the rate table shown on page 139.

The tax shown in Column 2 of the rate table is the sum of the Utah and Federal estate taxes. The difference (if any) between the taxes indicated in Columns 2 and 3 is the "net" Federal estate tax.

Suppose, for example, that a person domiciled in Utah dies leaving property subject to tax which, after the deductions, amounts to $300,000, all consisting of property in Utah. In that case the estate taxes would be:

Federal estate tax (before deducting Unified Credit)	$84,200
Utah estate tax	3,600
Total	$87,800

This data based on laws in effect February 1977.

Utah ESTATE TAX absorbs the maximum credit for State tax allowed by the Federal estate tax law.

RATES

Taxable Estate		Tax on Col. 1	Rate on Excess
(1) From—	(2) To—		
-0-	$35,000	$ -0-	5%
$35,000	85,000	1,750	8
85,000	balance	5,750	10

VERMONT

(Applicable to estates of decedents dying on or after January 1, 1971)

The tax is an amount measured by 30% of the Federal estate tax liability of the decedent's estate, reduced proportionately by the percentage of the Federal gross estate which is not Vermont gross estate. Vermont gross estate is the Federal gross estate, excluding real or tangible personal property which has an actual situs outside of Vermont.

The exemptions, deductions, and credits allowed under Federal estate tax law are allowed in computing the Vermont tax. A determination by the United States establishing the amount of the Federal taxable estate or estate tax liability is binding on the estate and the State for Vermont estate tax purposes.

Life Insurance Proceeds are includible in the gross estate if payable to the estate or if the insured possessed at his death any of the incidents of ownership.

Property Owned Jointly With Right of Survivorship. Federal estate tax rules apply.

Vermont ESTATE TAX absorbs the maximum credit for State tax allowed by the Federal estate tax law.

Vermont GIFT TAX is in an amount measured by 30% of the Federal gift tax liability, reduced proportionately by the percentage of all gifts which are not Vermont gifts. The exemptions, exclusions, and deductions allowed under Federal gift tax law apply for Vermont gift tax purposes.

VIRGINIA

The tax is computed at graduated rates on the value of the share passing to each beneficiary in excess of the applicable exemption. The exemption is taken from the lowest bracket.

Life Insurance Proceeds. There is no express provision in the statute. However, in practice insurance proceeds are generally taxable only if payable to the estate or to an executor or trustee to pay inheritance and estate taxes.

Property Owned Jointly With Right of Survivorship. Federal estate tax rule applies; except that where real property is owned by husband and wife as joint tenants or tenants by the entireties, and such property is a single family residence occupied as their home, not more than one-half the net value is taxed. (The exception applies to estates of persons dying on or after 7/1/64 and to estates of decedents which come into possession of beneficiaries by exercise or relinquishment of powers after such date.)

Federal Estate Tax is an allowable deduction in computing the State inheritance tax.

Virginia ESTATE TAX absorbs the maximum credit for State tax allowed by the Federal estate tax law

RATES

	Share	Tax	Rate on Next Bracket
Class A (father, mother, grandfather, grandmother, husband, wife, children by blood or legal adoption, stepchild, grandchildren, other lineal ancestors and descendants) *Exemption: $5,000 each.*	$ 5,000 $ 50,000 100,000 500,000 1,000,000	$ -0- 450 1,450 13,450 33,450	1% 2 3 4 5
Class B (brothers, sisters nephews, nieces) *Exemption. $2,000 each.*	$ 2,000 $ 25,000 50,000 100,000 500,000	$ -0- 460 1,460 4,460 36,460	2% 4 6 8 10
Class C (others) *Exemption $1,000 each.*	$ 1,000 $ 25,000 50,000 100,000 500,000	$ -0- 1,200 2,950 7,450 55,450	5% 7 9 12 15

Virginia GIFT TAX is computed on the value of gifts to each beneficiary during each year The classes, rates, and exemptions are the same as those set forth for the inheritance tax above.

WASHINGTON

The tax is computed on the total value of shares passing to EACH CLASS. One exemption per class is allowed—not one exemption per share. The exemption is taken from the lowest bracket.

Only one-half of community property is taxable in the estate of a married person.

Life Insurance Proceeds. $40,000 of the total proceeds payable to beneficiaries other than the estate is exempt If premiums are paid from community funds, only one-half of the proceeds are subject to tax, and the entire $40,000 exemption may be applied to the taxable half

Property Owned Jointly With Right of Survivorship. Federal estate tax rule applies, except that the tax does not apply to real property held in a tenancy by the entirety

Washington ESTATE TAX absorbs the maximum credit for State tax allowed by the Federal estate tax law.

RATES

	Value of Property Passing to Class	Tax	Rate on Next Bracket
Class A (lineal ancestors and descendants; spouse; stepchild or adopted child and their lineal descendants; adopted child of lineal descendants: son-in-law: daughter-in-law) *Exemption for class $5,000 plus an additional $5,000 on account of the surviving spouse, and $5,000 for each child, stepchild. adopted child, and their lineal descendants per stirpes. If none of above survives $10.000 or the class.*	$ 10,000 $ 25,000 50,000 75,000 100,000 200,000 500,000	$ -0- 150 650 1,400 2,400 9,400 36,400	1% 2 3 4 7 9 10

Note· The table shown assumes an exemption of $10,000. If exemption exceeds $10,000, reduce tax as computed from table by 1% of exemption between $10,000 and $25,000, 2% of exemption between $25,000 and $50,000.

	Value	Tax	Rate on Next Bracket
Class B (brothers and sisters) *Exemption for class $1,000*	$ 1,000 $ 5,000 10,000 30,000 50,000 100,000	$ -0- 120 320 1,720 3,720 11,220	3% 4 7 10 15 20
Class C (others) *Exemption None*	$ -0- $ 10,000 25,000 50,000	$ -0- 1,000 3,250 8,250	10% 15 20 25

Washington GIFT TAX rates are 9/10ths of the inheritance tax rates. The gift tax classes are the same as the inheritance tax classes, and total gifts to each class are taxed, after exemptions. There is a $3,000 annual exclusion for gifts of present interests to each person in each year There are also 'lifetime exemptions for gifts to each class Class A $10,000 Class B, $1,000 Clas C, none

WEST VIRGINIA

The tax is computed at graduated rates on the value of the share passing to each beneficiary Exemptions— applicable to the lowest bracket—are allowed on shares going to Class 1 beneficiaries There is no tax on shares going to a beneficiary if those shares total $100 or less

Life Insurance Proceeds payable to named beneficiaries are exempt Proceeds payable to the estate are taxable, except that there is an exemption in certain cases of premium payment by the beneficiary or assignment of the proceeds by the decedent

Property Owned Jointly With Right of Survivorship. In general, the Federal estate tax rule applies But not more than one-half is taxed if surviving owner is spouse, and, also, up to $2,500 of a joint bank account (or joint shares in Fed. sav. & loan or W. Va. bldg. & loan assoc.) is exempt if survivor is a Class 1 beneficiary.

The Federal Estate Tax is deductible in computing the State inheritance tax.

RATES

	Share	Tax	Rate on Next Bracket
Class 1 (spouse: child: stepchild: descendants of children: parents)	$ -0-	$ -0-	3%
	50,000	1,500	5
	150,000	6,500	7
Exemptions: (a) Widow	300,000	17,000	9
or widower, $15,000.	500,000	35,000	11
(Subtract $450 from tax as shown here.) (b) Father, mother. child, or stepchild, $5,000. (Subtract $150 from tax as shown here.) (c) Grandchild, $2,500. (Subtract $75 from tax as shown here.)	1,000,000	90,000	13
Class 2 (brothers and	$ -0-	$ -0-	4%
sisters, including those of	50,000	2,000	6
the half blood.)	150,000	8,000	8
Exemptions· None	300,000	20,000	10
	500,000	40,000	14
	1,000,000	110,000	18
Class 3 (relatives further	$ -0-	$ -0-	7%
removed from decedent	50,000	3,500	9
than brother or sister.)	150,000	12,500	11
Exemptions· None.	300,000	29,000	15
	500,000	59,000	20
	1,000,000	159,000	25
Class 4 (others)	$ -0-	$ -0-	10%
Exemptions None.	50,000	5,000	12
	150,000	17,000	14
	300,000	38,000	18
	500,000	74,000	24
	1,000,000	194,000	30

WISCONSIN

The tax is computed at graduated rates on the value of the share passing to each beneficiary in excess of the applicable exemption. The exemption is taken from the lowest bracket.

Life Insurance Proceeds. They are taxable if the insured held at his death any of the legal incidents of ownership, except that up to $10,000 of these otherwise taxable proceeds are exempt if payable to beneficiaries other than the insured's estate

Property Owned Jointly With Right of Survivorship. Federal estate tax rule applies

The Federal Estate Tax is deductible in computing State tax.

Wisconsin ESTATE TAX absorbs the maximum credit for State tax allowed by the Federal estate tax law.

RATES

	Share	Tax	Rate on Next Bracket
Class A			
(a) Surviving Spouse	$ -0-	$ -0-	2.5%
Exemption: $50,000.	25,000	625	5.0
(Subtract $1,875 from tax indicated by table)	50,000	1,875	7.5
Note: Reduce tax computed for surviving spouse by one half.	100,000	5,625	10.0
	500,000	45,625	12.5
(b) Lineal ancestor, lineal issue, adopted or mutually acknowledged child, his or her spouse or issue, wife or widow of son, or husband or widower of daughter *Exemption:* $4,000. (Subtract $100 from tax indicated by table)			
Class B			
Brother or sister, or a	$ -0-	$ -0-	5.0%
descendant of brother	25,000	1,250	10.0
or sister.	50,000	3,750	15.0*
Exemption: $1,000.	100,000	11,250*	20.0*
(Subtract $50 from tax indicated by table)	500,000	91,250*	25.0*
Class C			
Brother or sister of father	$ -0-	$ -0-	7.5%
or mother or descendant	25,000	1.875	15 0*
of such brother or sister	50,000	5,625*	22 5*
Exemption $1.000. (Subtract $75 from tax indicated by table)	100,000	16,875*	30.0*
Class D			
Others—*Exemption* $500	$ -0-	$ -0-	10.0%
(Subtract $50 from tax	25,000	2,500	20 0*
indicated by table)	50,000	7,500*	30.0*

*The tax on the share of any beneficiary shall not be more than 20% of the share

Wisconsin GIFT TAX The rates are similar to the Wisconsin inheritance tax rates. There is a $3,000 annual exclusion for gifts made to any person during any one year The tax on gifts to any donee in a year shall not be more than 20% of the gifts. In addition, there is a lifetime exemption to a spouse of $15,000—other Class A donees $4,000. No additional exemption for Class B, C and D donees

WYOMING

The tax is computed at a flat rate on the share of the estate passing to each beneficiary in excess of the applicable exemption

Proceeds of Life Insurance payable to the estate are taxable. Proceeds payable to named beneficiaries are exempt

Property Owned Jointly With Right of Survivorship. Not taxable.

Federal Estate Tax is deductible in computing the State inheritance tax (Supreme Court of Wyoming).

Wyoming ESTATE TAX absorbs the maximum credit for State tax allowed by the Federal estate tax law.

RATES

	Exemption Of Each Beneficiary's Share	Rate of Tax On Share In Excess of Exemption
Class A (wife, husband) .... (child, parent, brother, sister, adopted child, or adopted [adoptive] parent)	$60,000 $10,000	2% 2%
Class B (grandparent, grand-child, half-brother, half-sister)	$ 5,000	4%
Class C (other persons) **Class D** (gifts for state, municipal, charitable, educational, or religious purposes, or for preservation of wild fowl or game) .... (This class also includes proceeds of life insurance payable to beneficiaries other than the insured's estate)	None Entirely exempt if property is limited to use in State	6%
Class E (property transferred for charitable, etc., purposes if institution organized in Wyoming, limited to use in State, or there is reciprocal relationship between Wyoming and state or country where institution located or property to be used) .... Entirely exempt		

DISTRICT OF COLUMBIA

The tax is computed at graduated rates on the value of the share of the estate passing to each beneficiary in excess of the applicable exemption. The exemption is taken from the lowest bracket.

Life Insurance Proceeds are taxable if (a) paid to the estate; (b) if taken out to provide for the payment of taxes or other charges against the insured's estate, or to benefit the insured's estate otherwise; or if the named beneficiary predeceased the insured. Otherwise, proceeds are exempt.

Property Owned Jointly With Right of Survivorship. Decedent's fractional interest is taxed.

Federal Estate Tax is deductible in computing the District of Columbia inheritance tax.

District of Columbia ESTATE TAX absorbs the maximum credit for State tax allowed by the Federal estate tax law.

RATES

	Share	Tax	Rate on Next Bracket
Class 1 (spouse, children, parents, adopted children, lineal ancestor or descendants) *Exemption:* $5,000 each.	$ 5,000 25,000 50,000 100,000 500,000 1,000,000	$ -0- 200 700 2,200 22,200 52,200	1% 2 3 5 6 8
Class 2 (others) *Exemption:* $1,000 each.	$ 1,000 25,000 50,000 100,000 500,000 1,000,000	$ -0- 1,200 3,700 10,700 82,700 192,700	5% 10 14 18 22 23

COMMONWEALTH OF PUERTO RICO

(Applicable to estates of decedents dying after January 1, 1969)

The tax is computed at graduated rates on the value of the TAXABLE ESTATE, which is the gross estate reduced by exemptions and deductions.

Life Insurance Proceeds. They are included in the gross estate if the policies are payable to the estate; or, if payable to others, if decedent paid the premiums, directly or indirectly, or had ownership or control. However, the first $10,000 payable to the estate or to the surviving spouse or to heirs of the decedent is deductible.

Property Owned Jointly With Right of Survivorship. A rule similar to the Federal estate tax rule applies. (In general, the full value is included in estate unless surviving owner contributed to cost.)

Property of the Conjugal Partnership. In general, only the decedent's share is included in the gross estate. (The surviving spouse's share is included only for the purpose of allocating to such share some of the debts of the partnership.)

A Fixed Exemption of $60,000 is deducted from the value of the estate. There is no additional estate tax to absorb the credit allowed under the U.S. Federal estate tax law.

RATES

If the taxable estate is—	The tax shall be—
Not over $5,000	3%
Over $5,000 but not over $10,000	$150 + 6% over $5,000
Over $10,000 but not over $25,000	$450 + 10% over $10,000
Over $25,000 but not over $40,000	$1,950 + 15% over $25,000
Over $40,000 but not over $100,000	$4,200 + 25% over $40,000
Over $100,000 but not over $500,000	$19,200 + 30% over $100,000
Over $500,000 but not over $1,000,000	$139,200 + 35% over $500,000
Over $1,000,000 but not over $2,000,000	$314,200 + 40% over $1,000,000
Over $2,000,000 but not over $4,000,000	$714,200 + 50% over $2,000,000
Over $4,000,000 but not over $6,000,000	$1,714,200 + 60% over $4,000,000
Over $6,000,000	$2,914,200 + 70% over $6,000,000

PUERTO RICO GIFT TAX

(Applicable to gifts made
on and after Jan. 1, 1969)

The rates are 3/4ths of the Puerto Rico estate tax rates. There is a $30,000 lifetime exemption. Also there is a $500 annual exclusion (the first $500 given by a person in each year is exempt provided the gifts are not of future interests). Also there is a yearly exemption of the first $1,000 given to each incapacitated child of the donor.

Computation: For gifts made on or after 1/1/69, the tax is "cumulative." It is the excess of the tax on gifts in all years over the tax on gifts in the current year.

The Federal Tentative Tax and State Inheritance Tax table below should be used for computation for the states of Alabama, Alaska, Arkansas, Florida, Georgia, New Mexico and Utah.

1. ESTATE AND GIFT TAX COMPUTATION BASE	2. UNIFIED TRANSFER TAX before credit for State death tax		3. STATE DEATH TAX CREDIT* (IRC §2011)	
	Tax	Rate on next bracket	Tax	Rate on next bracket
Under $10,000	18% of amount		—	—
$ 10,000	$ 1,800	20%	—	—
20,000	3,800	22	—	—
40,000	8,200	24	—	—
60,000	13,000	26	—	—
80,000	18,200	26	—	—
100,000	23,800	30	—	0.8%
150,000	38,800	32	$ 400	1.6
200,000	54,800	32	1,200	2.4
250,000	70,800	34	2,400	2.4
300,000	87,800	34	3,600	3.2
500,000	155,800	37	10,000	4.0
700,000	229,800	37	18,000	4.8
750,000	248,300	39	20,400	4.8
900,000	306,800	39	27,600	5.6
1,000,000	345,800	41	33,200	5.6
1,100,000	386,800	41	38,800	6.4
1,250,000	448,300	43	48,400	6.4
1,500,000	555,800	45	64,400	6.4
1,600,000	600,800	45	70,800	7.2
2,000,000	780,800	49	99,600	7.2
2,100,000	829,800	49	106,800	8.0
2,500,000	1,025,800	53	138,800	8.0
2,600,000	1,078,800	53	146,800	8.8
3,000,000	1,290,800	57	182,000	8.8
3,100,000	1,347,800	57	190,800	9.6
3,500,000	1,575,800	61	229,200	9.6
3,600,000	1,636,800	61	238,800	10.4
4,000,000	1,880,800	65	280,400	10.4
4,100,000	1,945,800	65	290,800	11.2
4,500,000	2,205,800	69	335,600	11.2
5,000,000	2,550,800	70	391,600	11.2
5,100,000	2,620,800	70	402,800	12.0
6,100,000	3,320,800	70	522,800	12.8
7,100,000	4,020,800	70	650,800	13.6
8,100,000	4,720,800	70	786,800	14.4
9,100,000	5,420,800	70	930,800	15.2
10,100,000	6,120,800	70	1,082,800	16.0

*Note: Computation base for State death tax credit is gross estate (1) minus deductions (2).

FEDERAL GIFT TAX COMPUTATION

The amount of a donor's *net taxable gifts* in a calendar year is the total of all gifts less: (1) allowable charitable gifts; (2) an *exclusion* of the first $3,000 of gifts to each donee in the year, except gifts of a future interest; (3) a marital deduction equal to the first $100,000 of gifts made by a husband or wife to the other, and in addition one-half of gifts over $200,000 made by a husband or wife to the other. Gifts made by a husband or wife to third parties are taxed, with the spouse's consent, as though each gave one-half, thus in effect, doubling his or her annual exclusion to $6,000.

To find the tax on gifts made this year: compute the tax, using the Unified Tax Rate Table on page 115 and then apply the phased-in taxed credit as follows The balance will be the tax due and owing.

After December 31, 1976	before July 1, 1977	$ 6,000
After June 30, 1977	before January 1, 1978	30,000
After December 31, 1977	before January 1, 1979	34,000
After December 31, 1978	before January 1, 1980	38,000
After December 31, 1979	before January 1, 1981	42,500
After January 1, 1981		47,000

CARRYOVER BASIS—"FRESH START RULE"

Under prior law, the decedent's basis on all property in his estate was "stepped up" for income tax purposes to the fair market value of the property at the date of the decedent's death.

The 1976 Tax Reform Act introduced a new carryover basis tax, which provides that the basis of property acquired from a decedent shall be the same as the decedent's before his death. However, for all those assets purchased before December 31, 1976, the basis of the assets held by the decedent will receive a "stepped up" basis to the fair market value as of December 31, 1976.

Although this law was originally scheduled to cover the estate assets of all persons dying after December 31, 1976, the Revenue Act of 1978 postponed its effective date to cover all persons dying after December 31, 1979. The apparent reason for this postponement is that there are many practical difficulties in the application of this law. Congress therefore wanted to study possible amendments to the law. Some others have suggested that it be totally repealed. It is known however, that President Carter has announced his strong support for this new law.

The basic reason for the introduction of this law was to eliminate what certain legislators believed to be an income tax free transfer of property from decedent to beneficiary. It should be remembered however that the income taxable event does not occur at the death of an individual, it occurs when the beneficiary sells the asset which he or she receives from the decedent's estate.

This new law will cause considerable problems in the valuation of estates for income tax purposes in the years to come. It is suggested, therefore, that everyone value their assets as of December 31, 1976 and keep this information as part of their permanent records to aid in the administration of their estate.

As an aid in computing this tax, many tax publishers, including Dow Jones Books, have produced books listing the various publicly held stocks and bonds and their values as of December 31, 1976. The computation of the income tax gain or loss on these kinds of assets are then made relatively easy as compared to the computation of real estate which the decedent may have purchased many years ago.

For example, assume a decedent who dies on January 15, 1980 purchased a house in 1950 whose purchase price was $35,000. Assume further that at his death, this same real estate has a fair market value of $150,000 and under the terms of his will he specifically left this real estate to his son. The son decides to rent the property and a year later he decides to sell the property for $160,000.

Under the law in effect prior to December 31, 1979, the son would have a cost basis of $150,000 and the sale at a price of $160,000 would have produced a long term capital gain of $10,000. As a result of the Revenue

Act of 1978 only forty percent of the gain would be taxable. Under the new law the executor would be responsible for providing to the beneficiary at the time of the settlement of the estate an adjusted cost basis figure for this real estate as of December 31, 1976. This would be accomplished by doing the following. First, the total appreciation of the property would be determined.

1981 Sale Price	$160,000
1954 Cost	− 35,000
Total Appreciation	$125,000

The appreciation of $125,000 must then be computed on a daily basis by counting the number of days from the purchase date in 1954 to the sale date in 1981 and then dividing this number into the total appreciation in $125,000 to arrive at a per diem appreciation. The next step would be to count the number of days from the purchase date in 1954 to December 31, 1976 and multiply this number by the per diem appreciation. The result of this calculation would be added to the 1954 cost of $35,000 and the result would be the adjusted basis as of December 31, 1976. The difference between this figure and the sale price of $160,000 would be the long term gain. Again as a result of the Revenue Act of 1978, only 40 percent of this gain would be subject to tax.

At this point you may well have to start from the beginning and read this example over again. I must tell you however, that the example is an oversimplification in that there are several adjustments that should have been made for State Inheritance Tax and Federal Estate Tax attributable to this asset. Fortunately, the net result of these and a few other adjustments would be to further reduce the taxable gain.

The purpose of the foregoing illustration is twofold. First, to attempt to give you some information as to how the law will work and second, to show that the law is in dire need of amendment.

EXECUTOR, ADMINISTRATOR AND TESTAMENTARY TRUSTEE FEES

The following survey has been compiled by the author from various sources, including the statutes of the fifty states as of May 15, 1976. Laws are always subject to change; therefore, this survey should be used as a guide only and not as the final word on Executor, Administrator and Trustee fees. It is advisable to check your current state laws for a particular situation regarding fees rather than relying on the within survey.

The expanding use of fiduciaries, both corporate and individual, throughout the United States requires at least a general understanding of the charges and fees incident to such services. The fees and charges of fiduciaries not only vary from state to state, but in most instances there is little uniformity within the individual state.

There is currently some discussion in public or in the press usually by parties other than lawyers as to means and methods whereby property may be transferred at death other than through a will and applicable probate proceedings. One basic reason advanced for the use of non-probate methods is the avoidance of alleged "excessive probate fees and costs". It is not necessary to discuss these various methods and devices suggested by non-lawyers, including joint accounts with right of survivorship, in connection with bonds, stocks, bank and savings accounts, *inter-vivos* trusts and the like. Suffice it to say, every lawyer can cite numerous instances where the use of some of these methods has resulted in serious and expensive complications in the settlement of estates, with the actual intentions and desires of the decedent often being thwarted.

This study and review reveals that the fees of executors, administrators and testamentary trustees as charged and allowed vary in the fifty states. Actually, in the final analysis, the fees are based upon the reasonable value of the services rendered by the fiduciary. Where such fees are fixed by statutes, it can be assumed that the State Legislature considered the fairness and reasonableness of the fees before prescribing the same. Where not prescribed by statute, the court determines the reasonable value of the services rendered in approving the allowance for fees. In many instances, individual fiduciaries may waive all, or a substantial portion, of the applicable fees.

In no sense can the fees paid or allowed to the fiduciary be deemed an arbitrary assessment or tax not consistent with the reasonable value of the services rendered. In most estates, the executor or administrator performs continuing services, duties and responsibilities over a period of one to three years, and even longer. His duties include the collection of the assets and properties of the decedent; preserving and safeguarding property from waste, loss or deterioration; the determination and payment of claims and debts against the estate; the filing of any legal actions required or the defense of actions brought against the estate; the sale and liquidation of property; the filing of necessary tax returns, and the review and audit of the same; the payment of prior claims, legacies and bequests; the partition and distribution of the estate as directed in the will; and many other duties that might be mentioned. Except where extraordinary or unusual services are involved, the specified fees set forth in the statutes or as allowed by the court supervising the estate, cover all of these and many other services performed by the fiduciary.

Likewise, services rendered by a testamentary trustee usually extend over a long period of years and involve varied and often complicated services in carrying out the directions and wishes of the testator.

In considering whether the fees of fiduciaries result in an unnecessary or unfair burden on the estate, one should contrast the benefits obtained, and some of the difficulties avoided, by the use of a will and probate administration as compared to intestacy or use of non-probate devices and methods. For example,

1. The use of a will makes it possible for the individual to consider and provide flexible means of caring for needs and desires of the members of his family and of other persons entitled to his bounty.

2. Under the intestate statutes and informal methods for transmitting property, particular hardships and injustices often occur. Funds may be paid to designated persons or to those under the inheritance statutes, while under the existing facts and situation, other members of the family may be more needful of such financial aid and support. Substantial assets may be paid to persons so designated or entitled, whereas the full burden of paying debts and applicable taxes may fall on other heirs and be charged against their inheritance. Funds or property may accrue to minors which will require the institution of costly guardianship proceedings continuing until majority.

3. Estate and inheritance taxes may often be substantially reduced by careful estate planning and the execution of a will with proper provisions.

4. Testamentary trusts may be created to provide for the protection and administration of the bequest for the widow or for minor children, with detailed provisions as to the distribution of income for their benefit and the eventual distribution of the principal.

And also, only by a will may a person select the executor or trustee of his own choice and in whom he has confidence to administer his estate and thus make certain that his desires and wishes are to be carried out.

In most, but not all, of the states the fees of executors and administrators are specified by statutes. In the remaining states, the statutes merely provide for reasonable compensation or contain no provisions at all in regard to the fees. Even where statutory rates are prescribed, such rates may either by the terms of the statute or in the application thereof be considered as maximum rates. On the other hand, a majority of the statutes provide that additional compensation may be allowed for unusual or extraordinary services.

The fees for the testamentary trustee are usually not specified by statute except to the extent of authorizing reasonable compensation. In a few instances the statutes provide that the trustee shall receive the same compensation as the executor or administrator.

Banks and T ust Companies in the various states usually adopt a schedule of fees for services as fiduciary within the scope of the statutory provisions, if any, but in practice the fees actually charged are far from uniform. Corporate fiduciaries will usually enter into agreements providing specific fees for particular services, depending upon the circumstances involved. Usually in metropolitan centers the corporate fiduciaries follow a lower uniform schedule of charges. Furthermore, it must be kept in mind that in many instances the allowance of the particular fees, whether under the statutory provision for reasonable compensation or within the statutory maximum limits, rests upon the judgment of the court, depending upon the facts and circumstances of the particular case.

The property on which the fee rates are based also varies considerably from state to state. Tangible as well a intangible personal property in the possession of the fiduciary is usually included. On the other hand, real property is generally not included unless sold by the fiduciary. There is also involved the question of the valuation of the property on which the fee is based. Special rates are also applicable in many instances as to perpetual trusts, charitable trusts and other situations.

In presenting in this study so-called "customary rates, ' it is not meant to imply that such rates are established with any particular degree of uniformity. On the contrary, the rates thus given are examples of at least some of the typical fee schedules being used in practice. In many instances, such schedules refer to corporate fiduciaries. It is probably a general rule that fees charged by or allowed to individual fiduciaries are somewhat less than those to corporate fiduciaries.

A survey was made as to whether the executor, administrator or testamentary trustee is expected or required to pay attorney's fees out of the fiduciary fees allowed. The answer to this question is almost unanimously in the negative. In lieu of referring to this subject in the following schedule, we will briefly comment here, giving any reported exceptions to the general rule.

Generally, it is the rule that the fiduciary is not expected or required to pay his or its attorney's fees out of the fiduciary fees authorized or allowed. If the allowance must be made by the court, the application for attorney's fees is usually, but not always, made by the fiduciary but specifically for payment of the attorney's fees.

In Delaware, by rule of court, the executor or administrator is expected to pay attorney's fees out of the fiduciary's fees allowed, but upon petition the Registrar of Wills may allow additional compensation to an attorney for extraordinary services.

In Maine, with approval of the court, the executor or administrator may be required to pay for attorney's fees in part, and under proper circumstances the whole, out of the fiduciary's fees allowed.

In Maryland, the attorney's fee is not required to be paid out of the fiduciary's fee. By statute, upon the filing of a petition by either the personal representative or by the attorney, the court may allow a counsel fee to the attorney employed by the personal representative for legal services, which

148

compensation shall be fair and reasonable in light of all the circumstances. In allowing a counsel fee, the court is to take into consideration a fair and reasonable charge for the cost of administering an estate. The petition for approval of a counsel fee for the attorney and of commissions for the personal representative are considered by the court at the same time. Simple and standard duties of the personal representative, not requiring legal assistance, do not provide a proper basis for a counsel fee. There is some variation in the positions taken by various Orphan's Courts of the State.

In New Hampshire, usually the attorney receives one-half of a "combined fee" to the executor or administrator and attorney, but the fees are accounted for separately. The testamentary trustee is not expected or required to pay attorney's fees out of fiduciary's fees, and if the attorney is also the trustee, additional fees charged as attorney must be justified.

In Wisconsin and Colorado if the attorney is also the fiduciary, fees in both capacities are not allowed.

ALABAMA

EXECUTOR'S OR ADMINISTRATOR'S FEE.—Statute provides for fair compensation, not exceeding 2½% on "receipts" and 2½% on "disbursements" to be determined by the court. Same commissions as allowed on disbursements are allowed on "personal property" and "money and solvent notes distributed". For selling land "for division" (other than under the terms of a will), 2½% of amount received, but in no case more than $100.

Court approved additional compensation may be allowed for special and extraordinary services.

Example of customary rates follows. In average case involving estates of $50,000 or more, the following rates are used if they result in a lower fee than the statutory maximum:

2½% of first $200,000; 2% of next $800,000; 1½% of excess over $1,000,000, based on value of all property, real and personal, held in estate.

TESTAMENTARY TRUSTEE'S FEE.—No statutory rates. Examples of customary rates follow:

5% of gross income plus one-fifth of 1% of principal annually; or 10% of gross income annually; or one-half of 1% of principal annually. Minimum annual fee, $50.

ALASKA

EXECUTOR'S OR ADMINISTRATOR'S FEE.—Rates are as follows: 7% of first $1,000; 5% of next $1,000; 4% of next $2,000; 2% of excess over $4,000; based on "whole estate accounted for"

Additional compensation may be allowed for extraordinary and unusual services.

TESTAMENTARY TRUSTEE'S FEE.—Fees are negotiated at the time of accepting each trust.

The following fees of a corporate trustee in Anchorage are typical of other corporate trustees:

Acceptance fee: $75.00 to $500.00. Annual fee: ¾ of 1% of first $150,000 based on market value of assets at trust year end; ½ of 1% on next $850,000; negotiable over $1,000,000. Minimum annual fee is $50 to $500. Termination fee is 1% of market value of assets at last evaluation date or minimum of $250.

ARIZONA

EXECUTOR'S OR ADMINISTRATOR'S FEE.—Reasonable compensation for services.

TESTAMENTARY TRUSTEE'S FEE.—Statute provides for reasonable compensation. Example of customary rates charged by corporate fiduciaries follows:

Acceptance fee: 1% of corpus of trust estate where trustee has not acted as executor or administrator. No acceptance fee where trustee has acted as executor or administrator.

Annual fee: Three-fourths of 1% of portion of corpus which is productive real estate.

On portion of corpus which is not productive real estate: Six-tenths of 1% of first $250,000; four-tenths of 1% of next $250,000; three-tenths of 1% of next $250,000; two-tenths of 1% of all corpus over $750,000; minimum annual fee, $100.

ARKANSAS

EXECUTOR'S OR ADMINISTRATOR'S FEE.—As determined by the court.—Statute provides for reasonable compensation not to exceed: 10% of first $1,000; 5% of next $4,000; 3% of excess over $5,000; based on "personal property passing through the hands of the personal representative" which has been fully administered. Additional compensation may be allowed for substantial duties performed with respect to real property, and for services of accountants, engineers, appraisers, and other persons whose services are reasonably required.

TESTAMENTARY TRUSTEE'S FEE.—No statutory provision. Examples of customary rates follows:

Annual fee: On personal property, ½ of 1% of first $50,000 of principal, and ⅜ of 1% of excess, with minimum fee of $50 a year. On real estate, one to one and half times prevailing rental agent's fee. On unimproved real estate, a reasonable fee.

Distribution fee: 1% to 2% of principal, depending on circumstances and difficulties involved. Some slight modification will be made in exceptional circumstances. For example, if trust consists entirely or substantially of securities, annual charge may be reduced for portion of corpus in excess of $500,000.

CALIFORNIA

EXECUTOR'S OR ADMINISTRATOR'S FEE.—Statutory rates are as follows: 7% of first $1,000; 4% of next $9,000; 3% of next $40,000; 2% of next $100,000; 1½% of next $350,000; 1% of excess over $500,000; based on "amount of estate accounted for".

Additional allowance may be made for extraordinary services.

TESTAMENTARY TRUSTEE'S FEE.—Statute provides reasonable compensation. Examples of customary rates follows:

Acceptance fee of up to one-fifth of 1% of corpus where trustee has not acted as executor or administrator.

Annual fee of up to three-fourths of 1% of corpus.

Closing fee of up to one-half of 1% of corpus.

Where instrument specifies compensation, this is usually controlling.

Where the size or nature of corpus is out of the ordinary, the fees are subject to revision by negotiation.

Where an intervivos trust is used with a "pourover" will, the trustee's fees are usually lower due to fact that court accountings may not be required.

COLORADO

EXECUTOR'S OR ADMINISTRATOR'S FEE.—Under Colorado version of Uniform Probate Code, both fiduciaries and attorneys are provided "reasonable compensation" without reference to particular rates.

TESTAMENTARY TRUSTEE'S FEE.—No statutory provision. Example of customary rates, typical in metropolitan cities, is as follows.

Acceptance fee: No fee where trustee was executor or administrator. In other cases, more banks are basing acceptance fee on time and responsibility basis than on percentage of asset value.

Annual fee: on principal consisting of bonds, stocks and other personal property: $5 per $1,000 of first $100,000; $4 per $1,000 of next $400,000; $3 per $1,000 of next $500,000; $2 per $1,000 of excess over $1,000,000. For real estate mortgages, $7.50 per $1,000 of principal. Special fees apply to unimproved real estate, improved real estate and long term leases of real estate constituting a portion of the corpus of the trust

Distribution fee: 2% of first $50,000 of principal and 1% of excess, with banks tending to base fee on time and responsibility basis rather than percentage of asset value.

CONNECTICUT

EXECUTOR'S OR ADMINISTRATOR'S FEE.—No statutory provision. Should be reasonable but vary in different counties. The following have been suggested as reasonable minimum rates: 5% on first $10,000; 3% on next $40,000; 2½% on next $200,000; 2% on next $750,000; 1½% on next $1,000,000; 1% on excess over $2,000,000 Minimum fee of $200

A corporate fiduciary in Bridgeport computes the fees based on gross inventory plus additions and income: 3% of the first $100,000; 2½% of the next $400,000; 2% of the next $1,500,000; 1½% of all over $2,000,000. Minimum charge for settling an estate. $500.

TESTAMENTARY TRUSTEE'S FEE.—No statutory provision. The fee schedule of the various corporate fiduciaries vary so much that an applicable generalization cannot be made. The following charges made by one of the Hartford banks:

Annual fee: On principal: $5 per $1,000 on first $50,000; $4 per $1,000 on next $50,000; $3 per $1,000 on next $500,000; $1.50 per $1,000 on next $2,000,000. On gross rents or value of real estate: 3% of gross rents or one-tenth of 1% of gross value, whichever is larger. Minimum fee of $75.

Distribution fee: On partial or complete distribution of principal, based on market or sound value of amount distributed: 1% of first $100,000; ½ of 1% of all principal in excess of $100,000.

A corporate trustee in Bridgeport charges:

On gross income except rent: 5% of the first $10,000; 4% of the next $20,000; 3% of the remainder.

On gross rent, 8%. If no rental income fee is based on services rendered. Agent's fee deducted from bank's fees.

On market or sound value of principal, per $1,000: $3.00 on first $100,000; $2.00 on next $400,000; $1.00 on next $500,000; $0.50 on remainder.

If trust is fully invested in common trust funds, annual fee is reduced 20%. Additional charge of $2.50 per $1,000 face value for handling mortgages. Minimum fee of $250, if invested in common trust funds $150. Upon termination, charge of 1% of market value of distribution.

DELAWARE

EXECUTOR'S OR ADMINISTRATOR'S FEE.—No statutory provision. Fees are determined by Register of Wills in accordance with schedule established by him, but additional fees may be allowed on petition. Fee schedule of Register of Wills of New Castle County on gross estate is:

Less than $1,000, $100.00; $1,000-$5,000, $100.00 plus 10% over $1,000; $5,000-$10,000, $500.00 plus 6% over $5,000; $10,000-$20,000, $800.00 plus 5% over $10,000; $20,000-$30,000, $1,300.00 plus 4½% over $20,000; $30,000-$40,000, $1,750.00 plus 4% over $30,000; $40,000-$60,000, $2,150.00 plus 3½% over $40,000;

150

$60,000-$80,000, $2,850.00 plus 3¼% over $60,000;
$80,000-$100,000, $3,500.00 plus 3% over $80,000;
$100,000-$125,000, 4.0% Gross Estate; $125,000-
$150,000, 3.8% Gross Estate; $150,000-$175,000, 3.6%
Gross Estate; $175,000-$200,000, 3.4% Gross Estate;
$200,00-$250,000, 3.2% Gross Estate; $250,000-$300,000
3.0% Gross Estate; $300,000-$350,000, 2.9% Gross Estate;
$350,000-$400,000, 2.8% Gross Estate; $400,000-
$450,000, 2.7% Gross Estate; $450,000-$500,000, 2.6%
Gross Estate; $500,000 or over, 2.5% Gross Estate.

Fees represent total for personal representative and attorney.

Gross estate for fee purposes is based on total of inventory and appraisement, additional assets received and ½ of jointly owned personal property.

TESTAMENTARY TRUSTEE'S FEE.—No statutory rates. Fees are established by rules of Court of Chancery, subject to provisions of valid agreement and power of Court to increase or decrease for cause.

Rules of Chancery Court of New Castle County where great bulk of the estates in Delaware is administered provide:

(a) **Income Commissions:** An annual charge on gross income collected: 6% on the first $5,000; 5% on the next $5,000; 4.5% on the next $5,000; 3.5% on the next $10,000; 3% on the next $25,000; 2.25% on the next $50,000; 2% on all income over $100,000.

(b) **Principal Commissions:** An annual charge on the principal, computable and payable at the times and in the manner hereinafter set forth at the following rates: 5/10 of 1% on first $25,000 of principal; 3/10 of 1% on the next $75,000 of principal 1.10 of 1% on the next $100,000 of principal; 1/20 of 1% on all principal over $200,000.

The annual principal commissions shall be computed on the basis of the fair value, which shall be determined either (1) by appraisal by the trustee and certified to the Court as of the anniversary date of the trust; or (2) by value theretofore determined as part of a periodic review of trusts by the trustee, such review to be of a date not more than twelve months prior to the date of making such annual charge. Periodic reviews to be eligible for use for valuation purposes under clause (2) shall be made approximately at twelve month intervals and the date of such reviews shall not vary more than 60 days from one year to the next until the termination of the trust, as of which date a final valuation shall be made.

So far as practicable, and subject to the control of the Court, a trustee shall adhere to one or the other of such methods in computing successive annual principal commissions.

A trustee may elect not to compute or charge annual principal commissions in which event the trustee shall, at the time of distribution or of termination of the trust or of transfer to a successor trustee, be allowed principal commissions computed under the provisions of Paragraph (e) of the Rule, or in lieu thereof the trustee may at such time or times apply to the Court for appropriate commissions on principal, which the Court in its discretion may allow and which need not be limited to the amounts of principal commissions at termination set forth by Paragraph (e).

(c) **Additional Annual Charges in Special Cases:** When the trust includes one or more mortgages, an additional commission shall be allowed at the rate of ¼ of 1% of the total face value of all mortgages as of the times of the valuation of the trust assets or, if the trustee is not charging annual principal commissions, of the total face value of such mortgages held in the trust on the last business day of each fiscal year of the trust.

When the trust includes real estate, the annual income commission specified in Paragraph (a) shall apply to gross rents collected by an outside agent and paid to the trustee. If such rents are collected directly by the trustee, the trustee shall be allowed a commission of 8% of gross rentals received.

(d) **Decrease of Commissions in Certain Cases:** (1) If the direction and control of investments in any trust, the corpus of which exceeds $300,000 in value, rest solely with a person other than the trustee, the annual principal commissions set forth in Paragraph (b) shall be reduced by fifteen percentum (15%) so long as such condition exists. (2) Large Blocks of Securities: In a trust with limited diversification and a fair value of one million dollars or more, three-fourths or more of the fair value of which is invested in not more than two (2) blocks of stocks and/or bonds, the income commission set forth in Paragraph (a) shall be reduced by twenty-five percentum (25%), so long as such condition exists.

(e) **Principal Commissions Upon Distribution or Transfer:** Upon partial or complete distribution of any trust, or upon transfer to a successor trustee, the aggregate principal commissions allowable shall be calculated at the following rates: 5% of principal on the first $50,000; 3.6% of principal on the next $50,000; 2.3% of principal on the next $900,000; 1.0% of principal on all over $1,000,000.00.

Provided, however, that if at the time of distribution or transfer the trust shall have been administered by the trustee for a period less than ten years, such principal commissions shall be reduced to the following percentages of the rates hereinabove specified: 30% if termination occurs within 3 years; and with reduction increasing by 10% each year until there is a reduction of 100% if termination occurs after 9 years.

Such aggregate principal commission shall be computed on the basis of the fair value of the trust estate at the time of partial or complete distribution or of transfer to a successor trustee, by an appraisal made by the trustee.

(f) **Apportionment of Commissions:** Principal commissions shall normally be paid out of principal and income commissions shall normally be paid out of income. Additional commissions on mortgages and real estate shall be charged to income.

(g) **Perpetual Trusts:** If a trust is or becomes perpetual (a charitable trust, e.g.), the trustee shall be entitled to the total commissions set forth under Paragraph (a) and (b) of the Rule, which shall be charged entirely against income.

(h) **Co-Trustee:** The compensation to be allowed to each of two or more trustees shall be as the Court in its discretion may determine, considering the services rendered, etc. The compensation allowed in the aggregate may exceed the amounts allowed a single trustee.

(i) Certain Payments Income for Commission Purposes: For the purpose of determing commissions upon income allowable under this Rule, income shall be deemed to include (without being limited to) periodic payments of insurance, annuities, pensions, Social Security and Railroad Retirement Board benefits and the like, whether received from public, private or governmental sources, subject to review by Court in case of hardship.

(j) When a trustee receives property from an executor or administrator other than itself, or a successor trustee receives property from a former trustee, a fee equal to the reasonable costs actually incurred by the trustee shall be charged against principal and allowed to the trustee as compensation for review of the actions, administration and accounting of the former fiduciary, but shall not exceed the sum of $1,000 without special allowance of the Court.

(k) A trustee shall be entitled to a minimum commission of $200 for services in any one accounting year to be charged against income to the extent collectible as computed under Paragraph (a) and the balance, if any to be charged against principal.

DISTRICT OF COLUMBIA

EXECUTOR'S OR ADMINISTRATOR'S FEE.—Statute provides for commissions of not under 1% nor exceeding 10% of "inventory." The inventory does not include real estate unless directed to be sold by the will or by court order.

It is the practice to limit the combined executor's or administrator's commission and the attorney's fees to 10% in the absence of special circumstances. There are no scheduled rates in general use, but many executors and administrators claim 5% of an inventoried estate of $100,000, increasing the rate if the estate is substantially less than $100,000, and decreasing the rate if the estate is substantially more than $100,000.

There is too much variance in rates of commissions claimed to permit a more specific schedule to be used.

Where executor or administrator is practicing member of District of Columbia Bar, attorney's fees will not be allowed.

TESTAMENTARY TRUSTEE'S FEE.—No statutory provision. The customary rate of commission on income is 5% (in some cases, 6%).

The custom of charging an additional commission on principal at the termination of the trust has prevailed for many years, but this custom is apparently being replaced gradually by an annual commission on principal (in addition to above commission on income) varying in rate. Many trustees are charging an annual principal commission of one-fourth of 1% of the value of the principal assets.

FLORIDA

EXECUTOR'S OR ADMINISTRATOR'S FEE.—Statutory provisions provide for "reasonable compensation, additional compensation may be allowed for extraordinary services."

TESTAMENTARY TRUSTEE'S FEE.—No statutory provision as to fees. Customary rates vary widely. One example is as follows: On income 5% of income; On principal: Annual fee of: $3 per $1,000 on first $250,000; $2 per $1,000 on next $250,000; $1 per $1,000 on excess over $500,000. Closing fee of 1%.

A corporate trustee in Jacksonville charges: On income: No charge; On principal: Annual fee of: $5 on $1,000 first $200,000; $4 on $1,000 next $300,000; $3 on $1,000 on next $500,000; (Minimum annual charge $250); Special rates on over $1,000,000. 1% closing fee if trust terminates with ten years, otherwise no closing fee.

Another Jacksonville corporate trustee follows substantially the same schedule, but usually charges one-half of the usual fee against income, the other one-half against principal.

GEORGIA

EXECUTOR'S OR ADMINISTRATOR'S FEE.—Statutory rates are as follows: 2½% of cash received; 2½% of cash disbursed; and reasonable fee not exceeding 3% of property delivered in kind. Additional compensation may be allowed for extraordinary services.

Example follows of customary rates under agreement with testator: 2½% of cash received; 2½% of cash disbursed; 2½% of property delivered in kind.

TESTAMENTARY TRUSTEE'S FEE.—Statutory provisions are same as those for executors and administrators. Example follows of typical rates under agreement with testator: If trustee served as executor, 5% on income cash received, and 2½% on all other assets, based on the value thereof when distributed. No commission is charged upon the receipt of cash from the executor.

If trustee did not serve as executor: Annual fee: 5% on gross income and $1.00 per $1,000 on market value of assets held, with minimum of $150. Where trust is invested in common trust fund, minimum annual fee may be reduced to $75.00.

Distribution fee: 2½% on value of assets distributed.

HAWAII

EXECUTOR'S OR ADMINISTRATOR'S FEE.—Statutory rates are as follows: On income 7% of first $5,000; 5% of excess over $5,000, (computed on entire proceedings, not annually). On principal: 5% of first $1,000; 4% of next $9,000; 3% of next $10,000; 2% of excess over $20,000; based on appraised value of estate including real property. Additional compensation may be allowed for extraordinary services.

TESTAMENTARY TRUSTEE'S FEE.—On income: Same as Executor's, but rate recomputed annually. On principal: 1% of principal at inception of trust. 2½% of cash principal received after inception but not including principal upon which 2½% has previously been charged. One-tenth of 1% of principal annually, computed on values at expiration of each year. 2½% of cash principal paid out prior to termination of trust, (for example, principal paid to beneficiaries, capital gains, taxes paid, but not on investments made). 1% of principal upon final distribution of trust. Additional allowances may be made for extraordinary services.

IDAHO

EXECUTOR'S OR ADMINISTRATOR'S FEE.—Statute provides that the personal representative is entitled to reasonable compensation for his services and reimbursement of his expenses incident to the administration of the estate. No statutory rates exist. An example of typical rate structure is as follows: 5% of first $1.000: 4% of next $9,000: 3% of any over $10,000 based on 'estate accounted for.'

TESTAMENTARY TRUSTEE'S FEE.—Statute provides that the court shall allow trustee proper expenses and just and reasonable compensation. An example of customary charge on income producing commercial real property is as follows:

Annual fee of 1/10 of 1% of asset value with a minimum fee of $25. Annual fee of 5% of gross trust income with a minimum annual fee of $100. Distribution fee based on services with a maximum of 1% of market value of assets and a minimum of $100.

ILLINOIS

EXECUTOR'S OR ADMINISTRATOR' FEE.—

(1) Executors, Administrators and their attorneys are allowed reasonable compensation.

(2) In Cook County the Probate Division of the Circuit Court follows the following schedule based on the gross probate estate and gross income therefrom: 5% on first $25,000 and 4% on balance; 4% on first $50,000 and 3½% on balance; 3½% on first $100,000 and 3% on balance; 3% on first $250,000 and 2% on balance; 2½% on first $1,000,000 and 2% on balance. Based on the foregoing, the published fee schedule of one corporate fiduciary in Cook County calculates fees of $7,500 on an estate having a gross fair value of $250,000, $14,250 on an estate of $500,000, and $26,250 on an estate of $1,000,000.

(3) Courts in other counties generally follow the Cook County schedule, but vary from county to county. A corporate executor is generally allowed more than an individual executor. Executor's fee is generally somewhat less than the attorney's fee. In some counties a court schedule for determining the fee, of executor or administrator is not used.

(4) Fair value of retained real estate and proceeds from sale of real estate are to be taken into account, and an additional fee for extraordinary services may be allowed.

TESTAMENTARY TRUSTEE'S FEE.—Statute provides for reasonable compensation. Examples of some rates as follows:

(1) Cook County: Corporate trustee of stocks and bonds: Acceptance fee, if trustee did not act as executor, 1/10 of 1%. Annual fee: $600 base charge ($300 for accounts invested primarily in common trust funds). Plus 3/10 of 1% on the first $2,000,000; 2/10 of 1% on the next $4,000,000; 1/10 of 1% on the balance. Distribution fee: 1% on the first $500,000; 3/4 of 1% of the next $500,000; ½ of 1% of the balance. Additional charges are made for unusual duties.

(2) A corporate trustee outside Cook County quotes a minimum annual fee of $300 on the fair value of the trust assets, an acceptance fee of 1/10 of 1% if the trustee did not act as executor, and annual fees as follows:

Stocks and Bonds: 6/10 of 1% of first $100,000; 4/10 of 1% of next $300,000; 3/10 of 1% of next $600,000 and 2/10 of 1% of next $4,000,000.

Improved Real Estate: ½ of 1% of first $30,000; ¼ of 1% of next $30,000; 1/10 of 1% of next $40,000; 1/20 of 1% of next $400,000; 1/50 of 1% of excess over $500,000. The annual fee for unimproved real estate is ½ of the fee for improved real estate. For management and leasing 6% of gross income is charged except that 3% of the fair rental value is charged if the premises are occupied by the beneficiary. A distribution fee is charged on the fair value of the trust assets distributed: 1% of the first $100,000; ¾ of 1% of next $400,000; ½ of 1% of next $500,000; ¼ of 1% of excess over $1,000,000.

(3) Cook County corporate trustee, as to real estate: On improved real estate an annual fee for holding title is based on the latest full assessed value and one corporate fiduciary quotes ½ of 1% of the first $50,000, 3/20 of 1% of the next $50,000, 1/20 of 1% of the next $400,000, and 1/50 of 1% of all over $500,000. The annual fee for unimproved real estate is ½ of the fee for improved real estate.

For management and leasing, 6% of gross income, except 3 to 6% of gross income for office buildings, industrials, lofts, warehouses, hotels, etc., with reasonable annual fee to be charged if improved property is substantially or entirely unoccupied.

For sales of fees and leaseholds, charges as currently recommended by the Chicago Real Estate Board.

On farms, 8% on grain farms and 10% on cattle farms.

INDIANA

EXECUTOR'S OR ADMINISTRATOR'S FEE.— Statute provides for reasonable compensation. Fees vary greatly within the State. Examples of customary rates are as follows:

(1) Indianapolis (corporate fiduciary): 5% on first $25,000; 4% on next $25,000; 3% on next $50,000; 2% on next $650,000; 1½% on next $250,000; 1% for any excess.

Minimum fee is $500. Reasonable fee for property not included in probate estate but included in taxable estate or requiring other services is usually 1%.

For extraordinary services, additional reasonable fees may be allowed. Fees as co-executor or administrator will be the same.

Another corporate fiduciary in Indianapolis normally charges between 2% and 5% of the overall estate, depending on complexities and size. Courts have the prerogative of setting fees of executors, administrators and attorneys.

(2) Fort Wayne: One corporate fiduciary: 5% of the first $25,000; 4% of next $25,000; 3% next $50,000; 2% of next $650,000; 1½% of next $250,000; 1% of excess.

Minimum fee $500. Reasonable fee (usually 1%) of property in taxable estate, but not probate estate. Fee for extraordinary services may be charged.

Another corporate fiduciary: 4% on first $100,000; 1% on each additional $100,000.

Another corporate fiduciary; 5% on first $25,000; 4% on next $25,000; 3½% on next $50,000; 3% on next $75,000; 2½% on next $100,000; 2% on next $250,000; 1% on next $1,000,000. Based on taxable estate. Also 1% on nonprobate but taxable property.

Many counties allow the fiduciary to receive one-half of the fee which attorney receives; others perhaps 60%; while most of the counties allow the same fee as the attorney, except for some extraordinary matters.

By statute, if an attorney acts as executor or administrator, he is entitled to a full fee for legal services and a one-half fee for acting as personal representative.

TESTAMENTARY TRUSTEE'S FEE.—Statute provides for reasonable compensation. Two examples of customary rates are as follows:

(1) Indianapolis: (corporate fiduciary): Annual fee: ½ of 1% of first $100,000; ¼ of 1% of next $400,000; 1/5 of 1% of next $500,000. To be negotiated for any excess.

Minimum annual fee is $125 except for trust wholly invested in common trust funds of Bank, where minimum is $75.

On termination, distribution or revocation (wholly or in part) ½%. Special rates for retention and management of real estate, improved and unimproved. Fees for extraordinary services may be claimed. The same fees apply to co-trustee.

(2) Fort Wayne: One corporate fiduciary (annual fee): ⅝ of 1% of first $25,000; ½ of 1% of next $75,000; ¼ of 1% of next $400,000; ⅛ of 1% of all over $500,000.

Minimum fee is $125. Exceptions may be made if circumstances require. Another corporate fiduciary (annual fee): ½ of 1% on first $50,000; ¼ of 1% on excess over that amount. Termination fee ½ of 1% and ½ of 1% distribution fee on principal.

IOWA

EXECUTOR'S OR ADMINISTRATOR'S FEE.— Statute provides that rates are not to exceed the following for ordinary services: 6% of first $1,000; 4% of next $4,000; 2% of excess over $5,000; based on "gross assets of the estate listed in the probate inventory for Iowa inheritance tax purposes". Life insurance payable to named beneficiaries is excluded. Additional allowance may be made for extraordinary services. Attorney's fees are fixed independently of the executors fees and are not paid out of executor's fees. If each item of the estate is in joint tenancy and no need exists for clearance of debts and liabilities by exposure to probate, CIT (Clearance of Inheritance Taxes) proceedings are quicker, simpler and about half as expensive. In Des Moines area at least, if attorney is also executor, the fee is one and one-half times the usual executor's fee.

TESTAMENTARY TRUSTEE'S FEE.—No statutory rates. Example of rates by some corporate trustees in Des Moines:

Annual fee: One-fourth of 1% on government bonds; ¾ of 1% on mortgages; 1% on principal except real estate; 3% to 10% on gross income from real estate depending on nature of interests and management involved, such

as 5% on downtown leases, 7½% on mortgages, 10% on farm income. Some corporate trustees charge ½ of 1% on corpus other than real estate.

Distribution fee: No uniform custom. All compensation to be allowed by court from time to time.

KANSAS

EXECUTOR'S OR ADMINISTRATOR'S FEE.—Statute provides for reasonable compensation. Customary rates in the Wichita, Kansas, area are as follows: 5% on first $20,000 (with a minimum of $250,000); 3½% of the next $30,000; 3% of the next $150,000; 2% of the next $800,000; 1% of the excess over $1,000,000; Plus ½ of 1% of the value of property held in joint tenancy. Plus a fee for the sale of real estate of 2%, if negotiated by the administrator, and ½ of 1% if negotiated by a broker.

Provision is usually made, also, for the payment of additional fees for unusual and extraordinary services.

In the Shawnee County and Kansas City areas, the breakdown is somewhat different than the foregoing but the customary fees are generally in the same range, although perhaps slightly higher.

In the outlying counties the customary fees would be somewhat lower than the foregoing.

TESTAMENTARY TRUSTEE'S FEES.—The statute provides for reasonable compensation. Customary rate is in the range of ½ of 1% of the first $500,000, and 3/10ths of 1% of the next $500,000, plus ¼ of 1% of the excess, with a minimum annual fee of $200.00 for the first year, and $150.00 for each year thereafter.

Approximately the same variations up and down would be encountered in the area of Trustee's fees as are set forth above with respect to executor's and administrator's fees.

KENTUCKY

EXECUTOR'S OR ADMINISTRATOR'S FEE.—Statute provides that compensation shall not exceed 5% of "personal estate", plus 5% of income collected. Additional allowance may be made for extraordinary services. Example of customary minimum rates follows:

On Income: 5% of income collected.

On principal: 5% on first $25,000; 3% on next $75,000; 2% on next $200,000; 1½% on excess over $300,000. Minimum fee of $350.

TESTAMENTARY TRUSTEE'S FEE.—Statutory rates are as follows:

On income: 5% of income collected.

On principal: One-fifth of 1% annually, or in lieu of annual commission, a commission not in excess of 5% of principal distributed. Additional compensation from income or principal may be allowed for extraordinary services.

Customary minimum annual charges on principal are as follows: One-fifth of 1% of first $250,000; One-tenth of 1% of excess over $250,000. Minimum annual fee $200.

LOUISIANA

EXECUTOR'S OR ADMINISTRATOR'S FEE.—Statute provides for allowance of 2½% of amount of "inventory' which may be increased by the court upon proper showing that usual commission is inadequate. For estates of $2,000 or less, maximum rate of 5% of gross assets.

Provisional administrator or administrator of vacant succession shall be allowed reasonable compensation. Public Administrators (who act in intestate succession in parishes of over 100,000 population where no heir is present or represented in State) receives 5% of all funds administered (not applicable to Caddo, Ouachita, Orleans and Calcasieu Parishes).

TESTAMENTARY TRUSTEE'S FEES.—Statute provides for reasonable compensation.

Note: In 1973 the Louisiana State Bar Association has repealed suggested minimum fee schedules.

MAINE

EXECUTOR'S OR ADMINISTRATOR'S FEE.—Statute provides that executors, administrators, and trustees may be allowed $1 for every 10 miles travel to and from court, and $1 for each day's attendance, and also a commission not exceeding 5% on amount of personal assets that come into their hands.

TESTAMENTARY TRUSTEE'S FEE.—Statutory provisions are same as for executor or administrator. except that additional allowance may be made for care and management not exceeding in any one year 1°o of principal of trust. Said additional sum so allowed is to be charged against principal or income, or both, and if charged against both, to be charged in such proportions as the Court shall determine.

MARYLAND

EXECUTOR'S OR ADMINISTRATOR'S FEE.—Statute provides for commissions not exceeding 10% of the first $20,000.00 of the 'probate estate' and on the balance of the estate, no more than 4%, such fees to be determined, however, in the exclusive jurisdiction of the Orphans Court. These maximum fees are applicable unless the Will provides for a larger measure of compensation. Probate estate' does not include life insurance or other death benefits payable to others, jointly held property or joint and several annuities. While the 'probate estate' does include real property owned by the decedent, no commissions are payable with respect to such real property unless sold and in the event of sale, the Court may allow such commissions on the proceeds not exceeding 10°o thereof.

Taxes payable on commissions in the following amounts, whichever is greater: (a) One percent of first $20,000.00, and One fifth of one percent on balance of estate, or (b) Ten percent of total commissions allowed.

TESTAMENTARY TRUSTEE'S FEE.—Statutory rates are as follows as to each separate trust:

Annual commission on principal: One-third of 1% on first $250,000; one-fifth of 1% on next $250,000: one-eighth of 1% on next $500,000; and one-twelfth of 1% of excess over $1,000,000

Annual commission on income: 6% on all income from real estate, ground rents and all mortgages collected.

As to all other income: 6% of first $10,000; 5% of next $10,000; 4% of next $10,000; 3% of excess over $30,000.

For selling real property or leasehold property, commission on proceeds of sale at rate allowed by rule of court or statute.

On final distribution, allowance commensurate with labor and responsibility involved in distribution, in absence of special circumstances equal to one-half of 1% of principal being distributed.

MASSACHUSETTS

EXECUTOR'S OR ADMINISTRATOR'S FEE.—No statutory rates. Example of customary rate for non-professional fiduciaries is 3% of gross personal estate, plus 3% on any real estate that is sold. Some fiduciaries reduce rates as size of estate increases.

In Boston most corporate executors follow this schedule subject to specific approval in each specific case and based generally upon the probate property: 5% on the first $40,000; 4% of the next $60,000; 3% of the next $400,000; 2½% of the next $500,000; 2% of the next $500,000; 1% of the next $500,000; 1% of the value in excess of $2,000,000: Plus reasonable charge in connection with nonprobate property included in estate tax returns or for which other services are rendered.

If there is a professional co-executor or if we are agent for an executor or administrator, fee will be 75% of the executor's compensation charged.

TESTAMENTARY TRUSTEE'S FEE.—No statutory rates. Example of customary rates are as follows:

Annual fee on income: 6% of gross income.

Annual fee on principal: Four-tenths of 1% of first $200,000: three-tenths of 1% of next $300,000: two-tenths of 1% of next $500,000: one-tenth of 1% on excess over $1,000,000. Distribution fee: 2°o of principal distributed. Some trustees reduce rates as value of principal distributed increases.

MICHIGAN

EXECUTOR'S OR ADMINISTRATOR'S FEE.—New statutory rates shall apply where the certification of death of the decedent occurred after January 1, 1975. Rates on estates of those dying prior to that date are not affected. New rates are as follows: For the first $5,000.00, at the rate of 5%; for all above that sum and not exceeding $20,000.00, at the rate of 4%; for all above that sum and not exceeding $50,000.00, at the rate of 4%; and for all above that sum and not exceeding $50,000.00 at the rate of 3% and for all above $50,000.00 at the rate of 2°o. The judge of probate, upon petition of the fiduciary, may also allow the foregoing commissions upon the amount of real property, or any portion thereof, inventoried and accounted for by the fiduciary. Additional allowances may be made for extraordinary services.

TESTAMENTARY TRUSTEE'S FEE.—Statute provides for reasonable compensation. Two examples of customary rates are as follows:

(a) **Western Michigan:** Annual fee of one-half of 1% of principal.

(b) **Detroit Area:** Corporate trustees generally charge a percentage of income collected plus a percentage of the value of the corpus of the trust. These vary from 7/10 of 1% of the first $100,000.00 principal, with a minimum fee of $500.00. Others charge on a basis of 3/10 of 1% of the market value of the entire trust assets plus a charge of 5% on the corpus income collected with a minimum fee of $550.00 to $600.00. Some trust companies charge additional fees for opening and closing of the trust, while others do not make such a charge. Separate fees are charged for real estate management and for unique assets.

MINNESOTA

EXECUTOR'S OR ADMINISTRATOR'S FEE.—Statute provides for just and reasonable compensation. Fees computed on gross appraised value of estate before liens plus gross income received by executors. When fees allowed to individual representatives, such fees are usually limited to one-half the fees charged by corporate fiduciaries. Four examples of customary rates charged by corporate fiduciaries in Twin Cities area for uncontested probate administrations requiring no extraordinary services are as follows:

(1) One corporate fiduciary: 3% of first $300,000; 2% of next $700,000; 1% on excess over $1,000,000; ½ of 1% of non-probate assets. If minimum responsibility, fee may be reduced. Minimum fee, $2,000.

(2) Second example: 4% of first $50,000. Minimum fee, $600. For estates over $50,000: 3% of first $100,000; 2% of next $400,000; 1% of next $500,000. Over $1,000,000 fee is dependent on amount and type of assets unless bank handles this property.

(3) Third example: 3.50% on first $100,000; 3% on next $100,000; 2.50% on next $100,000; 2% on next $200,000; 1.50% on next $500,000; 1% on excess over $1,000,000. Minimum fee, $750.00. On non-probate assets: life insurance, based on time and responsibility. Other assets, 1.5% of value up to $1,000,000; above $1,000,000 to be negotiated. Minimum fee, $100.00.

(4) Fourth example: 3% on first $250,000; 2% on next $250,000; 1½% on next $500,000; 1% on next $9,000,000; ½% on excess over $10,000,000. Fees for administering jointly held property and other non-probate assets, except life insurance or employee benefit proceeds naming bank as beneficiary, requiring services of bank shall be one-half the basic fee schedule. Administration fee on trust assets of which the bank is trustee shall be one additional trustee's fee not including distribution fee. Minimum fee $3,000. Additional charge for extraordinary services.

TESTAMENTARY TRUSTEE'S FEE.—Statute provides for reasonable compensation. Four examples of customary annual rates charged by corporate fiduciaries in Twin Cities area for ordinary trust services are as follows:

(1) First example: $10.00 per $1,000 of first $50,000; $5.00 per $1,000 of next $250,000; $4.00 per $1,000 of next $300,000; $3.00 per $1,000 of next $900,000; $2.50 per $1,000 of next $1,000,000; $2.00 per $1,000 of next $1,000,000. Minimum fee of $750. No distinction between common trust funds and individual securities as to minimum fees or rate schedules. Additional charges for real estate in collection of rentals. 5% of gross rentals of business properties and 7% on residential. For supervision of repairs, 5% of first $5,000 expended and 2% of excess. Minimum fee for each property, $100. An annual fee of 1% is charged on all special situation investments. Acceptance fee, based on time and responsibility, where bank did not act as executor. Distribution fee on principal, 2% of first $50,000 and 1% on excess; 2% on all discretionary distributions.

(2) Second example: $7.50 per $1,000 on first $100,000; $5.00 per $1,000 on next $200,000; $4.00 per $1,000 on next $200,000; $3.00 per $1,000 on next $500,000. Over $1,000,000 to be negotiated. Minimum annual fees: fully utilizing common trust funds, $400; not invested in common trust funds, $500.

(3) Third example: Annual fee for ordinary services computed on market value at beginning of account year: $5.00 per $1,000 on first $300,000; $4.00 per $1,000 on next $500,000; $3.00 per $1,000 on next $700,000; $2.00 per $1,000 on next $500,000. Minimum annual fee, $250 on fully utilizing common funds and $350 otherwise. Distribution fee of 2% of value of principal after the 6th year. If distribution represent final distribution and occurs within six years, fee is ½ of 1% of principal if in first year of trust and ¼ of 1% for each additional year up to a maximum of 2%.

(4) Fourth example: Minimum fee is $200 per year plus basic fee which is $100 per year. For court qualified trusts, there is fee of $75 per court hearing attended. For co-trustee accounts, an additional fee of $25 per year. Management of stocks, bonds, savings and other property, annual fee: $5.00 per $1,000 on first $300,000; $4.00 per $1,000 on next $200,000; $3.00 per $1,000 on next $500,000. Over $1,000,000 rate is based on factors involved. On real estate mortgages, contracts and notes: $8.00 per $1,000 on first $500,000 of balance; and additional to be negotiated. Closing or distribution fee is based on time involved ($20-25 per hour), minimum $200. Additional charges for unusual services.

MISSISSIPPI

EXECUTOR'S OR ADMINISTRATOR'S FEE.—Statute provides for compensation of not less than 1% nor more than 7% on amount of "estate administered".

Example of customary rates follows: 3 to 5% of first $100,000; 3% of next $400,000; 2% of excess over $500,000.

TESTAMENTARY TRUSTEE'S FEE.—No statutory provision. Example of customary rates follows: ½ of 1% of market value of corpus annually on first $250,000; 4/10 of 1% of next $750,000; 2/10 of 1% of excess over $1,000,000. Minimum fee is $150.

MISSOURI

EXECUTOR'S OR ADMINISTRATOR'S FEE.—Statutory minimum rates are as follows: 5% of first $5,000; 4% of next $20,000; 3% of next $75,000; 2¾% of next $300,000; 2½% of next $600,000; 2% of excess over $1,000,000; based on "personal property administered" and "proceeds of all real property sold under order of the probate court". Additional allowance may be made to provide reasonable compensation. Trust company may have minimum fee, e.g. $500-$2,000.

TESTAMENTARY TRUSTEE'S FEE.—No statutory provision. Two examples of customary rates follows:

(1) Example of customary rates in Kansas City: Annual fees on principal: 0.4% of first $500,000; 0.35% of next $500,000; 0.3% of next $2,000,000; .25% of excess over $3,000,000. Another example: $75 per year plus 3/10 of 1% of principal, if funds are invested in fiduciary common trust. $100 per year plus 3½% of income, if funds are in general investments.

(2) Example of customary rates in St. Louis: Acceptance fee is charged if trustee did not act as executor, amount depending on work and responsibility involved in auditing and taking over assets from executor. Annual fee of 5% of income, plus 1/5 of 2% of first $100,000 of principal, and 1/10 of 1% of balance, with minium annual fee of $200 to $400. Fees are reduced if assets include trust company's common trust funds. Distribution fee of 3% of first $100,000 or principal, and 1½% of balance, plus 5% of accrued income. Distribution fee is reduced by 50% if distribution takes place within first five years of trust period, provided trustee also acted as executor

MONTANA

PERSONAL REPRESENTATIVE'S FEE.—Statutory rates are as follows: 3% of the first $40,000 of the value of the estate as reported for federal estate tax or state inheritance tax purposes, whichever is larger, and—2% of the value of the estate in excess of $40,000.

Additional allowance may be allowed for extraordinary services. Extra allowance must not exceed total amount allowed for original compensation at above rates. (Section 91A-3-719, R.C.M. 1947)

TESTAMENTARY TRUSTEE'S FEE.—When a declaration of trust is silent upon the subject of compensation, the trustee is entitled to the same compensation as an executor. If it specifies the amount of his compensation, he is entitled to the amount thus specified, and no more. If it directs that he shall be allowed a compensation, but does not specify the rate or amount, he is entitled to such compensation as may be reasonable under the circumstances. (Sec. 86-511, RCM 1947)

Three examples of customary rates are as follows:

(1) First example:

Acceptance fee: 1/5 of 1% of first $250,000; 1/10 of 1% of excess over $250,000. Minimum $50. (None if trustee is also executor)

Annual fee: $5 per $1,000 par value of bonds; $5 per $1,000 market value of stocks; $7.50 per $1,000 par value of mortgage contracts; $7.50 per $1,000 miscellaneous; $7.50 per $1,000 fair value real estate. If total accounts exceeds $250,000, fee is $1 per $1,000 less on excess above $250,000, and fee is reduced another $1 per $1,000 on excess over $500,000

(2) Second example:

Annual fee: $4 per $1,000 on government bonds; $5 per $1,000 on other bonds and stocks; $6 per $1,000 on mortgages and contracts; 5% of rents from city real es-

tate; $6 per $1,000 on city non-rental; 10% owners share crop on farm property; $6 per $1,000 on miscellaneous property.

Closing fee: Depends on work involved. In most cases about 1% to 1½%.

(3) Third example:

Acceptance fee: None.

Annual fee: $5 per $1,000 of the first $100,000; $4 per $1,000 of the next $150,000; $3 per $1,000 of anything over $250,000. If there is rental property, 5% of rent.

NEBRASKA

EXECUTOR'S OR ADMINISTRATOR'S FEE.—Statutory rates are as follows: 5% of first $1,000; 2½% of next $4,000; 2% of excess over $5,000; based on "personal estate collected and accounted for", and upon "proceeds of real estate sold" under court order for payment of debts. Additional allowance may be made for extraordinary services.

TESTAMENTARY TRUSTEE'S FEE.—No statutory provision. Some customary rates are as follows:

Acceptance fee: ½ of 1% of principal unless trustee was also executor.

Annual fee: On securities and other personal property, 3/8 of 1% of value of property, except that on real estate mortgages, the fee is ½ of 1%. On real estate for management or sale the regular fee charged by recognized property management agencies upon like property in the community where real estate is located plus (as to management only) 1/8 of 1% of value of property. Minimum annual fee is $50.

Closing and distribution fee: 2% of value of property distributed.

The above annual fees are only approximate, as there is considerable variance among corporate trustees as to fees. Generally, many charge fees starting at one-half of one percent minimum to a certain stated amount, and thereafter ¼ of 1%.

NEVADA

EXECUTOR'S OR ADMINISTRATOR'S FEE.—Statutory rates are as follows: 6% of first $1,000; 4% of next $4,000; 2% of excess over $5,000, based on "personal estate accounted for". Additional allowance may be made for service in regard to real property, and for extraordinary services.

TESTAMENTARY TRUSTEE'S FEE.—Statute provides for reasonable compensation. Example of customary rates follows:

Acceptance fee: (If trustee did not serve as executor) 1/5 of 1% of principal, with minimum charge of $100.

Annual fee: ½ of 1% of personal property, and ¾ of 1% of real property. Minimum charge of $100.

Distribution fee: 1% of principal. Minimum charge, $100.

Above fees apply where there are no contrary provisions in will; and apply in the further event, if there are other provisions in the will, the fiduciary waives the same.

NEW HAMPSHIRE

EXECUTOR'S OR ADMINISTRATOR'S FEE.—No statutory provision. Probate Court usually allows not to exceed these maximum fees for fiduciary and attorney (combined): Reasonable compensation on estate up to $10,000; 5%, $10,000-$100,000; 4% on excess over $100,000-$500,000; 3% on excess over $500,000-$1,000,000; 2% on excess over $1,000,000. Counsel advises that rates are applied to property owned solely by decedent, excluding life insurance not payable to estate, and that real estate is generally excluded, unless sold by fiduciary.

TESTAMENTARY TRUSTEE'S FEE.—Statute provides for reasonable compensation. Annual compensation allowed by Probate Courts is usually limited to 5% of income plus 2/10 of 1% of principal. Termination fee is usually limited to 1% of principal prior to distribution, at fair market value.

NEW JERSEY

EXECUTOR'S OR ADMINISTRATOR S FEE.—Statutory rates are as follows·

Income: 6% on income, without court allowance.

Corpus: 5% on "all corpus that comes into the fiduciary's hands" not exceeding $100,000, and on the excess, such percentage not in excess of 5% as court may determine, according to actual services rendered. If there are two or more fiduciaries, court may allow additional corpus commissions at rate not exceeding 1% of corpus for each additional fiduciary. If administration of fiduciary extends beyond a period of 25 years, corpus commissions for such additional years are allowed at rate not exceeding 1/5 of 1% per annum, irrespective of number of fiduciaries. Real estate coming into possession of fiduciary and remaining unsold may be considered in fixing corpus commissions. Further compensation may be allowed for services as to property not coming into fiduciary's hands but included in estate for tax purposes.

Example of rates: 5% on first $100,000 and not exceeding 5% on excess in discretion of the court. Where more than one fiduciary, not to exceed 1% for each additional fiduciary.

TESTAMENTARY TRUSTEE'S FEE.—Statutory provisions for executors and administrators are applicable.

The court may, on an intermediate or the final settlement of the fiduciary's accounts, allow corpus commissions in addition to those provided by this section, on a showing that unusual or extraordinary services have been rendered by the fiduciary for which the fiduciary should receive extra compensation.

Fiduciaries may annually, without court allowance, take sums as follows on account of corpus commissions: if there is but one fiduciary, the amount so taken may equal 1/5 of 1% of the first $100,000.00 of corpus and 1/10 of 1% of the value of the corpus in excess of $100,000.00, or $1 100.00, whichever is less· and, if there are two or more

fiduciaries, the amount so taken may equal the commissions which may be taken pursuant to this subsection when there is but one fiduciary, plus 1/5 of such commissions for each fiduciary more than one. In computing the amount of commissions which may be taken annually pursuant to this subsection, the value of any item of corpus at the time when such item came into the hands of the fiduciary or fiduciaries, herein in this section referred to as the "presumptive value" of such item, may be used as the value of such item, or, at the option of the fiduciary, the value of such item at the end of the period for which such commissions are taken may be used. The failure of a fiduciary or fiduciaries to take commissions in any year as provided in this subsection shall not constitute a waiver of the right of such fiduciary or fiduciaries to take in a subsequent year the commissions not taken for such year. Commissions taken as provided in this subsection shall be subject to review on intermediate and final accountings, and to the extent that aggregate commissions so taken exceed the commissions allowable under paragraphs (2) and (3) of subsection a. of this section, they shall be disallowed.

In the event of a dispute as to the value of corpus on the settlement of the account of a fiduciary or fiduciaries, the burden of proving that the value of any item of corpus differs from the presumptive value of such item shall be upon such fiduciary or fiduciaries or other party claiming such difference. Amended by L.1957, c. 80, p. 152 § 2; L.1964, c. 25, § 1; L.1972, c. 147, § 1, eff. Sept. 7, 1972.

NEW MEXICO

EXECUTOR'S OR ADMINISTRATOR'S FEE.—Statutory rates are as follows: On "property . . . which shall come into their hands" (subject to below provisions): 10% on first $3,000; 5% on excess over $3,000; provided that if said property consists of "proceeds of life insurance policies, or cash, including checking accounts, time deposits, certificates of deposit, savings accounts, Postal Savings certificates and all United States Government Bonds," compensation shall not exceed: 5% of first $5,000; 1% of excess over $5,000; and provided, further, that no compensation is paid on account of real estate, except as followed by court upon proper cause.

TESTAMENTARY TRUSTEE'S FEE.—No statutory provision. Customary rates vary from 5 to 10% of income, or ½ of 1% of principal, annually.

NEW YORK

EXECUTOR'S OR ADMINISTRATOR'S FEE.—Statutory rates for receiving and paying out all sums of money 4% on amounts not exceeding $25,000; 3½% on additional amounts not exceeding $125,000.00; 3% of additional amounts not exceeding $150,000.00; all sums above $300,000.00 at the rate of 2%.

Percentage is taken ½ as receiving and ½ as paying out. For example, assume an executor receives $8,000, but because of depreciation, pays out $7,000. He would be entitled to 2% of $8,000 as receiving commission and 2% of $7,000 as a paying out commission. If principal amounts to $100,000 or more, each representative, not exceeding three, is entitled to full compensation at above rates. Additional commission of 5% of gross rents collected where representative is required to collect rents of and manage real property, but only one such additional commission is allowed regardless of number of representatives

TESTAMENTARY TRUSTEE'S FEE.—Statutory rates for trustees under wills of persons dying after August 31, 1956, are as follows:

Annual commissions on principal: $5 per $1,000 on first $300,000; $2.50 per $1,000 on next $500,000; $2 per $1,000 on excess over $800,000; 6% of gross rents collected where trustee is required to collect rents of and manage real property, but only one such additional commission is allowed regardless of number of trustees.

Paying out commissions: 1% of principal paid out.

If principal amounts to $100,000 or more, each trustee, not exceeding three, is entitled to full compensation at above rates.

In trust solely for charitable, etc. purposes, annual commission is 7% on first $2,000 of income and 5% on balance. If income amounts to $4,000 or more, each trustee receives full commissions, but if more than two trustees, two full commissions are apportioned among them.

NORTH CAROLINA

EXECUTOR'S OR ADMINISTRATOR'S FEE.—Statute provides for commissions to be fixed in the discretion of the Clerk of Superior Court not to exceed 5% on receipts including value of all personalty, and 5% on expenditures. No commissions are allowed on real estate except for the proceeds of the sale of real estate actually used to pay debts or legacies. No commissions are allowed on payment of legacies or distributive shares. The above maximum rates apply only to estates of more than $2,000.

Example of customary rates for ordinary services follows: 5% of first $100,000; 4% of next $200,000; 3% of next $400,000; 2% of next $2,300,000; 1½% of excess over $3,000,000; based upon receipts of all assets including real estate and life insurance payable to the estate, subject, however, to the above statutory maximum rates. Additional charges may be made where unusual services are required. No charge is made on life insurance payable to a named beneficiary. The annual charge on income, other than real property income, is 5% of first $50,000 of annual income and 3% of balance. The charge on real property income and disbursements is 5% of income and 5% of disbursements. Minimum charge for settling estate, $1,000.

TESTAMENTARY TRUSTEE'S FEE.—Above statutory provisions re maximum rates are applicable.

Example of customary rates for ordinary services (based on value of real and personal property) follows:

Acceptance charge: If trustee did not act as executor, 1% of principal.

Annual principal charges: ¼ of 1% for first $100,000; 1/10 of 1% for next $400,000; 1/20 of 1% of excess over $500,000. Minimum annual charge, $200. Total of commissions on principal shall not exceed statutory maximum.

Annual income charges: 5% of first $50,000; 3% of excess over $50,000.

Termination charge: If trustee did not act as executor, 1% of principal. Additional charges may be made where unusual services are required.

NORTH DAKOTA

EXECUTOR'S OR ADMINISTRATOR'S FEE.—Statutory rates are as follows: 5% of first $1,000; 3% of next $5,000; 2% of next $44,000. On excess over $50,000 compensation is fixed by court, at rate not in excess of 2%. Rates are applied to "whole estate accounted for". Extra allowance may be made for extraordinary services. Total amount of such extra allowance may not exceed commission at above rates.

TESTAMENTARY TRUSTEE'S FEE.—Statute provides for allowance by District Court of reasonable compensation and necessary expenses. If trust instrument specifies compensation, that shall be the full compensation for services.

Customary rates range from ½ of 1% of the average principal balance annually to ⁴/₅ of 1% of the average principal balance annually plus 5% of annual income received. If Trustee's duties include management of real property, fees range to 10% of income from such property and no charge against the principal value of such property.

OHIO

EXECUTOR'S OR ADMINISTRATOR'S FEE.—Statutory rates are as follows: 6% of first $1,000; 4% of next $4,000; 2% of excess over $5,000; based on "personal estate . . . received and accounted for", and to "proceeds of real estate sold" under authority contained in a will. Additional allowance may be made for extraordinary services.

TESTAMENTARY TRUSTEE'S FEE.—No statutory rates. A typical fee is the following one established by the rules of the Franklin County Probate Court (Columbus). Annual charges on income: 6% on first $10,000; 5% on next $10,000; and 4% on the balance. Annual charges on principal: $4 per $1,000 on first $100,000, $3.50 on next $200,000, $3 on next $200,000, $2 on next $500,000, $1.50 on next $500,000, and $1 on the balance. One-time principal distribution fee upon termination; 1% of fair market value.

OKLAHOMA

EXECUTOR'S OR ADMINISTRATOR'S FEE.—Statutory rates are as follows: 5% of first $1,000; 4% of next $5,000; 2½% of excess over $6,000; based on "whole estate accounted for". Further allowances may be made for extraordinary services. Extra allowance may not exceed commission at above rates.

TESTAMENTARY TRUSTEE'S FEE.—Statute provides for reasonable compensation. Example of customary rates follows:

Acceptance fee: None, unless Trustee must audit accounts of predecessor Executor (other than Trustee) or Trustee, then fee based on; 1% on first $250,000; ½ of 1% on next $500,000; ¼ of 1% on next $2,250,000; ⅛ of 1% on next $5,000,000; 1/10 of 1% on excess of $8,000,000.

Annual fees: Exclusive of real estate, mortgages and oil and gas assets: 6/10 of 1% on first $100,000; ½ of 1% on next $300,000; ⅜ of 1% on next $600,000; ¼ of 1% on next $2,000,000; ⅛ of 1% on next $5 000,000; 1/10 of 1% on excess of $8,000,000.

There are special schedules for real estate, property management, mortgages, and oil and gas matters. Minimum annual fee where assets all in common trust fund, $150; individually invested (no real estate or mortgages), $250; and containing real estate, $300.

Distribution fee: 2% on first $250,000; 1% on next $750,000; ¾ of 1% on next $1,000,000; ½ of 1% on next $3,000,000; ⅜ of 1% on excess of $10,000,000.

Above fees are reduced ½ if corpus is distributed within five years from date of creation.

OREGON

PERSONAL REPRESENTATIVE'S FEE.—Statutory rates are as follows: 7% of first $1,000; 4% of next $9,000; 3% of next $40,000; 2% of excess over $50,000; based on "whole estate accounted for". Further compensation may be allowed for extraordinary services.

One percent of the property, exclusive of life insurance proceeds, not subject to jurisdiction of the court but reportable for Oregon inheritance tax or federal estate tax purposes.

TESTAMENTARY TRUSTEE'S FEE.—No statutory provision. Variation exists as to customary rates charged by corporate trustees.

One corporate trustee in Portland:

An opening charge is made only when the bank or trust company has not also served as Executor and such opening charges are as follows: 1/10 of 1% on first $100,000; 1/20 of 1% on assets over $100,000.

Annual principal charges: Stocks, bonds and other securities: 6/10 of 1% on the first $100,000; ½ of 1% on the next $900,000; ¼ of 1% on assets over $1,000,000.

Real estate: 1% on the first $50,000; ¾ of 1% on values over $50,000.

Mortgages, contracts and notes: ¾ of 1% plus $5 for each item. Minimum fee is $250,000 per year.

Distribution fee is 1% of principal. For revocation of a living trust, a fee of 1/10 of 1% is charged.

Another corporate trustee charges: An opening charge is based on reasonable compensation for time involved with a minimum opening charge of $150.

Annual principal charges: Stocks, bonds, and other securities: ⅝ of 1% on the first $250,000; ½ of 1% on the next $250,000; ⅜ of 1% on the next $500,000; ¼ of 1% on assets over $1,000,000.

Real estate: ¾ of 1% on the first $250,000; ½ of 1% on values over $250,000.

Mortgages, contracts and notes: ¾ of 1% plus $35 per receivable. Minimum fee is $250 per year.

Distribution fee is 1% with a minimum fee of $150. Revocation of living trust, 1/10 of 1%.

PENNSYLVANIA

EXECUTOR'S OR ADMINISTRATOR'S FEE.—No statutory provision. All fees are subject to control of court which must find them to be reasonable as to each case. Custom-

ary rates vary widely. Many corporate fiduciaries have established their own fee schedules by agreement with testator.

In absence of agreement between testator and fiduciary, following are examples of fees normally approved:

(1) Pittsburgh—One corporate fiduciary:

On principal: 5% of first $150,000; 4% of next $200,000; 3% of next $650,000; 2½% of excess over $1,000,000. (Somewhat lower if estate is quite large).

On income: 6%.

Another corporate fiduciary:

On principal: 5% of first $100,000; 4% of next $200,000; 3% of next $300,000; 2½% of next $400,000; 2% of excess over $1,000,000.

On income: 5% of first $25,000 per annum; 4% of next $25,000 per annum; 3% of excess over $50,000 per annum.

(2) Philadelphia—One corporate fiduciary:

On principal: Estates under $50,000, 5%; (Minimum fee, $1,000).

Estates over $50,000: On the first $100,000, 4%, (Minimum fee $2,500); On the next $400,000, 3%; On the next $500,000, 2½%; On the next $1,500,000, 2%.

On gross income: 5%. Amounts in excess of $2,000,000 to be determined by special analysis.

Another corporate fiduciary:

Income: 5% on the income collected.

Personalty: 5% on the first $50,000; 4% on the next $50,000; 3% on the next $150,000; 2⅔% on the next $250,000; 2% on the next $500,000; 1½% on the next $2,000,000; 1% on the excess.

Real estate: 1% on specifically devised real estate; 2% on generally devised real estate; or 3% on proceeds of real estate sold through a broker, or 6% on proceeds of real estate sold without a broker.

(3) Other counties: Vary greatly but generally fall between rates allowed in Pittsburgh and Philadelphia.

TESTMENTARY TRUSTEE'S FEE.—Statute provides for reasonable compensation. Customary rates vary widely. Many corporate fiduciaries have established their own fee schedules by agreement with testator. In absence of agreement between parties, following are examples of fees which customarily may be allowed:

(1) Pittsburgh—One corporate fiduciary·

On income: 6% per annum.

On principal (where interim compensation is permitted either by agreement or with court approval): 2/10 of 1% per year on market value of principal up to maximum of 5% at 25 years or longer, depending on duration of trust.

Another corporate fiduciary (annual fee):

(On interim basis): ½ of 1% on first $100,000; 4/10 of 1% on next $400,000: 3/10 of 1% on next $500,000; 2/10 of 1% on next $1,000,000; 1/10 of 1% on next $18,000,000; (basis in market value of assets [Principal personalty] on each anniversary date—5% of above rates normally charged to income, balance to principal).

In pre-1945 trusts, testamentary trustee who was also executor will not be allowed a second commission in principal. Above examples applicable to post-1953 trusts

(2) Philadelphia—One corporate fiduciary:

Annual compensation: (Based upon principal. There is no compensation based on income). On the first $300,000, $5 per $1,000: On the next $400,000, $4 per $1,000: On the next $300,000, $3 per $1,000; On the next $1,000,000, $2 per $1,000.

Another corporate fiduciary: From such time as the trust becomes active, 5% on income, as collected, and an annual fee based on the original market or fair value of the principal of each account and as revalued annually at the following rates: $3 per $1,000 on the first $250,000 of principal; $2 per $1,000 on the next $500,000 of principal; $1 per $1,000 on the next $500,000 of principal.

(3) Other Counties: Vary greatly, but generally between rates allowed in Pittsburgh and Philadelphia.

Also note that, on principal, in pre-1945 trusts, if testamentary trustee was also the executor of the will, he will not be allowed a second commission on principal as trustee if he received a commission on principal as executor.

RHODE ISLAND

EXECUTOR'S OR ADMINISTRATOR'S FEE.—Statute provides for just compensation. An example of customary charges follows: 3% to 3½% of principal value, depending upon complexity of administered estate.

TESTAMENTARY TRUSTEE'S FEE.—Statute provides for reasonable compensation. An example of annual customary rates is as follows:

4% of gross income plus $3 per $1,000 on first $200,000 principal; $2 per $1,000 on next $300,000 principal; $1 per $1,000 on next $2,500,000 principal; $0.50 per $1,000 on balance. Minimum annual fee is $200.

SOUTH CAROLINA

EXECUTOR'S OR ADMINISTRATOR'S FEE.—Statute provides maximum fees of $2.50 for every $100 of appraised value of all personal assets paid away in credits, debts, legacies, or otherwise, except for sums retained by fiduciaries for payment of debts or legacies to themselves; and $10 for every $100 arising from moneys let out to interest. The same commissions are provided for the sale of real estate when directed by will or court order Additional compensation may be allowed for extraordinary services.

Customary rates charged by corporate fiduciaries in Charlestown:

(1) On personalty: 4% on first $100,000; 3% on next $150,000; 2.5% on next $250,000; 1.5% on next $500,000; 1% on all over $1,000,000. On life insurance, 1%.

On real estate, no fee unless sold by fiduciary under will or court order. If sold, proceeds are added to appraised value of other probate property and scheduled applies.

Minimum commission on principal is $1,000. Income charge, 5%.

(2) Another corporate fiduciary charges no fee on income. On personalty: 4% on first $100,000; 3% on next $300,000; 2% on next $500,000; 1% on excess over $900,000. Minimum commission is $750. Life insurance, 1%. Real estate not included where specifically devised to individuals.

(3) There are other variations as to rates charged. Additional charges may be made for extraordinary services.

TESTAMENTARY TRUSTEE'S FEE.—Customary rates vary among corporate fiduciaries.

(1) One corporate fiduciary:

Annual charge on principal: 1/5 of 1% on first $100,000; 3/20 of 1% on next $400,000; 1/10 of 1% on all over $500,000; based on current value of principal.

Annual charge on gross income: 5%.

Termination: ½ of 1% of fair market value of principal. Minimum annual fee of $100.

Where fiduciary did not serve as personal representative, additional charge is made of 1% of value of personal property received

(2) A corporate fiduciary.

No charge for acceptance or on income. Annual charge on principal: ½ of 1% on first $100,000; ¼ of 1% on next $200,000; 1/5 of 1% on next $200,000; 1/10 of 1% on excess over $500,000. On removal, transfer or termination, charge of 1% of current value.

Minimum fee is $200 per year, or $100 if entirely invested in common trust funds.

If real estate, business enterprise or similar activity managed, reasonable compensation is charged.

(3) Another corporate fiduciary·

Annual charge on principal ¼ of 1% on first $100,000; 1/5 of 1% on next $100,000, 1/10 of 1% on all over $200,000

Annual charge on income· 5% on first $10,000; 2% on all over $10,000. Minimum annual charge is $250, or $125 if entirely invested in common trust funds.

Acceptance charge: None if acted as executor. Otherwise, charge of· 1% on first $100,000; ½ of 1% on next $400,000; ¼ of 1% on all over $500,000. Minimum acceptance fee, $250.

Termination fee, on same basis as acceptance fee and minimum $250.

Flat charge of ¼ of 1% on invested common funds.

SOUTH DAKOTA

EXECUTOR'S OR ADMINISTRATOR'S FEE. Statutory rates are as follows: 5% on first $1,000; 4% on next $4,000;

2½% on all sums in excess of $5,000, based on "personal property accounted for by him, excluding personal property not ranked as assets" Real property sold as part of proceedings in probate is considered as personal property. On other real property accounted for, statute provides for reasonable compensation for services performed, to be fixed by the court (SDCL 30-25-7)

TESTAMENTARY TRUSTEE'S FEE.—Statute provides that "when a declaration of trust does not specify the rate or amount of the trustee's compensation, the trustee is entitled to and shall receive reasonable compensation for the performance of his duties. If such declaration specifies the amount or rate of his compensation, he is entitled to the amount or rate thus specified and no more " (SDCL 55-3-14)

TENNESSEE

EXECUTOR'S OR ADMINISTRATOR'S FEE.—Statute provides for reasonable compensation. The following customary rates are believed to be typical for banks in Nashville.

5% on first $50,000; 4% on next $50,000; 3% on next $200,000; 2% on next $700,000, 1% on amounts in excess of $1,000,000.

In estates of more than $500,000, fee may be determined by special agreement. Minimum fee is $500 to $1,000. Rates are applied to property passing through fiduciary's hands. No charge is made on life insurance payable to estate except portion used to pay debts, etc., nor on real property unless it must be sold. Additional charges are made for other than average services.

Rates are not uniform in state. In some counties, 5% of gross personal assets, subject to adjustment by court.

In Memphis, by rule of the Probate Court of Shelby County, Tennessee, the Court will be guided, but not bound, by Section 3273(a) (9) of Shannon's Tennessee Code (1917) which provides:

Gross Estate	Minimum	Maximum
Not exceeding $1,000	5%	10%
$1,000-$3,000	5%	7½%
$3,000-$10,000	4%	6%
All amounts in excess of $10,000, add	2%	4%

TESTAMENTARY TRUSTEE'S FEE.—No statutory provision. The following customary rates are typical for banks in Nashville; annual fee based on market value of assets in trust·

$5 per $1,000 for first $100,000 of assets; $4 per $1,000 on next $250,000 of assets; $3 per $1,000 on next $250,000 of assets, $2.50 per $1,000 on amounts over $600,000 Minimum annual charge $125 to $750. For trusts over $500,000, fee may be determined by special agreement. Additional compensation may be charged for extraordinary services. Rates are not uniform in state.

In Memphis, an example of fees of a corporate fiduciary

Acceptance fee: None if Trustee is the original Trustee and has served as Executor; otherwise a fee of ¼ of 1% of the principal amount in the trust

Annual principal charge: On the first $200,000, $2 50 per $1,000; next $300,000, $2 per $1,000 on next $500,000, $1 per $1,000; over $1,000,000, $0.50 per $1,000

Annual income charge: 5% of all income up to $20,000 3% of all over $20,000

Minimum annual fee: $100, or if assets are all in common trust fund, $75

Distribution fee: None, if corporate fiduciary receives all assets as executor or trustee, otherwise During first year of trust, 1½%; during second year of trust, 1¼%, during third year of trust, 1%; during fourth year of trust, ¾ of 1%, during fifth year of trust, ½ of 1%, after fifth year, ¼ of 1%

Notwithstanding the foregoing, the fees of a trustee for "selling and collecting" are limited by statute (TCA §35-119) to a minimum of 5%

TEXAS

EXECUTOR'S OR ADMINISTRATOR'S FEE.—Statutory rate is 5% on all sums received in cash, and 5% on all sums paid out in cash. This rate is applicable only if there is no contrary stipulation in the will nor an agreement by testator and the Executor. No commission is allowed for receiving cash on hand at time of decedent's death, nor for paying out cash to heirs or legatees as such In no event shall commission exceed 5% of the gross fair market value of the estate subject to administration. If compensation as calculated above, is unreasonably low, court may allow reasonable compensation for services

TESTAMENTARY TRUSTEE'S FEE.—No statutory provision. Absent provisions for compensation in the will, presumably court would have jurisdiction to allow a reasonable fee.

As a guide the following schedule of basic annual charges (for corporate trustees) based on the reasonable value of the trust, may be used· Three-fourth of 1% on first $50,000; One-half of 1% on next $450,000; One-third of 1% on remaining value of trust. Minimum fee of $100

In larger cities, corporate trustees usually charge ½ of 1% on first $500,000.

The above charges are fairly standard for securities and like assets. It is somewhat customary for trust departments to consider a basic charge computed on the above schedule. However, this fee is subject to adjustment in individual cases. Charges for handling oil interests are not standardized in the least, and it is impractical to give an example. Where the income of the trust is largely based on rents from real property, the fee is frequently based upon a percentage of the rents collected, such as 3% to 6% depending upon the circumstance

UTAH

EXECUTOR'S OR ADMINISTRATOR'S FEE.—

Statutory rates are as follows 5% on first $1,000; 4% on next $4,000; 3% on next $5,000, 2% on next $40,000; 1½% on next $50,000; 1% on excess over $100,000; based on "estate accounted for" including property included in gross estate for purpose of Utah Inheritance Tax Further allowance may be made for extraordinary services bu·

aggregate amount of commission and extra allowance shall not exceed twice commission at above rates.

TESTAMENTARY TRUSTEE'S FEE.—Statute provides for reasonable compensation. Example of customary rates charged by trust company is as follows: Where trustee has full responsibility, annual fee of three-fourths of 1% of principal with the exception of mortgages; 1% of principal on mortgages; and additional charges where assets include real estate as follows: 10% of the gross rents received on residence properties; 5% of the gross rents received on apartment houses; 5% of the gross rents received on business and industrial property. 1/20 of 1% of assessed value of vacant property annually, with a minimum fee of $5 for each piece of vacant or nonproductive property separately set.

Some corporate fiduciaries charge a flat 7% of the gross rents received on any real property. Some fiduciaries do not provide a minimum fee for unproductive property.

VERMONT

EXECUTOR'S OR ADMINISTRATOR'S FEE.—Statute provides fee of $4.00 for each day's attendance by executor, administrator, or trustee. Probate court may allow, in cases of unusual difficulty or responsibility, such further sum as it judges reasonable.

In practice, charges may approximate 5%-3% depending on the size of the estate and other factors.

TESTAMENTARY TRUSTEE'S FEE.—Statutory provisions are the same as for executors and administrators. In some cases, a charge is made on principal, two-tenths (2/10) of one per cent approximately, and a charge is made on income collected, 6% approximately.

VIRGINIA

EXECUTOR'S OR ADMINISTRATOR'S FEE.—Statute provides for reasonable compensation. Example of corporate fiduciary charges follows: Principal: 5% on first $50,000; 4% on next 50,000; 3% on next $900,000; 2% on excess over $1,000,000: Income: 5% of gross income.

1% on foreign assets and assets passing outside the will but includable in the estate for tax purposes.

TESTAMENTARY TRUSTEE'S FEE.—Statute provides for reasonable compensation. Example of corporate fiduciary charges follows:

Where trustee has acted as executor: Annual commission on principal: 4/10 of 1% on first $100,000; 2/10 of 1% on next $400,000; 1/10 of 1% on excess over $500,000; Income: 5% on annual gross income.

Where trustee has not acted as executor: Annual commissions on principal and income same as where trustee has acted as executor. Acceptance fee of 1% is usually required.

Note: each case governed by its own facts.

In addition, Commissioner of Accounts approves fees requested, which approval is subject to court approval

WASHINGTON

EXECUTOR'S OR ADMINISTRATOR'S FEES.—Statutes provide for reasonable compensation. Where the attorney acts also as executor or administrator, minimum attorney's fee of bar association may be increased by 50% and no additional fee is allowed as fiduciary.

Rules of Superior Court of King County prescribes provisions for allowance of fees to fiduciaries and attorneys. If fee requested by noncorporate representative is greater than one-half of minimum fee allowed to attorney, representative must file detailed statement as to services rendered. If will provides for compensation for representative, that shall be his full compensation unless he files renunciation before qualifying. Additional compensation may be allowed representative who also serves as attorney.

Example of customary charges by a Seattle corporate fiduciary: 3% of gross inventoried value of first $200,000; 2% of values over $200,000; Additional compensation for extraordinary services. If co-fiduciary, charges made as if sole fiduciary.

If bank serves as executor and trustee, its fee as executor is the same as its annual trustee's fee based on inventoried value; plus in addition a "once only" fee of 1% of first $500,000 and ½ of 1% in excess thereof of appraised values, both separate and community, reported for state and federal tax purposes, whichever is higher

In settlement of "small estates" which do not require filing of federal tax return, the charge is 2% of gross inventoried value, separate and community. Minimum fee $200. Additional charge of 1% of gross value of real estate or real estate mortgage without deduction for encumbrances. Additional compensation for extraordinary services. These charges are applicable only where bank acts as sole executor or administrator.

TESTAMENTARY TRUSTEE'S FEE.—No statutory provisions. Customary charges of a Seattle bank follows:

Annual fee: (1) Personal Property ¾ of 1% of first $250,000; ½ of 1% of next $750,000; ⅜ of 1% of next $500,000; ¼ of 1% of the balance. Fee reduced by ⅛ of 1% on common trust fund units. Maximum additional fee of ¼ of 1% on individual mortgages, loans or contracts secured by real and/or personal property. (2) **Real Property:** ½ of 1% of value without reduction for encumbrances on first $100,000 each parcel, then ¼ of 1% on balance.

For management, 5% of gross income. If outside management is employed, 3% minimum.

For sales: improved, not exceed 6%; unimproved, not to exceed 10%. If broker is employed, 1% up to maximum 3%. Minimum $100.

For collection of ground rents or leases over 15 years: 3% of first $10,000 of annual rent; 2½% of next $40,000; and 2% of excess of $50,000 rent. Where undivided interests are involved, fee computed on value and income of entire property.

One-half of total annual fee is charged to income and one-half to principal

WEST VIRGINIA

EXECUTOR'S OR ADMINISTRATOR'S FEE.—Statute provides for reasonable compensation "in the form of a commission on receipts or otherwise". Example of customary rate is 5% on receipts. Real property not sold is excluded from computation, unless devised to Executor to be sold.

TESTAMENTARY TRUSTEE'S FEE.—Same fee as executor or administrator.

WISCONSIN

EXECUTOR'S OR ADMINISTRATOR'S FEE.—New Probate Code Section 857.05 provides that personal representative (executor, administrator etc.), subject to approval of court, shall be allowed commissions based on inventory value of property less mortgages or liens plus net corpus gains in estate proceedings at rate of 2%: and such other sums for extraordinary services as are reasonable. If representative or any law firm with which he is associated also serves as attorney for estate, court may allow him either executor's commissions (including sums for extraordinary services) or attorney's fees; or may allow both executor's commissions and attorney's fees where justified, and shall pay both where will so directs.

TESTAMENTRY TRUSTEE'S FEE.—No statutory provision, except as to apportionment of annual fee between income and principal. Fees vary from bank to bank. Fees are usually based on negotiation on trust size and nature of assets and duties of investment.

(1) Milwaukee:

Following is schedule of one bank:

Annual fee: ½ of 1% of first (minimum $250) $100,000; 4/10 of 1% of next $150,000; ¼ of 1% of next $750,000; 2/10 of 1% of excess over $1,000,000; If all assets are in its common trust fund, annual charge is reduced 20%. On outstanding balances of mortgages and notes ¾ of 1% in first $100,000; 5/10 of 1% on excess over $100,000.

Termination or distribution fee: Upon termination of trust, in addition to fee. Inclusive of such services as are performed by trustees in connection with court proceedings on the hearing for termination, income tax returns, plan of distribution, final account, transfer of assets, tax clearance, and the like as follows: not to exceed: 1% of first $100,000; ¾ of 1% of next $150,000; ½ of 1% of next $750,000; ⅛ of 1% of excess over $1,000,000.

No succession fee if bank was executor or agent of executor. If bank has not so acted, a succession fee is charged: $50,000 or less, $100; $50,000 to $150,000, $200; $150,000 to $300,000, $300; $300,000 to $500,000, $400; over $500,000, $500.

If title to real estate is held but without management duties, annual fee is charged per parcel based on fair market value of improved property: On first $20,000 or less, $100; On next $30,000 ¼ of 1%; On next $50,000, 1/10 of 1%; On next $400,000, 1/20 of 1%; Over $500,000, 1/50 of 1%. If management duties are involved, 6% of gross income. Basic charge may be increased or decreased by unusual services.

(2) Madison:

Three examples of customary fees are:

(1) ¾ of 1% on 1st $200,000; 4/10 of 1% on next $800,000; 2/10 of 1% on next $4,000,000; 1/10 of 1% on remainder; slightly less if invested in common trust funds; full fee plus 30% if a co-trustee.

(2) ½ of 1% on 1st $200,000; 4/10 of 1% on next $500,000; 3/10 of 1% on next $300,000; 2/10 of 1% on remainder.

(3) ½ of 1% on 1st $300,000; 4/10 of 1% on next $700,000; 2/10 of 1% on all over $1,000,000. Most have minimum rates, varying from $200 to $750. Acceptance fees are charged by two of the three unless the Trust Company has acted as personal representative. Termination or distribution fees vary from an extra annual fee to a straight 1% fee. Special fees are charged for sale of real estate, rental of real estate, and extraordinary management duties.

Some items are usually "negotiable."

WYOMING

EXECUTOR'S OR ADMINISTRATOR'S FEE.—Statutory rates are as follows: 10% on first $1,000; 5% on next $4,000; 3% on next $15,000; 2% on excess over $20,000; based on "amount of the estate accounted for." Additional allowance may be made for extraordinary services, but extra allowance must not exceed one-half amount of commission at above rates.

TESTAMENTARY TRUSTEE'S FEE.—No statutory provision. Rates vary in different counties and depend on facts of particular case.

INDEX